Thinking Hands –
the power
of labour in
William Morris

By Philip Katz

The moral right of the author to be identified as the originator of this work has been asserted under the Copyright, Designs and Patents Act 1988.

Published by Hetherington Press

First pressing October 2005
Design Toby Issacs
Cover Photo courtesy Telegraph Science Library
Typeset in Joanna 11/13 pt
Printed in the UK by PhilTone Litho

British Library Cataloguing-in-Publication Data
A catalogue record for this book is available from the British Library.

Display as: History; Employment; Industrial History; Economics; Trade Unions; Future of Work.

For those wishing to use sections for extensive quoting, development, adding testimonials or bulk reproduction for academic purposes, the book is available in Word text only format - Mac or PC - or PDF on CDrom at a cost, including postage of £10 or $15.
Orders can be made at reprints@hetheringtonpress.co.uk

Copies of Thinking Hands – the power of labour in William Morris can be purchased via orders@hetheringtonpress.co.uk priced £11 or $17.50 including postage and packing.

Those wishing to contact the author may do so at philkatzone@mac.com

ACKNOWLEDGMENTS

For John Clarke and Jeffrey Rosen who illuminated the way. And for Sam, Bella-Rosa, Betty and Hugo.

Writing, whilst working full time at a different craft, is difficult. So my thanks go primarily to those who in their various ways made my path a little easier. I extend thanks to John Dixon, Assistant General Secretary of the New South Wales Teachers' Federation (Australia), Brian Revell and Chris Kaufman, National Secretaries of the Transport and General Workers' Union, Dave Smith Regional Recruiter, Transport Salaried Staff Association and Richard Stainton Principal Officer for Continuing Professional Development at the National Union of Teachers who brought experience and wisdom to their analysis of the sections of the draft.

Thanks also go to the following people. To the librarians who left the doors open for one who did not keep conventional hours. To the researchers who shared their ideas through numerous websites. To those who helped with picture and illustration research including: Katherine Hill, Matthew Slocombe and Philip Venning of the Society for the Protection of Ancient Buildings; the archivists of the International Institute of Social History of Amsterdam who made it possible for me to work in a number of instances from original and in a few cases unpublished manuscripts; to Pryor Publications for permission to reproduce illustrations from 'A Boys Book of Trades'; to the Masters and Fellows of Trinity College Cambridge who helped with picture research and gave permission for use; and the Newcomen Society for the Study of the History of Engineering and Technology. Special thanks go to Chris Coome who swiftly answered my enquiries and who, together with Nick Salmon, have done so much to make Morris available to a new audience.

I thank the volunteers of Marx Memorial Library who maintain a superb collection of Morris's work which you do not have to be a PhD student to access and to Keri Myers, researcher, Chris Coates and Alex Bromley, TUC librarian who project manage TUC History Online (www.unionhistory.info) housed as part of the TUC Library Collections at London Metropolitan University.

Thanks to: Harry Braverman, Dr. Kate Bronfenbrenner, Director of Labor Education Research, Cornell University, Professor Philip Bagwell, Emeritus Professor of History, University of Westminster, Edward Thompson, Gareth Steadman Jones, Peter Linebaugh and Ellen Meiksins Wood who inspired a generation of worker-writers to look that bit deeper and to Jenny who typed my manuscript. Thanks go to Diana for her encouragement and criticism and for being a brilliant mum, who managed to convince the little ones that their dad was doing something worthwhile. And to the little ones for believing her.

Special thanks go to Ros Anderson who edited this and my last book *The Long Weekend – Combatting Unemployment in the Inter-War Years* (2001) who brought to each, an application of brain and hand, of which William Morris would have been proud.

So what Morris said is true – nothing is the work of an individual alone – all is collective.

CONTENTS

Intelligence enough to Conceive, ~~Power to Compel~~ courage enough to will, power enough to Compel. If our ideas of a new Society are any thing more than a dream, these three qualities must animate the due Effective majority of the working people: and then, I say, the thing will be done

Thinking Hands

William Morris had an abundance of ideas that were a constant challenge to workers in the nineteenth century and remain so for the twenty-first. Morris changed the way workers looked at their world. To him, work was central to life. It determined both its character and quality. It was the prism through which people came to discover social relations and develop an understanding of nature and the place of people in it. Life could be changed for the better.

Morris delighted in the uncertainty and uniqueness people brought to life at a time when an industrial system was being put in place that rested on certainty, uniformity, standardisation, predictability, and repeatability. It was to become a mechanical age with the worker literally worked by the machine owner until he was of no further physical use, that is if he was not replaced altogether by a machine, producing standardised goods, inferior in quality and bereft of art.

Morris glorified the craftsman of the Middle Ages as an independent free thinker, who could more or less control his own work and life space. He was aware that during this 'golden' time, a huge quantity of knowledge and careful thought had gone into the development of production processes. He was therefore horrified to see its nineteenth century descendants crushed under a tide of commerce, alienated from the means of production, and herded from home and land into soulless factories. Rather than take pride in their knowledge and skill, they were merely expected to work their machines and do their detailed task. This was Victorian civilisation and Morris spent his life trying to undo it.

An unpredictable worker was a dangerous element, a human obstacle to producing the perfect item for sale in the perfect market. So the market keeper alone should be responsible for producing goods and putting them up for sale. These goods were primarily for profit; use came second, where it came anywhere at all. Workers were reduced to human material labouring alongside raw material. Intuition and subjective judgement was eliminated from production. All the time and space hitherto allocated to the worker to enjoy a childhood, or his family, or his community, or to learn, was now considered better spent making goods for sale. All were drawn into the vortex of commercialism. Even Nature itself was uncertain and had to come second to making profit. Capital, once generated internally, was provided by financiers. Externalising capital, or depersonalising it, went hand in hand with dehumanising the worker and reducing him to a machine part. To Morris this could never mean more than an engagement to meaningless toil.

In its place he advocated 'Useful Work'. He stressed the need for physical pleasure from work to give pleasure to both mind and body and for it to be performed without compulsion, free from a mind-numbing routine. Morris saw a need to bring the skills of both brain and hand to the work, so that theory and practice could unite and be enriched by the acquisition of extensive learning and increased dexterity. He believed in learning by doing and established mechanisms for passing on 'deep knowledge' through and across generations. He showed the impossibility, let alone the futility, of separating the artistic elements of production from the functional ones. He believed that everyone could acquire a range of crafts and that they should seek out work best suited to their talents, rather than let work define them. All were artists. Art was but work done well.

Those entrenched in commercialism resented their workers taking an interest in production, seeing their involvement as disruptive. Morris believed that the production of quality goods being exchanged for other high quality goods, directly between producers, required the complete involvement of workers from all stages of the production process. Designers should be able to weave, print and make things, with no separation between the concept and the finished article. Everyone should master not just a small part of the job, but the whole process and would also be expected to perform that greatest and least predictable function in production – experimentation. They would first need to conceive, then apply themselves to the process before giving thought to the materials – their mass, shape and form. And then, and only then, conjure up the tools to do the job. To carry this out the worker would need space and time, and these were resources that capitalism would never supply.

In the 1970s there was constant conflict between workers and employers in car plants over seemingly tiny issues such as allowing thirty seconds at the end of a shift for a worker to wash himself, or a ten-minute tea break. These were but small oases of humanity, where a worker could briefly reconnect with himself before rejoining the dehumanised desert of production. Only those who worked in such places could comprehend how important these glimpses of a different world were. The car plants of the 1970s have given way to the call centres of the 2000s, these being the worst example of a disease that afflicts most of our places of work.

Morris showed that only by actively enlisting the natural inquisitiveness, intuition and creative energy of workers could production be made real. Otherwise all that was produced was dross. He asserted that people had to think deeply about the power of the machines and the kind of production processes they had allowed to grow up. He warned against seeing things through the eyes of a 'consumer', which was forever to play in to the hands of capitalism. For it is capitalism that on the one hand makes throwaway products whilst at the same time preparing to appropriate the natural resources of others. The problem was not with consumption but with production and then the interrelationship of the two. Morris made no predictions and certainly was not a person to lay down schemes as to how others should live. He only asked that they think and act, rather than just drift aimlessly and let things happen. "What should guide these workers?" Morris answered "Nature and History." But life will only change when the majority of people want it to.

To all those who complain today about work stress, overwork, underwork, lack of work, inferior quality, poor management, little power in the workplace or absence of consultation, I would say "Don't read Morris. You'll find him challenging and unsettling." Of course it is possible to read his work and still remain supine, feeling powerless to make any changes. To people who feel like this, Morris wrote, "It is for him that is lonely or in prison to dream of fellowship, but for him that is of a fellowship, to do and not to dream."

Morris was a visionary at a time when industrial development was profound and thoroughgoing, when capitalism was rapacious and intruded into every aspect of the nation's life. Morris first saw its impact in architecture and the arts and concluded that where the so-called 'civilisation' conflicted with community, fellowship at work, or craft and skill, civilisation would have to move over. This made him very unpopular in some quarters but an icon to millions more. He remains one, today.

Morris saw the intrusion of production solely for profit and sought to change the ways that it impacted on people by crowding their space, burdening their lives, distorting their sense of time, self worth and community culture. He reasoned that not everything that was new was good or what was old, so bad. What was so special, he asked, about being able to travel more swiftly between a and b, if one missed seeing everything on the journey? Or how could art be of any value if it was restricted to a narrow circle cut off from reality, where it had once been the preserve and social duty of every worker?

What was it that enabled Morris to look so differently at the Industrial Revolution? He had a unique knowledge of the England of the Middle Ages. This allowed him to reflect upon how different things had been before the commonweal and the fellowship of production and community had been subverted by land enclosure, forced emigration and the shift from cottage industry to 'satanic mills.' He was horrified to see a man stripped of his individuality to become a mere appendage to a machine. Visits to Iceland gave him glimpses of a communal pre-industrial nation still existing in the modern age.

In studying the Renaissance, he found a model that demonstrated that man was a natural polymath, whom capitalism sought to reduce to a mere cog in it's machine. He also noted, with concern, that work, once performed with pride and skill, was now endured rather than enjoyed. He was aware that year on year, the numbers, concentration and consciousness of workers was growing and sought to give expression to the resurgent power of Labour.

Morris's aim was not to do away with industrialism, but to see it develop in an alternative form and direction. His socialism came only minimally from the idea of equality – he used the concept quite differently from the way we would today – nor was he primarily concerned with the downtrodden people who laboured under terrible conditions in the first half of the Nineteenth century. This was a concern to a broad range of social reformers. His main concern, and this separated him out, was with the content of work itself. Social advance beyond capitalism would come as a result of workers using firstly their education and intelligence, then their collective power. The power of the worker derived from his skill, and his ability to cooperate with colleagues using similar or related skills. These were the workforces who built the biggest cathedrals of their day, as well as castles, harbours, roads and universities. All were commissioned by Kings or Queens, but were remembered 500 years on, for the artistry and skill of the builder. These were the workers who constantly strived to maintain dignity and a sense of community in their search for a better way of life.

To fully employ their skills, which provided self-confidence and an arena for the kind of experimentation that drove 'real' civilisations forward, the worker, who Morris saw as "the real organic part of society" needed:

- Time
- Space
- A sense of history, craft combination and purpose
- An understanding of nature
- Education
- Culture
- No fear of using initiative or expressing creativity
- A love of freedom
- Freedom from undue pressure and compulsion.

In fact all those things that the wasteful hierarchies of capitalism could not tolerate.

The core of the problem with capitalism was the division of labour and Morris was neither the first nor the only one to see this. This effectively took a highly skilled craftsman accustomed to working through entire processes at his own pace and in his own way and reduced him to powerlessness in the production process. He could work as long as he could hire out his labouring power to an owner of capital, but his contribution to the end product was reduced to a minor bit part, controlled by the overseers in the factories. Morris sought a way to remedy this and was convinced, as were many other social commentators of the time, that there could be a more satisfactory solution.

The division of labour lay at the root of the enormous rise in productivity that was the Industrial Revolution. In opposing it, Morris had to come up with something that was different yet at least as productive. He concluded that even though there were alternatives that maintained productivity, a society no longer working under compulsion might decide to produce the same at a slower pace, or less at a faster one, or something completely different. He knew that under the profit system, the producers had little influence over what was produced, when, where, how and at what pace. Take away the profit motive and they might just decide to surprise everyone.

The issues he examined and the challenges he threw out continue to be fought over in nearly every workplace in Britain today. Work is the big issue of the last two hundred years. Morris was right in that. Many people work too hard and for too long, others do too little and some do no work at all. How many respect, let alone are proud of what they do? Much work today is soulless and we simply go through the motions. Where hawkers once sold matchboxes door-to-door, today, we sell advertising, insurance and timeshare over the phone and on the web. We are spammed out of our heads and waste precious minutes wading through piles of junk mail or junk phone calls we neither want nor need.

The problems that occur at work influence both our local community and the nation as a whole – all too often adversely. It is still the case, as Morris contended, that many of the good things that occur in life do so as a result of collective effort in the face of those who employ labour and who do so little to let skill and ingenuity, creativity and innovation, shine through. For as long as the capitalism exists, that Morris described as setting worker against worker and workers against themselves, those seeking change and progress in the world, do so with one hand tied behind their backs.

It is possible to become resigned to this, but far better to address the mess we meet in our working lives. Morris would never be content to just moan as many do today for he had a fearsome temper to boot. His search for a path beyond the division of labour sets him apart and makes him still relevant today. He set about developing a concept of 'Useful Work' that he counterpoised to useless toil. 'Useful Work' gave an opportunity to dissociate from the division of labour, using new ways, but with echoes of a distant past when craftsmen ruled industrial life. It aimed to bring together mental and manual labour, hand skills and machine work, time for rest, time for practice and space for self awareness and experimentation. There would be time to labour and to build a family and a community in both town and countryside. All these would raise work into art. His vision was to turn the 'satanic mills' into 'palaces of industry' and urban spaces into garden cities. He envisaged houses fit to be called homes: simple yet beautiful in the way they reflected the relationship between history and nature.

Through a notion of 'thinking hands' he attempted to strike an organic balance between 'thinking' and 'doing' based on labour free from compulsion. 'Thinking hands' aimed to make all who work masters of crafts rather than masters of people. Each worker would be expected to try to master at least three crafts. The emphasis would be on understanding complete processes rather than one stage or how to work a specific piece of machinery. The space created would allow art back into workers' lives, for art was simply work done well, resulting in products to be proud of.

Today, we have to try to achieve some of this 'multi-skilling' in order to remain employable, yet the compulsion to labour remains and the pressures of work are having a direct impact on workers' health, family life and the wellbeing of the community. British workers work really long hours – far too long to achieve quality – yet productivity stagnates. There is a message for us in there somewhere. Morris would have had a field day with butter mountains, wine lakes, call centres, shoddy goods dumped on inner cities and developing countries, the abandoning of apprenticeships, production quotas and trade restrictions, subsidies in farming alongside high food prices, the destruction of our fish stocks, paying out for predatory wars abroad whilst failing to adequately fund rail, health or education at home, and the abdication from industrial strategy. However, he is not here to speak for himself and given his temper it is probably just as well.

Morris's legacy lies, not in having provided us with a blueprint of the best way to live, but by understanding that all workers have the intelligence and independence to take control of their lives, if they so wish. As the quotation at the front of this book illustrates, once the mind of the majority was made up, Morris believed 'the job would be done'. Then, he reckoned, "Socialism would melt into society."

Why is Morris still relevant today? There is a sense in which we have become mesmerised by technology. Essential that it is, we must always remember two things. First, that machinery only mimics things that humans have always done: push; pull; mould; hammer; rotate; wind; fuse; break up; fold; twist; weave or stitch. Second, that they are supposed to improve our lives not replace them. We live in a time when one part of the world is grappling with such challenges whilst others cannot provide enough water and food to get them through a summer or a winter. Machines may be exciting, and interesting, and raise productivity, but let's keep a sense of perspective. We would be closer to the 'problems' if we were to focus, not on the tools of production, but the social relations of production. What is it we make and why? The challenge to us all remains on the table.

In the nineteenth century the concern, the great sacrifice of those who built the unions, acted to end slavery in plantations abroad and factories at home, and made elementary education compulsory, was with the dignity of labour. But with the dignity of labour secured what of the creativity, the inner substance of labour? Why do we go to work? What do we produce and why? Morris felt that production workers, today we could say most workers, were being dealt automation when they were mature enough together to handle autonomy. Making real decisions about real production of goods that were of use. Even the unions believed that what was necessary was to emphasise the production of more and then argue about how it was spread round. As if more alone, would lead to equality and respect. Maybe we had what was once called a national cake and it remained only to make a bigger one and cut the slices up differently. Well this is the hard world of capitalism and that approach has not worked.

In the later Middle Ages capitalism emerged as a new way of organising the means of existence, within feudalism. It became the material reality. Political revolution ensued. It may well be that, in the twenty-first century we can set about establishing a new way of organising the means of existence as a new material reality. Morris thought such new ways: co-operatives; state and municipal owned units of production and services; and combinations of producers, would constitute 'tokens of hope'. They would act as an example and beacon of higher, better ways of doing things. But for any or each of these to reach full maturity, political change – fundamental and radically separated from what had gone before – would have to occur.

Today, we produce so much more than we can handle and the inequality between classes continues to grow. For too long we have contented ourselves with the contradictions of distribution and consumption. Now is the time to grapple with the contradictions of production. It is both possible and necessary to go beyond the quantity and look at the quality. William Morris would not rest at condemning *useless toil*. The challenge of replacing this with useful work, based on 'Thinking hands' was his life work. It remains a challenge today.

Timeline 1701-1901

Taking in selected developments in science and the arts, industry and technology, society and the life of William Morris

---

1701-50

1701 Jethro Tull uses mechanical seed sower

1702 Halley produces a world navigation chart

1709 Abraham Darby uses coke in place of charcoal to smelt iron ore

1712 Thomas Newcomen builds first commercial steam engine with Thomas Savery who invented the steam pump in 'miners friend'

1714 Gabriel Daniel Fahrenheit invents mercury thermometer

1721 Lady Mary Wortley Montagu introduces smallpox inoculation

1733 John Kay introduces the Flying Shuttle

1740 Transfer printing of pots begins to replace hand printing

1745 Benjamin Huntsman develops crucible steel

1751-1780

1756 John Smeaton rediscovered hydraulic cement

1758 First threshing machine used

1759 British Museum opens

1760 Wedgwood opens pottery works

1761 Bridgewater canal built by James Brindley

1762 John Harrison's No. 4 Chronometer wins longitude prize

1765 Spinning Jenny automates weaving of cloth, James Hargreaves

1769 Water powered frame automates weft, Richard Arkwright

1774 John Wilkinson produces a boring mill for cannon later used for cylinders for steam engines

1774 Joseph Priestley isolates oxygen

1775 James Watt introduces his first steam engine

1776 *Wealth of Nations* published, Adam Smith

1776 American War of Independence – colonies declare independence

1777 Grand Trunk Canal, connects Trent and Mersey with main ports including Hull and Bristol

1778 Jean-Jacques Rousseau and Voltaire die

1779 First steam-powered mill

1779 Samuel Crompton's Spinning Mule combines Hargreaves' and Arkwright's machines to automate weaving

1781-1799

1786 Albion Cotton Mill uses a Watt steam engine

1787 Edmund Cartwright builds a power loom

1789 Thames and Bristol Channel linked by canal

1789 Bastille falls and French Revolution begins

1789 The metre defined by the French Academy of Sciences

1791-2 *Rights of Man* published, Tom Paine

1792 First home lit with coal gas

1792 *Vindication of the Rights of Women* published, Mary Wollstonecraft

1793 *Justice* published, William Godwin

1795 John Loudon McAdam revolutionises road-building

1796 First iron-framed factory built (cast-iron)

1796 Edward Jenner develops smallpox vaccination

1796 Alois Senefelder develops lithographic process in printing

1798 *Essay on Population* published, Thomas Malthus

1799 Humphrey Davy discovers first anaesthetic

1799 Nickolas Robert develops paper-making machine

1800-1834

1800 Robert Trevithick demonstrates his steam locomotive

1801 Union of Great Britain and Ireland

1801 First Census reveals women outnumber men

1802 First Factory Act – "The Factory Health and Morals Act" of 1802 applied principally to apprentices

1803 M. Brunel and Maudsley produce woodworking machines to make pulley blocks

1803 Horsedrawn public railway started in South London

1803 Start of the Caledonian Ship canal cutting across Scotland

1804 Richard Trevithick produces first high pressure steam locomotive

1804 *Jerusalem* published, William Blake

1803 Stanhope and Walker produce a printing press made of iron

1805 Battle of Trafalgar

1805 London Docks opened

1811 Luddite uprisings begin in the Midlands

1813 Waverley published *Walter Scott*

1813 Westminster streets lit by gas

1813 *Pride & Prejudice*, Jane Austen

1813 New Lanark industrial community formed by Robert Owen

1815 Battle of Waterloo

1815 Corn Laws passed

1817 *Principles of Political Economy* published, David Ricardo

1819 Massacre of corn law protesters in Manchester Peterloo

1819 Second Factory Act passed

1819 *Ivanhoe* published Walter Scott

1819 Walt Whitman born

1819 John Ruskin born

1820 *Prometheus Unbound* published Percy Byshe Shelley

1821 Michael Faraday demonstrates electro-magnetism, principle of the electric motor

1821 John Keats dies

1822 Shelley dies

1823 London Mechanics Institute founded

1823 John Stuart Mill jailed for distributing pamphlets on birth control

1823 Fiftieth English town lit by gas

1824 Byron dies

1824 Macintosh opens first factory to produce rubberised raincoats

1825 Stockton – Darlington railway link opened

1825-1843 M Brunel builds first subaqueous tunnel under the Thames

1827 Tongue and groove making machine is manufactured

1829 Catholic Emancipation Act restores civil liberties to Catholics

1829 Louis Braille produces a reading method for the blind

1829 George Stephenson launches the Rocket steam locomotive

1829 Cammel Laird begins building iron ships at Birkenhead

1830 Richard Roberts perfects a self-acting spinning mill

1830 Liverpool-Manchester railway opens

1831 Faraday discovers electro magnetic current

1831 British Association for Advancement of Science is formed

1831 Hobhouse's Factory Act passed – setting age limit for night work

1832 First Reform Bill passed

1833 Slavery abolished throughout the British Empire

1833 Factory Act passed to part protect female and juvenile labour

1833 First education grant – first government involvement in education

1834 Charles Babbage designs an analytical engine, forerunner of the computer

1834 William Morris born at Elm House, Clay Hill, Walthamstow

1834 Trial of the Tolpuddle Martyrs

1834 Poor Law Amendment Act – system of workhouses established

1835-50

1835 William Henry Fox Talbot produces his first photographs

1835 Municipal Corporations Act opens up local government

1836 Chartism begins to grow

1836 Marriage Act – civil wedding ceremonies permitted

1836 Tithe Commutation Act ended payment of tithes to the church

1836 Stamp Duty reduced resulting in growth of printed popular journals

1836 *Pickwick Papers* published, Charles Dickens

1836 Tolpuddle Martyr's sentences quashed

1837 Samuel Morse develops the telegraph and Morse code

1837 William IV dies and Victoria ascends throne

1837 Registration Act introduced – now possible to prove age and secure protection under the law

1837 *French Revolution* published. Thomas Carlyle

1837 Government School of Design (later Royal College of Art) established

1839 Jamaica Act finally secures the ending of slavery and freedom for apprentices in the colonies

1839 Building begins on first ocean going iron screw-driven ship, the Great Britain

1839 James Nasmyth designs a steam hammer to work on axles for Brunel's *Great Britain*

1839 Clydeside build more iron ships than wooden

1839 A tea clipper sails Shanghai to London in 90 days

1840 Sir Rowland Hill's Penny Post started

1840 Grammar Schools Act passed

1840 Corrugated iron roof invented

1841 *Punch* begins publication

1841 Workers rebuilding Houses of Parliament go on strike

1841 Joseph Whitworth establishes standardised sizes for screw threads

1841 Miners' Association of Great Britain and Ireland formed

1842 Literary Copyright Act passed

1842 Railway Act – protecting travellers using rail

1842 Mines Act – prevented the employment underground of women and boys under 10 years old

1843 Typewriter invented

1843 Launch of first iron-built ocean-going steamship with screw propeller for propulsion, the Great Britain

1843 *Modern Painters* (1) published, Ruskin

1843 William Wordsworth appointed Poet Laureate

1844 Bank Charter Act – ties issuing of money to gold reserves

1844 Companies Act passed to try to control speculation and forcing companies to register

1844 Miners' Association strike defeated

1845 Potato famine hits Europe, starvation in Ireland

1845 Corn Laws repealed – these had artificially raised the price of grain

1845 Artist and designer Walter Crane born

1845 Robert Owen forms National Association of United Trades for the Protection of Labour

1846 First telegraph cable laid under Channel

1846 Elias Howe invents sewing machine

1846 Gauges Act made the standard gauge compulsory for all new railways

1847 'Ten Hours' Factory Act passed – an unsuccessful attempt to restrict hours of male and female working aged 13-18

1847 Chloroform first used in child-birth

1847 Morris's father dies

1847 Rivet hole punching machine developed by Roberts for use in construction of the Menai Bridge

1847 Architectural Association founded in London

1848 Revolutions across Europe

1848 Last Chartist rally on Kennington Common

1848 Queens College for higher-education of women opened

1848 First Public Health Act passed

1848 The Pre-Raphaelite Brotherhood is formed

1848 *Communist Manifesto* published – translated into English by Helen MacFarlane and serialised in the *Red Republican*

1849 Navigation Act repealed – goods could henceforth be imported to Britain in foreign owned ships

1849 Epidemic of cholera in London (and again in 1854)

1850 Isaac Singer produces commercial sewing machine

1850 Coal Mines Inspection Act – sought greater safety in coal mining – coal owners in the Lords opposed all attempts to regulate conditions

1850 Alfred Lord Tennyson appointed Poet Laureate

1851-1875

1851 Great exhibition at Crystal Palace

1851 *The Stones of Venice* begun by Ruskin

1851 Petition on women's suffrage presented to parliament

1851 Census shows for first time, more people living in towns than countryside in England

1852 Samuel Fox builds first umbrella with a steel frame

1853 Morris is at Exeter College, Oxford (until 1855). The Brotherhood is formed

1853 Mass production of watches begins

1854 Crimean War begins

1854 Henry Bessemer invents steel converter

1854 *Hard Times* published, Charles Dickens

1854 Morris visits Belgium and France with his sister Henrietta

1855 Abolition of stamp duties on newspapers – the *Daily Telegraph* was produced priced 1d

1855 *North and South* published, Elizabeth Gaskell

1855 Morris wrote his first poem

1856 Bessemer converter allows mass production of steel

1856 Crimean War ends

1856 William Henry Perkin produces aniline dyes allowing for mass produced colour-dyed cotton

1856 Morris articled to GE Street, architects

1856 At year end, Morris abandons architecture for painting

1857 Matrimonial Causes Act passed allowing divorce through the law courts

1857 South Kensington museum opens

1858 Transatlantic cable laid

1858 Jewish Disabilities Act established allowing Jews to be MPs

1858 Property qualifications for members of parliament abolished

1858 Cathode rays discovered

1858 *Defence of Guenevere* published, William Morris

1859 *The Origin of Species* published, Charles Darwin

1859 Molestation of Workmen Act passed allowing some moderated forms of picketing

1859 *Self-Help* published, Samuel Smiles

1859 William R. Lethaby, architect and designer, born

1859 Morris marries Jane Burden

1859 Philip Webb builds 'Red House' for Morris leading to formation of The Firm

1859 Titus Salt builds Saltaire, a model Victorian industrial village

1860 Food and Drugs Act passed to prevent adulteration of food

1860 Mines Regulation and Inspection Act banned underground mine work to the under 12s

1860 *Unto This Last* published, Ruskin

1860 Work begins on an underground rail system for London

1861 *Utilitarianism* published, John Stuart Mill

1861 Universal milling machine invented

1861 Machine gun first produced

1861 American Civil War begins

1861 Excise duty on paper abolished, leading to growth of publishing

1861 *Great Expectations* published, Charles Dickens

1861 Morris, Marshall, Faulkner & Co. founded

1861 Jenny Morris born

1862 May Morris born

1862 The Firm exhibits at London International Exhibition of Art and Industry

1862 Jean Bertraud-Leon Foucault measures speed of light

1863 Rotation press allows continuous printing

1864 Clifton suspension bridge built by Isambard Kingdom Brunel

1864 Workers' First International founded in London

1865 Use of lead in manufacture of ceramic glazes prohibited

1866 Sanitary Act forced local government to take responsibility for sewers, water and street-cleaning and tackled overcrowding in homes

1866 The Firm decorate the armoury and tapestry room at St James's Palace

1867 *Capital* published by Karl Marx

1867 Alfred Nobel produces dynamite the first stable high explosive

1867 Second Reform Bill introduced by Disraeli extended franchise to skilled workers

1867 Master and Servant Act partly removed threat of criminal proceedings against trade unionists

1867 Morris publishes *The Life and Death of Jason*

1867 The Firm decorate the green Dining Room at the V&A museum

1868 Morris publishes *The Earthly Paradise*

1868 In league with Eirikr Magnusson Morris begins work on the Icelandic Sagas

1868 First congress of the TUC

1869 Suez Canal opened

1869 *The Subjection of Women* published, John Stuart Mill

1870 Right to vote in municipal elections extended to single women ratepayers

1870 The lathe is automated

1870 Education Act provides for women to serve on elected school boards

1870 Morris begins work on illuminated manuscripts

1870 School reform leading to education for all

1871 *Descent of Man* published, Charles Darwin

1871 North East engineers strike for the nine-hour day

1871 Germany unified

1871 University Tests Act opened Universities to all regardless of religion

1871 Civil service reform allowed access to employment based on exam rather than 'connections' – except in foreign office

1871 Trade Union Act legalised trade unions and allowed them to hold funds and conduct strikes

1871 Criminal Law Amendment Act all but outlawed strike action

1871 *Fors Clavigera* is published, John Ruskin

1871 Morris purchases Kelmscott Manor, Oxfordshire

1871 Morris visits Iceland for first time

1872 Licensing Act allowed magistrates to license public houses

1872 Ballot Act made voting secret

1873 Judicature Act brought together legal apparatus of the country under one High Court of Justice

1873 Morris visits Italy and Iceland

1874 Factory Act limiting number of hours worked in a day to ten and banned full time employment to those under 14

1875 Artisans Dwelling Act allowed local authorities to clear out slums

1875 Conspiracy and Protection of Property Act legalised certain types of picketing again and remove conspiracy threat against unions

1875 Employers and Workmen Act put workers and employers on equal legal footing in cases of breach of contract – henceforth to be dealt with in civil law

1875 Morris takes up dyeing and carpet weaving

1875 The Firm is dissolved

1876-1884

1876 Alexander Graham Bell produces the telephone

1876 School attendance made compulsory – some state support with education fees

1876 Merchant Shipping Act – the Plimsoll line (maximum loading line) drawn up to help sailors forced on to ships not seaworthy

1876 Morris appointed Examiner at the School of Art, South Kensington

1876 Morris becomes treasurer of the Eastern Question Association

1877 Morris founds Society for the Protection of Ancient Buildings

1877 Morris gives his first public lecture on *'The Decorative Arts'*

1877 Morris opens a showroom in Oxford Street

1878 Factories and Workshops Act all factories with 50 or more workers to be subject to government inspection

1878 Morris moves to Kelmscott House, Hammersmith

1878 Universal Postal Union founded by 22 countries

1878 London's main drainage system complete

1879 Thomas Edison perfects the first incandescent electric lamp

1879 Morris becomes Treasurer of National Liberal League

1880 Morris & Company decorate the Throne Room at St James's Palace

1880-89 Work begins on Panama Canal

1881 Morris and Company move to Merton Abbey Works, Surrey

1881 Morris takes up high-warp tapestry weaving

1882 First electric flat iron produced

1882 Robert Koch isolates tuberculosis

1882 Married Women's Property Act

1882 Morris works for the Iceland Famine Relief Committee

1882 Morris publishes *Hope and Fears for Art*

1882 Morris gives evidence before the Royal Commission on Technical Instruction

1883 Hiram S. Maxim invents the world's first automatic machine gun

1883 Fabian Society formed

1883 Morris becomes honorary fellow of Exeter College, Oxford

1883 Morris joins the Democratic Federation soon known as Social Democratic Federation

1883 Morris reads Marx's *Capital* in French, Marx dies in March

1884 Koch isolates cholera

1884 Third Reform Act extends vote to most adult males

1884 Art Workers Guild formed

1884 Morris leaves the SDF to become leader of the Socialist League

1885-1901

1885 Karl Benz invents first vehicle to run on internal combustion engine

1885 Redistribution Act The Commons made more representative especially of the cities

1885 Morris edits the Socialist League newspaper, *The Commonweal*

1885 Morris publishes *Pilgrims of Hope*

1885 Morris arrested in court disturbance following free speech meeting

1885 International Standard Time established

1886 Morris publishes A *Dream of John Ball*

1887 Morris acts as pall bearer at funeral of Alfred Linnell who died during the riots of the unemployed

1887 Foundation of the Arts and Crafts Exhibition Society

1888 Ball point pen patented

1888 Local Government Act – elected councils replace government boards – London County Council established

1888 Morris publishes *Signs of Change*

1888 Morris is delegate to an international socialist congress in Paris

1888 *A Dream of John Ball* is produced in book form

1888 Hertz demonstrates existence of radio waves

1888 Scottish Labour Party formed

1888 Match Girls form a union and strike

1889 Lumiere brothers develop the Cinematographe

1889 Dockers Strike

1889 Eiffel Tower completed

1889 Labour and Socialist (second) International formed

1889 Miners' Federation of Great Britain is formed

1890 Morris removed as editor of *The Commonweal* and resigns from Socialist League

1890 Morris publishes *News From Nowhere* in instalments

1890 Morris speaks at the first Great May Day demonstration (which also includes Lenin speaking from a nearby platform)

1890 Hammersmith Socialist Society formed

1890 Firth of Forth bridge completed

1891 Free Education Act made all elementary education free

1891 Kelmscott Press begins printing and publishing

1891 Morris is taken ill

1891 Crystal Palace Electrical Exhibition

1892 Morris is elected Master of the Art Workers' Guild

1892 Morris writes preface to Kelmscott edition of Ruskin's *The Nature of Gothic*

1892 Morris rejects the chance to become Poet Laureate

1892 Artificial silk made from wood pulp

1893 Independent Labour Party (ILP) formed

1893 Morris and Ernest Belfort Bax write *Socialism: Its Growth and Outcome*

1893 Morris helped to draft the *Manifesto of English Socialists*

1894 Morris publishes the *Wood Beyond the World*

1894 Morris is reconciled with the SDF but does not rejoin

1895 William Roentgen discovers X-rays

1895 Morris publishes his translation of *Beowulf*

1896 Marconi patents a wireless telegraph

1896 Morris publishes *The Well at the World's End* and *The Sundering Flood*

1896 Morris speaks at his last public meeting at the Society for Checking Abuses of Public Advertising

1896 The Kelmscott edition of *Chaucer* is published

1896 William Morris dies 3 October and is buried at Kelmscott

1896 Central School of Arts and Crafts formed, Lethaby and George Frampton as joint principals

1897 Workmen's Compensation Act – compensation for injury or loss of life at work to be paid by employers

1898 *Tomorrow: A Peaceful Path to Real Reform* reprinted in 1902 as *Garden Cities of Tomorrow*, written by Ebenezer Howard

1899 Aspirin is developed and introduced

1900 Planck develops quantum theory

1900 John Ruskin dies

1900 Labour Party is formed

1900 Oscar Wilde dies

1901 Queen Victoria dies

'Si Je Puis'
'If I Can' was the personal motto of William Morris

William Morris – an extraordinary, ordinary man

William Morris was an extraordinary man making his mark on an extraordinary century. Yet in so many ways his life was a quest for the simple, the ordinary and the 'truth'. Even now, more than one hundred years after his death, his work is known and admired by millions throughout the world, no small achievement in a century that gave us Darwin's *Origin of the Species*, John Stuart Mill's *Utilitarianism*, Marx's *Capital* and countless works of art, industry and science alongside feats of engineering that set the world alight.

Three developments occurred during Morris's lifetime that would lead to more change than had been experienced in the previous thousand years. Firstly, animal and mineral gave way to man-made resources. Then with the coming of the steam engine, power became independent of and separated from the physical limitations of the human form. Lastly, these machines brought a dull certainty, dependability and endless means of production. The result was that a new man emerged, a new class, for whom the joy that could be gained through work was but folklore or a distant memory.

Morris had to grapple with these changes, analyse them and draw an understanding from them that he could share with others. While it took his whole life to refine that understanding, he grasped its essence very quickly, before most of his contemporaries were out of the starting blocks. "A man" he wrote, "in his short lifetime can see but a little way ahead, and even in mine, wonderful and unexpected things have come to pass. I must needs say that therein lies my hope rather than in all I see going on round about us." He perceived change as a sign of vitality. In his first public lecture *The Decorative Arts* (1877) he said, "Whatever I may blame or whatever I may praise, I neither, when I think of what history has been, am inclined to lament the past, to despise the present or despair of the future; that I believe all the change and stir about us is a sign of the world's life." But who would benefit from this change? And who would not?

Morris was amongst those who saw that Labour was not a preparation for living, but the essence of life itself. All workers were concerned about

33

their product and its quality. Everything made by man, through labour, has a form. This can be either beautiful or ugly, and may or may not conform organically to the conditions that brought it about. To Morris, there could be no such thing as an absence of design, as all things are made for a reason or function. There could only be good or bad design. In allowing a workman to apply intelligence and enthusiasm to what he was making he was simply being allowed to make with his hands what was in his mind and soul. Only then could labour be sanctified. All else, he reasoned, was slavery. This is true for all workers. No one can remain immune to the product of his or her labour, then or now. Did not Einstein say that if he had known the impact of the atom bomb he would have become a watchmaker? And Mikhail Kalashnikov said recently that he would have preferred to make something other than a semi-automatic assault rifle – "something of use to farmers, for example a lawn mower."

William Morris with life-long friend and companion Edward Burne-Jones. Burne-Jones, an influential painter met Morris at Oxford, joined his company and designed figures for the stained glass and tapestries. He illustrated for the Kelmscott press and followed Morris into the Socialist League.

Throughout his life Morris conducted an intense struggle against 'civilisation'. Of course this term meant something quite different from the way we use it today. In Morris's time it was a term of cultural and political superiority and economic domination not just by the western 'civilisers' of 'darkest Africa' but of the working classes of 'darkest England' too. "… I had thought" Morris wrote, "that civilisation meant the attainment of peace and order and freedom, of goodwill between man and man, of the love of truth and hatred of injustice … that was what I thought it meant, not more stuffed chairs and more carpets and gas, and more dainty meat and drink – and therewithal more and sharper differences between class and class … "

One constant, throughout Morris's life, was the struggle against this civilisation. He fought it in different ways at different phases of his life and across different disciplines; in design, in politics, in culture. In this struggle he was far from alone. The influential Professor Huxley, who could hardly be considered a socialist, wrote in 1886, that he would "rather be born a savage in a Fijian Island than be born to a London slum."

Morris thought that an average adult could easily learn and master three or more crafts in a lifetime. Yet he is acknowledged as a master in a far greater number than this. Much was exceptional about him. He was one of the most accomplished writers in a century when Britain dominated the literature of the industrialising world. He was a poet, writer of prose and journalist. As a poet he ranked amongst the very best, refusing an offer to become Poet Laureate at the death of Tennyson, though becoming Professor of Poetry at Oxford University. According to Oscar Wilde, "To Morris, we owe poetry whose perfect precision and clearness of word and vision has not been excelled in the literature of our century." As a storyteller he has been compared to Walter Scott and Homer. He gave inspiration to Holst, Shaw, Yeats and Wilde. Even JR Tolkien claimed he could not have written *Lord of the Rings* without the overwhelming influence of Morris. To this day he is considered the best English-speaking interpreter and translator of the Icelandic sagas – a very influential body of literature in Victorian England.

Morris is a dominant figure in the creative style of the decorative arts in the United Kingdom, continental Europe and parts of America. His influence is acknowledged in the work of Mackintosh, Gaudi and the prairie style of Frank Lloyd Wright. He was a dominant figure in the Arts and Crafts Movement and in no small measure influenced those who went on to make Britain a centre of the Modern Movement. In Europe, Morris was acknowledged by Van Der Velde and Walter Gropius, as an inspiration for the Bauhaus. He was an accomplished designer and manufacturer and his knowledge of the historical evolution of manufacturing processes was, and perhaps remains, unrivalled. Morris as a scholar and authority on such historical processes was a key figure advising the Victoria and Albert Museum on the purchase of a wide range of artefacts. Of

Morris as a master craftsman, AA Purcell, the chairman of the Trades Union Congress in 1924, who had actually worked with him at Merton Abbey, thought "there was none better."

If that was not enough he went on to lead his own revolutionary political party and establish the Society for Protection of Ancient Buildings (SPAB) a forerunner of the English Heritage movement and an outpost of concern for the environment in an era of smokestack and decay. It is rare for one individual character to so influence his times whilst laying down a legacy that continues to influence long into the future. Today, if anything his popularity is greater than ever.

For a centenary exhibition in 1996, the Special Collections Library at the University of Michigan wrote of Morris, "rarely do we find someone in our midst who excels in many fields, whose seemingly unending vigour reflects vision, intellect, learning, skill and craft". It listed the fields where his talent met these standards as: painter, poet; translator; designer; decorator; craftsman; manufacturer; businessman; printer; socialist and reformer. To these we can add husband, father and friend. Most of his family contributed in some way or other to his work. May, his youngest daughter was in charge of the embroidery section of the Firm, shared her father's political commitment and, in later years, edited his Collected Works. But Morris was essentially a renaissance figure in an era that measured contribution in pounds, shillings and pence.

One of Morris's best known and most controversial quotes is " have nothing in your house that you do not think beautiful". It was a comment less on the home and more on Victorian society. Morris's simplicity and quest for ordinariness marks him out – he was a designer who lived a life uncluttered by needless decoration and his observations on society are similarly uncluttered. Later in his life he wrote,'I decorate houses for people but the house that would please me would be some great room where one talked to one's friends in one corner, and ate in another, and slept in another, and worked in another.'

His was a life of contradictions: a political party man yet a non-politician who eschewed office, a critic of capitalism who owned factories and companies, a designer who developed a consciousness for workers whilst working exclusively for the rich, a man skilled at detail and decoration who himself lived in very simple and what we would today call minimalist habitat. And all the time a man who would probably have liked nothing better than to withdraw to his factory where he could study handicraft and in the evening write poetry. But it was always clear from early days that his life was going to be more eventful than that. There is an aspect to Morris of sheer doggedness whatever he turned his hand to. In 1872 for example, he began a translation of the Icelandic saga *Heinskringla*. It was not completed until 1895.

Above all else he was a deeply thoughtful man who valued knowledge, treasured an audience and gave his all to any cause in which life or circumstance pushed him to enlist. He was a visionary in reverse. Most utopians seek to take their audience out and away from themselves and their current predicaments; Morris used the utopian method to draw people back into their reality and to encourage them to change it. As a republican he took up the commission to design wallpaper for Queen Victoria's new house in Balmoral in Scotland but spurned approaches to become her Poet Laureate, as it would mean, at least technically, that he was accepted as part of her family. To him, these were commissions to design in which he retained a degree of sovereignty. Whereas, to write poetry would be to give the monarchy access to, and control over, his very soul. On a more personal note he once said to a friend, he would not contemplate, "sitting down in crimson plush breeches and white stockings to write birthday odes in honour of all the blooming little guelflings and Battenburgs that happen to come along."

William Morris's birth on 24 March 1834 at Elm House in Walthamstow, east London, set him up for a torturous relationship with the capital that would last a lifetime. At that time, and readers who currently live in the east of London may find this difficult to believe, Walthamstow was 'a quiet picturesque village' and a preserve of the well-to-do. It was situated just above the Lea Valley where he could look at London and watch it grow into an enormous metropolis, at the time the largest concentration of people in the industrialising world, with an unparalleled display of great wealth and poverty.

Morris was born into a wealthy family, the third of nine children and the oldest son of a father who made his money in one of the quick-killings of the early industrial revolution, the result of successful share dealing in copper mining in the south west of the country. His first home was Woodford Hall, a sizeable estate of some one hundred acres on the edge of Epping Forest. He was a very bright child captivated by all things medieval and chivalrous – by the age of nine he had read all of Sir Walter Scott's *Waverley* novels and would ride around Epping Forest which he came to know '"yard by yard", in a specially made suit of Medieval armour. Scott was, along with Shelley, Byron and Wordsworth, a critic of the excesses of early capitalism. At the age of twenty-one Morris was awarded an annual income of £900, a considerable sum for that time.

CAUTION.

WHEREAS it has been represented to us from several quarters, that mischievous and designing Persons have been for some time past, endeavouring to induce, and have induced, many Labourers in various Parishes in this County, to attend Meetings, and to enter into Illegal Societies or Unions, to which they bind themselves by unlawful oaths, administered secretly by Persons concealed, who artfully deceive the ignorant and unwary,—WE, the undersigned Justices think it our duty to give this Public Notice and Caution, that all Persons may know the danger they incur by entering into such Societies.

ANY PERSON who shall become a Member of such a Society, or take any Oath, or assent to any Test or Declaration not authorized by Law ---

Any Person who shall administer, or be present at, or consenting to the administering or taking any Unlawful Oath, or who shall cause such Oath to be administered, although not actually present at the time ---

Any Person who shall not reveal or discover any illegal Oath which may have been administered, although not actually present at the time ---

Any Person who shall not reveal or discover any illegal Oath which may have been administered, or any illegal Act done or to be done ---

Any Person who shall induce, or endeavour to persuade any other Person to become a Member of such Societies, WILL BECOME

Guilty of Felony,

and be liable to be

TRANSPORTED FOR SEVEN YEARS.

ANY PERSON who shall be compelled to take such an Oath, unless he shall declare the same within four days, together with the whole of what he shall know touching the same, will be liable to the same Penalty.

Any Person who shall directly or indirectly maintain correspondence or intercourse with such Society, will be deemed Guilty of an Unlawful Combination and Confederacy, and on Conviction before one Justice, on the oath of one Witness, be liable to a Penalty of TWENTY POUNDS, or to be committed to the Common Gaol or House of Correction, for THREE CALENDAR MONTHS; or if proceeded against by Indictment, may be CONVICTED OF FELONY, and be TRANSPORTED FOR SEVEN YEARS.

Any Person who shall knowingly permit any Meeting of any such Society to be held in any House, Building, or other Place, shall for the first offence be liable to the Penalty of FIVE POUNDS; and for every other offence committed after Conviction, be deemed Guilty of such Unlawful Combination and Confederacy, and on Conviction before one Justice, on the oath of one Witness, be liable to a Penalty of TWENTY POUNDS, or to Committment to the Common Gaol or House of Correction, FOR THREE CALENDAR MONTHS; or if proceeded against by Indictment may be

Convicted of Felony, and be Transported for SEVEN YEARS.

COUNTY OF DORSET.
DURHAM DIVISION.
February 20th, 1834.

JOHN BOND.
JOHN H. CALCRAFT.
JAMES C. FYLER.
GEORGE PICKARD, Junior.
NATHANIEL BOND.

C. Groves, Printer, Wareham

1834 – the year of Morris's birth. Local magistrates – most of whom were also local employers – issue a chilling threat to those seeking to form trades' unions. Shortly after, in Dorset, the six martyrs of Tolpuddle were arraigned.

CHARTIST DEMONSTRATION!!

"PEACE and ORDER" is our MOTTO!

TO THE WORKING MEN OF LONDON.

Fellow Men,—The Press having misrepresented and vilified us and our intentions, the Demonstration Committee therefore consider it to be their duty to state that the grievances of us (the Working Classes) are deep and our demands just. We and our families are pining in misery, want, and starvation! We demand a fair day's wages for a fair day's work! We are the slaves of capital—we demand protection to our labour. We are political serfs—we demand to be free. We therefore invite all well disposed to join in our peaceful procession on

MONDAY NEXT, April 10,

As it is for the good of all that we seek to remove the evils under which we groan.

The following are the places of Meeting of THE CHARTISTS, THE TRADES, THE IRISH CONFEDERATE & REPEAL BODIES:

East Division on Stepney Green at 8 o'clock; City and Finsbury Division on Clerkenwell Green at 9 o'clock; West Division in Russell Square at 9 o'clock; and the South Division in Peckham Fields at 9 o'clock, and proceed from thence to Kennington Common.

Signed on behalf of the Committee, JOHN ARNOTT, Sec.

Henry Hetherington, Printer, 5, Edward Street, Hampstead Road.

The mass appeal of Chartism. A call to join one of its largest demonstrations held in 1848. Note the link of a 'We are the slaves of capital' and ' we are political serfs.'
(Reproduced courtesy of the TUC unionhistory.info)

Through his 62 years, years that closely follow what has become known, rather by way of laziness or short hand, as the Age of Victoria, Morris was to experience change at a rate never previously thought possible. He was born in the same year as the trial and transportation of the Tolpuddle labourers arraigned for conspiring to form an illegal combination or trade union and when Chartism, and the agitation against the Corn Laws was gathering muster. He experienced the growth of the state and its intervention in industrial and political life from the Factory Acts progressively restricting child labour, to the Reform Act of 1867, that widened the franchise to the working class for the first time and the Secret Ballot Act of 1872. Morris died as the internal combustion engine was being applied to motorised transport and just a few years before man took to flight in an aeroplane.

He was educated, first at Marlborough College at the age of fourteen then at Exeter College, Oxford. Whilst there, he continued his quite extraordinary voyage of inquiry piecing together fragments of medieval literature, of political and ecclesiastical records, theological tracts and collections of legends, that allowed him to reconstruct a unique knowledge of the lives of ordinary people in the fourteenth and fifteenth centuries. Amongst the books he is recorded as reading during that time are: Gibbons *Decline and Fall of the Roman Empire* (six volumes), Milman's *History of Latin Christianity* (four volumes), Cobbett's *History of the Protestant Reformation* (two volumes), Holinshed's *Chronicles* (six volumes), Stowe's *Annales Of England*, Neale's *A History of the Holy Eastern Church* (five volumes), Sismondi's *A History of the Fall of the Roman Empire* (two volumes), Mallet's *Northern Antiquities*, Percy's *Reliques*, Thorpe's *Northern Mythologies* (three volumes), Carlyle's *French Revolution* (three volumes), Ruskin's *Stones of Venice* (three volumes), Commyne's *Memoirs*, Froissart's *Chronicles*, and Caxton's *Recuyell of the Historyes of Troy and Golden Legend*. In addition he studied Malory and established a lifelong interest in Chaucer reading *Troilus* and *The Canterbury Tales*.

Morris did much more than read history books and studied countless volumes which related the technique of crafts such as woodworking or weaving. In 1876 on a trip to Paris, he was delighted to have been able to purchase ancient books on dyeing techniques including Joseph Macquer's *Art de la Teinture en Soie*.

He immediately assumed a leading role amongst the student body at Oxford gathering to him characters such as Edward Burne-Jones and Dante Gabriel Rossetti. Morris roomed at 'Hell's Quad' which overlooked Fellow's garden and the Bodleian library. Burne Jones wrote to Cornell Price, "I have set my heart on our founding a Brotherhood. Learn Sir Galahad by heart. He is to be the patron of our Order." In 1848, these three formed a fraternity that they called, the Brotherhood. Here under the influence of Tennyson's Arthurian poems, Carlyle's *Past and Present*, and works of Ruskin, such as *Stones of Venice*, they sought to comprehend the fast changing industrial landscape and make-up of Britain. But they never tried to come to terms with it, preferring instead, to dream of war 'against the hated civilisation'. They saw in the fraternity of the Brotherhood an opportunity to develop influence that could change the direction of the country. These were lofty aims of the kind found in and encouraged at Oxford University at the time. In 1850, he bankrolled *The Germ*, and wrote for this important organ for the Pre-Raphaelites.

Inspired by an encyclopedic knowledge of medieval history, culture and architecture The Brotherhood set about a project that was to last each of them, in different ways and in varying degrees, all of their days. Burne-Jones went on to become the most important of the pre Raphaelite painters. These were men who were destined, because of birth and schooling, to play an important part in the life of the country. What the country could not know or the authorities at Oxford expect, was quite how they would use their influence and to what purpose. But it was certainly not the orthodoxy expected of men born into wealth. Indeed the conspicuous consumption of Victorian Britain repulsed them. As soon as he began his inheritance Morris and Burne-Jones embarked on a walking tour of the great gothic cathedrals of Northern France. It was a cathartic experience. Within a year Morris had abandoned any thoughts of become an Anglican clergyman, left Oxford, and dedicated himself to a life of art. That same year, he enrolled at the offices of G E Street where he was articled to become an architect, but soon left to follow his friend Burne-Jones into painting. A year on and he was married to an eighteen-year-old working class beauty Jane Siddal. He took up carving, clay modelling, illuminating and wood engraving. For their honeymoon, Morris and Jane who had never seen the sea before – visited Paris, Bask, Liege, Mainz, Cologne, Ghent, Bruges, Antwerp and Brussels.

The Brotherhood was first influenced by religion and then by romanticism. Its members thought in terms of a holy war against the prevailing culture and art of the time. This holy war was not limited to ideas but had its material base in opposition to the ecclesiastical authorities who commissioned so much of the visible architecture of the time, owned extensive land and sponsored a wide range of art from decorative stained glass windows and tapestries, to illuminated books. The Brotherhood fell under the influence of John Ruskin. In the mid century Ruskin was developing a critique of capitalism that looked back to medievalism as an alternative.

At the centre of the medieval world was the craftsman. It was a world rich in community with a set of social norms and rules enshrined as a code of chivalry. It was the craftsman who created the physical architecture of the time and, as a free agent, much of the thinking architecture too. This craftsman was related to the worker of the later industrial period but existed in quite different relation to the system of production. The former had control of the labour process and ownership of his tools, as the means to life. The latter had neither. Ruskin saw in all aspects of culture and, in particular, in the prominent artists and architects of the day, sustainers of the hated industrial age. So those who wanted to oppose such change had to do so across the range of cultural disciplines. Morris was thus drawn to painting, poetry and the writing of prose. Along with Burne-Jones and Rosetti, all obviously big talents from an early age, Morris was taken on to paint frescoes for the Oxford Union. His first major work, *The Defence of Guenevere and Other Poems* was published in 1858.

After leaving their studies, the Brotherhood set about putting the theory into practice, coming together to build the Red House for Morris. Together they decorated it and used the experience to experiment with styles and techniques, making all the furnishings, designing stained glass windows, painting murals and weaving tapestries. By 1861 they came together formally to establish a company Morris, Faulkner, Marshall and Co. It was arguably one of the most innovative and influential companies ever in Britain. Along with the painter Ford Maddox Brown and the brilliant architect Philip Webb who Morris had met when at Street's, the company evolved a new style, translated into mediums ranging from stained glass, wood carving, furniture, wall hangings and wallpaper, to carpets and tapestries.

The Company revolutionised public tastes and had influence in a bewildering array of directions, for example, in the formation of the Victoria and Albert Museum where in 1867 Morris designed and built the Dining Room, to the formation of what we today call English Heritage. He designed and built the Armoury and Tapestry room in St. James's Palace. He also found time to lead a campaign to save St. Mark's Square in Venice enlisting along the way, perhaps uniquely given their personal enmity, the support of both Disraeli and Gladstone. In 1875 the partnership dissolved and Morris and Company was formed.

Whilst the Company was developing and then began to fragment, Morris's mind was at its most active. So was his pen. "I do not believe", he wrote "in the possibility of keeping art vigorously alive by the action, however energetic, of a few groups of specially gifted men." In 1867 he wrote *The Life and Death of Jason*, in 1868 his influential *The Earthly Paradise* and, in 1870, the first of his translations in collaboration with Eirikr Magnusson of the Icelandic Sagas – the *Volksunga Saga*. In the next year he took his first of two visits to Iceland, a country that was to have a very deep impact on him. This visit lasted a year. As one who sought alternatives to capitalism, at first in romanticism and medievalism, he found a quite different approach as a result of his contact with Iceland, a country that had yet to develop industrially. There, social class was unformed and community still dominated – a sort of primitive communism. This experience led to a radical turn in his political outlook; a result of greater insight into what he already knew about his much loved England – that things were not as they should or could be.

Morris sought to establish a company in the same vein as he established The Brotherhood; to act as a shopfront for superior craftsmanship and progressive thought. Each fell short of his expectations.

In the same period, Morris's life was to take a further turn – from radical thoughts to radical action – as a result of the aggressive and aggrandising foreign policy of Prime Minister Disraeli. He became agitated by the Eastern Question and began to work for the Liberal Party under Gladstone, who opposed Turkish expansion and atrocities against the Bulgarians. Gladstone's famous pamphlet, *The Bulgarian Horrors and The Question of the East* (1876), which opposed lining Britain up with the Turks and demanded the evacuation of an entire Bulgarian province, is said to have sold 200,000 copies in a single month. It was during this agitation and as a result of his work for the Liberals that Morris first came into contact with workers and, in particular, the skilled workers who were class conscious, organised into trade unions and the Labour Representation League. Of this time, Ruskin wrote of his hope that, "It seems to me especially a time when the quietest men should be disquieted, and the meekest self-asserting." In 1875 he dissolved the Company and reconstituted it as sole proprietor into Morris and Co. His name alone was big enough to carry on the trade. It would not close until 1939.

In 1877 he formed the first substantial environmentalist organisation in Britain, The Society for the Protection of Ancient Buildings, SPAB, whose work continues today. The Society, in true Morris fashion, was 'established to counteract the highly destructive restoration of medieval buildings being practiced.' But it did not wait for them to be knocked down. He put together a highly successful team of some of the finest architects of the day, to so work out plans that the buildings could be retained in their original form. Morris's way was not to moan but to act. It was to think ahead so as to avoid being put on the back foot. He protested, "all 'restoration' that means more than keeping out wind and weather."

A facsimile proof drawn from Morris who wrote of the founding of Kelmscott Press, "I began printing books with the hope of producing some which would have a definite claim to beauty, while at the same time they should be easy to read and should not dazzle the eye, or trouble the intellect of the reader by eccentricity of form in letters."

His disillusion with liberalism grew. He resigned as treasurer of the National Liberal League in 1881 as he gravitated to what was then called socialism. In 1882 he became treasurer of the Icelandic Famine Relief Committee. Later that year he published the seminal collection of lectures *Hopes and Fears for Art*. In January 1883, along with Burne-Jones he was elected an honorary fellow of Exeter College Oxford. This rare privilege was all the more significant as he was not a Privy Councillor, Bishop or other such rank. In the same year he embraced Marxism.

Socialism was in its infancy and Morris brought to it a sense of the historical and an innovative mind. He read a French translation of Marx's *Capital* – the first of the three volumes was not yet translated into English and his German was not too good. In the same year he joined the Democratic Federation, soon renamed the Social Democratic Federation, leaving it in December 1884 at the ripe age of fifty, to form the Socialist League. Even though it included amongst its followers, the likes of Frederich Engels, Marx's closest collaborator, and his eldest daughter Eleanor Marx Aveling, Morris was the main public face and acknowledged leader. He also served as editor of the party journal *Commonweal*.

Over the next years he travelled the length and breadth of the country and abroad, to Dublin and Paris and Brussels, agitating on behalf of socialism. Many of the generation who put trade unionism and socialism on a permanent basis in this country were converted at meetings addressed by Morris, from printers in Glasgow to striking coal miners in Northumberland. Many more came as a result of reading his pamphlets. He took part in demonstrations and was active on behalf of those arrested for defending the right to free speech, especially in the east end of London. He was himself arrested. In 1883 his only foray into music – though as we shall see later he influenced many a musician including Gustav Holst – resulted in the publication of *Chants for Socialists*. Some of his best-known works were yet to come. The author of the *Earthly Paradise* now wrote of *The Pilgrims of Hope* (1885), the brilliant *Dream of John Ball* (1888) and the serialised *News from Nowhere* the following year. As far as working class literature goes the latter two are amongst the most read in Britain and are still in print in popular editions 120 years on. Morris's stamina was legendary. It took him 516 hours to complete one tapestry – *Cabbage and Vine*.

With dissolution of the League, Morris took the bulk of active members into a kind of holding organisation – the Hammersmith Socialist Society. He spent his last years working towards unity of the socialists in Britain. In 1891 he was diagnosed with a kidney disease. Characteristically, in the same year he began one of his most influential endeavours setting up the Kelmscott Press. He made his last public speech at the Society for Checking the Abuses of Public

Advertising. He continued to write and campaign though was much more choosy about his engagements. In 1893 he co wrote *Socialism, its Growth and Outcome, Manifesto of the English Socialists* (1893) *The Wood Beyond the World* (1894) and the *Well at the World's End* (1896). In the same year he became reconciled with the Social Democratic Federation, regretting the original split.

Kelmscott edition of News from Nowhere.

He began one of the great achievements of his life, publishing the Kelmscott Chaucer which he designed and Burne-Jones, truly a lifelong colleague, illustrated. Kelmscott was a kind of parting thanks to those he admired. It published works by Coleridge, Keats, Shelley, Tennyson and Swinburne. It was his last practical attempt to retain the old relationship between artist, his art and society and to establish an ideal relationship between author and reader, text and craftsman printer. He died on 3 October 1896.

Morris died as he lived, buried following a journey of great simplicity. Laid to rest in the little churchyard at Kelmscott, his body was taken to its grave in an open hay cart, gaily covered with vines, alders and bulrushes, and driven by a countryman.

Kelmscott Manor a limestone manor established in the sixteenth century in Oxfordshire. Morris lived there for a number of years from 1871. He loved the manor even though it had unhappy personal memories for him. It looked as if "it had grown up out of the soil". He returned there for his last journey and is buried in a nearby church.

Such was the influence that Morris had. But who influenced him? Morris drew from a range of sources and relationships. Some involved individuals he knew and others he could not. He worked much out for himself. Other influences included those things around him. Looking back over 40 years in his lecture *The Aims of Art* he said "I first saw the City of Rouen, then still in its outward aspect a piece of the middle ages: no words can tell you how its mingled beauty, history and romance took a hold on me." His range of languages was a great help, from the classical Greek – many key books from the medieval period were translated into English from scripts originally written in Greek and imported from Italy – to reading *Capital* in French. Iceland confirmed the theories about class society that he was developing. He insisted on reading as close to the original as possible. Better still, he visited first hand, whether it was the trip to Iceland, or to Italy, or to the Staffordshire potteries when he turned his mind to ceramics.

The written and printed word was key to Morris and influenced him greatly. He read throughout his life. He was a voracious letter writer. He was democratic to the core. At the centre of his formative influences was the actual *exchange of thinking*: he knew he did not have all the answers. He was drawn to those challenging established ideas and, where possible, exchanged his own with them. He read to stretch himself, his library including – Tommaso Campanella's *City of the Sun* and Thomas More's *Utopia*. But he found time to read a range of literature from the most up to date fiction to Shakespeare. "Chaucer was my master," he once wrote.

He was influenced by events and by his own studies. He was influenced by leading figures of his age. Certain characters stand out. Fourier, Owen, Ruskin and Marx. Ruskin was perhaps the greatest of the early influences. With Ruskin he found a common admiration for the architects and masons of the medieval period. He found in him, a consistent critic of capitalism and the smashing up of country life which had arisen as a result of land enclosure and the imposition of city slums. Both were champions of work, done well as a form of Art. Work, reasoned Ruskin should be an essential part of one's self respect, it should be such that the worker cares about what he makes and it should be done to the best that his abilities allow. These points became the foundation of Morris's definition of socialism. But although Ruskin shared the analysis he did not share the conclusions. There was always great mutual affection and respect between the two. It is said that, when Ruskin described Morris as the 'ablest man of his time' he opened a bottle of his favourite port to celebrate. But Ruskin only travelled part of the way with Morris and so should be considered an influence on him more for his early rather than later years.

Fourier developed a doctrine based on the necessity and possibility of making labour attractive. This became central to Morris's concept of socialism and social living. Carlyle was an influence too. In *Past and Present* He wrote, " What is the use of your spun shirts? They there by the million unsaleable; and here, by the million, are diligent backs that can get no hold of them … " Morris differed with Carlyle who saw a future in a kind of modern medievalism with the industrialist playing the role of feudal lord. His scheme was based, not on exchanging one set of overseers for another, but doing away with class altogether.

Morris was strong on the concept of natural, historical and inalienable rights. In this sense he could draw from a rich vein of domestically spun political theorists. He read William Godwin who, wrote in *Political Justice*, " From the simple principles we may deduce the moral equality of mankind. We are partakers of a common nature, and the same causes that contribute to the benefit of one contribute to the benefit of another … We are all of us endowed with reason, able to compare, to judge, and to infer. The improvement therefore which is to be desired for the one, is to be desired for the other … " Ernest Jones, a leader of Chartism took the concept and gave it a partisan, class dimension. In 1851 he wrote, "Distinctions have been drawn between divine right, natural right, social right, political right and conventional right. I believe all the rights of man to be founded on one – *the right to live* – but how is man to live? We are told he is to eat his bread in the sweat of his brow? Therefore, he is to live by work. We are further told, he that will not work, neither shall he eat? Therefore, it is his duty to work. But there never was a duty that did not imply a right – consequently it is his further *right to work*. But it is a mockery to tell a man 'he has a right to work', if you do not also concede to him the MEANS of working. Therefore, man has a right of free access to the means of work. What are those means? Land and Machinery. Therefore man has a right of free access to land and machinery. He is not bound to owe his access to them to the will of any other man ..." Morris agreed, it was the emerging working class who would act as the custodians of such ideals. George Loveless one of the Tolpuddle martyrs, writing in the year of Morris's birth, expressed this sense of historical right, "God is our guide! No swords we draw, We kindle not war's battle-fires, By reason, union, justice, law, we claim the birthright of our sires; We raise the watchword Liberty – We will, we will, we will be free!"

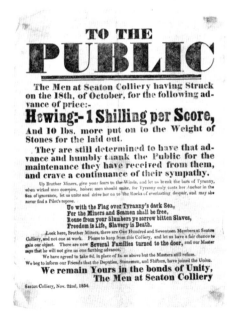

According to Morris, socialism was the "intelligence of Labour plus the coal miners". This handbill at once demonstrates the bitter relationship between workers in the pits and their employers, mid nineteenth century. It also shows that the unions were gathering all grades and trades to their ranks.

In Robert Owen he saw similarities with his own calling and a beacon of ideas. To him, Owen was "lifter of the torch of socialism amidst the dark days of confusion, when commerce ran riot, working and town conditions were truly terrible and workers' hope seemed lost because localised, spontaneous and isolated revolt had not yet settled in to Chartism." In Owen he saw more than just quality ideas. He saw a manufacturer, one who did rather than just talked. One who grappled with nature in order to transform it. Central to Owenism is a culturally alert and intelligent working class, organised for production, but on non – exploitative lines. Owen is greatly underestimated.

Morris loved and admired the work of William Blake, one of the most celebrated artists and poets in the English-speaking world. Blake has now become accepted, for all his brilliance, but his true feelings are often hidden or moderated. For example he wrote of 'bow of burning gold' and 'arrows of desire.'. But he also wrote, "Let the slave grinding at the mill run out into the field. Let him look up into the heavens and laugh in the bright air: Let the enchained soul, shut up in the darkness and sighing, Whose face has never seen a smile in thirty years, Rise and look out; his chains are loose, his dungeon's doors are open, And let his wife and children return from the oppressor's scourge. For Empire is no more, and now the Lion and Wolf shall cease."

John Stuart Mill, economist, philosopher and exponent of Utilitarianism wrote, "The social problem of the future we considered to be, how to unite the greatest individual liberty of action, with common ownership in the raw material of the globe, and an equal participation of all in the benefits of combined labour." Indeed one need not look too far to grasp just how rich was the well of political thinking that Morris could draw from. In later years a whole new generation of thinkers – perhaps more earthy and gritty than those who influenced him early on, came in to his life. When they did he was well equipped to develop his thought as he was as comfortable in the role of student, as he was of teacher.

There are three specific and interlinked aspects of the thinking of Morris that are explored in this book. Each raise in its own way issues that touch on the way we live now. I first look at the changes that took place in his lifetime to give us a measure and sense of perspective and change. Life was not always as it is now. And work has changed in more ways and more profoundly than other aspects of life. I, then turn to the question of skill and machinery, their organisation into factories, and the impact of the division of labour. The third and most important contribution that Morris made was to make us consider the way in which we work and why?

Work is the big issue of the coming century and in Morris we are equipped with one of the most original and deepest thinkers in the field. A quintessential Englishman imbued with a worldview, one of modernity's most talented and enduring craftsmen-designers and an original thinker who anticipated socialism and much of Marx too. He makes a special contribution. In unravelling the historical and technical evolution of the division of labour he gives us an insight into how we may take such division and go beyond it. A new, better and more productive society awaits us.

Everyone claims Morris, from the decorative artists and the Victoria and Albert Museum to English Heritage, the revolutionary socialists and the Societies' of designers. That they all have a right to make such a claim is a testament to the extent of Morris's activity and interests. But his first love was Art. In Art, Morris saw the opportunity for ordinary people to grapple with and depict their love of life. It was an expression, in a diversity of forms, of the workingman's interest in and expectation of their realities.

Art was a product of the many, throughout the ages, not the preserve of the few. What is more, 'good art' was at its best when humans were at their best, fully enjoying their labour free from compulsion and 'drudgery'. He believed capitalism broke with that. Through the profit motive it infected every aspect of life including Morris's much loved art, separating artist from people and people from the means of life and artistic expression.

Although his first love was Art, he was mainly interested in the links that existed between architecture, sculpture, painting and the decorative arts, particularly in an organic sense. In capitalism he perceived a threat to this unity, which he felt also applied to literature, music, poetry and language.

Today we are still deeply concerned with the conditions of work, but, to his last breath, Morris was convinced that people would only be able to fundamentally and radically alter the condition of their labour by changing the character of it from profit-centred to socialistic. He thought that a combination of 'life's necessities', manual skill, increased technical and general education, together with sufficient leisure time, would surely rekindle ordinary people's love of art, thereby guaranteeing its renaissance.

Time and space played a big part in Morris's scheme. Given enough space and time he reasoned, people would naturally map out their own path to art, but only if they could work unhindered by compulsion and profit motive. Art would become a measure of the state of labour's health. Whilst labour remained forced for the sole means of making easy money, work would be rushed and corners cut. This would lead to diminished quality. The worker would become mentally and physically exhausted. He could work till he dropped, but his work would go unlamented, possibly despised. However, with space and time and freedom from constraint many workers would seize the opportunity to perfect themselves in the "niceties of their craft, or in research as to its principles." Others would aim to extend themselves through study and development of their general knowledge. The degree to which people could commit themselves to art and life beyond work would thence be in their own hands. It is an awesome thought.

Quality would be their responsibility, determined by the amount of time and space individually and collectively apportioned to it and would illustrate the degree of organisation of labour, its socialisation and the amount of control it had over working life. So in Morris, presence of Art reflects the newly discovered power of workers and the level of their culture and consciousness. Yes, they would willingly adorn their factory with art, pictures and sculpture, but more importantly, the output of their labour would be transformed from a commodity for sale in the marketplace to a true artefact. It is somewhat ironic that many have characterised socialism as insipid and lacking in individuality whereas William Morris's concept of socialism was full of colour, involving nature, art and the written word and the latent creativity of Everyman.

According to GDH Cole, Morris "made pictures in his mind; but he was never happy until he had set them out for others to see." He did not believe in supermen and women changing the lives of others. In his eyes, change was to be self-propelled by the majority, or it was no real change at all. Morris was practical and visually oriented. Even his prose is written in a graphic style, designed to tease the imagination. He had taken to heart William Hogarth's belief that "ocular demonstration will convince ... sooner than ten thousand volumes." Visionaries are few and far between, but usually their visions are placed at the disposal of others and often adopted, long after their lifetime. Morris was a different kind of modern visionary. He asked "What shall we do? How shall we live? I don't know, nor do you, and we cannot know ... " He was asking as much as telling and left the door open for his ideas to be developed. His Utopianism was tempered by a need to demonstrate that his was a project lofty in ideals but based on a practical core. Socialism would triumph over capitalism if it could unpick the division of labour and reconstruct work on a new basis. In the search to reclaim time from 'useless toil' and return it to workers, he became a supporter of the demand for eight hours work, eight hours rest and eight hours for enlightenment. In the margin to his notes for the lecture *How Shall We Live?* he had scribbled "... more simply and consequently more interesting life."

For those who speculate that Morris was too Utopian and lacked what today would be 'hardball' politicking, he finished *Monopoly or How Labour is Robbed* in the following way. "The necessities of the miserable and the aspiration of the intelligent, will outrun the slower processes of gradual conversion, anti-monopolists will find themselves in a position in which they will be forced to try to get hold of the executive, in order to destroy it and thus metamorphose society, not in order to govern by it and as they are now governed; in other words, they will have to sweep away all the artificial restrictions that stand in the way of free labour, and they will have to compel this step by some means or other." He acknowledged that, "those who set before them this necessity will doubtless differ at present as to the means whereby this will be done; but they should at least agree … that any means that are means, and are not inhuman, are good to use."

Fascia of one of twelve watch cases struck in the 1860s, to mark the first meeting in London of the International Working Mens' Association (First International). Pride of place was given to the demand for a redivision of the working day.
(Reproduced courtesy of the TUC unionhistory.info)

Morris was a kind of prophet of a new industrialism and visionary of a new way of setting society to really work. Our future government, he wrote, "would be rather an administration of things than a government of persons." He was a prophet, not in the biblical sense, but in the pragmatic English sense. He may have been a visionary, but he was of this world and wanted to change it for present good. He identified himself closely with John Ball, the unseen and most humble theoretician of the Peasants' Revolt, who travelled the length and breadth of the country preaching the simple message, of fellowship and the commonweal. Although knights in shining armour inhabited Morris's early reading and imagination, in real life he opted to play the man in sackcloth.

The range of influence and application is unrivalled. Wallpaper, tiles, stained glass windows and in 1866 a commission to design a public dining room – The Green Room – in South Kensington Museum.

In terms of his motivation and inspiration he can speak for himself "For your teachers, they must be in Nature and History."

He made furniture, designed wall hangings, printed books and wove tapestries. He excelled at carpet making, upholstering and type manufacture. With just a few followers he became, through the Arts and Crafts movement, a father figure to the rediscovery of calligraphy and ceramics in the modern age. He had tenacity and commitment to doing things well. When, in the 1870s, it became clear that in the space of ten years, natural vegetable based dyes had been supplanted by inferior man-made chemical ones, he set about rediscovering ancient recipes and traditions, using dye-vats at his own works in

Queen's Square to make inks with which to print textiles. He was at one point using walnuts to make dyes for silk printing, cutting poplar trees to make a yellow dye and even looked into using recipes, based on insects, gleaned from France a century before. When the paper was not right for a Kelmscott edition he made it out of linen. When the type was not right he designed and had cut, his own fonts. He was artist, designer, revolutionary and craftsman. In his hands all four were as one. He could have rested comfortably on his laurels and we could have treasured him as one of our greatest artists, but he insisted that what worked for him could work for anyone. It was less a question of intelligence and more one of training, opportunity and resource. His birth gave him access to all of these, but he also wanted others to reach their full potential.

None of Morris's crafts necessarily relate. How can the skill of weaving at a loom be transported to designing the cut of a type font? In what way would the sketching of a stained glass window relate to upholstering a chair? And yet he seemed to move effortlessly through and between a range of crafts. How was this so?

Natural talent aside, and we must remember that Morris believed that with the right type and amount of training, most people could acquire a range of skills to a high level, he approached each craft in two interrelated ways. The first was to see each as a contributor to a greater purpose: architecture, for example, was in essence the engineering of the human landscape. In this sense there would be a little of each craft in the others. There would be no point producing two items that would jar the human senses because they were so discordant. Each product of his craft had then to 'stand alone' and interrelate. Architecture was, in the nineteenth century, an imposing and very real statement of historical evolution and of the state of human life.

The second way was in mastering not only individual crafts, but knowing how to acquire and sustain each one. These techniques *are* transposable. Morris would follow a similar path whether working on tapestries and carpets or the illumination of a book page. He would research the history of the medium and, in particular, the historical evolution of the tools used. He would analyse and was constantly experimenting with new materials – he was amongst the first to work with linoleum and pioneered a return to the natural and organic development of dyestuffs and printing inks. He would then go to the artisans to learn how a craft was practised and, wherever possible, (for example spending time with workers in the potteries), learn how methods had evolved and how they were developing. When this was not possible, as when he was developing Abbey Mills or the Kelmscott Press, he gathered the best workers around him. He would research first hand, travelling far and wide to study architecture, and spending countless hours in libraries and especially the South Kensington Museum, analysing past attempts at doing what he now wanted to do himself. What could he learn? How would it need to be adapted? How could it be improved? If the right machinery or tools did not exist, he would either make them or import them and invariably used the best and often the most modern machinery available.

To Morris, acquiring a craft required a team effort with rank accounting for little. In this sense, the one that did things the best or who grasped the essence of a problem was the master craftsman. As a team player and also a brilliant practitioner he was humble and hungry to learn. Indeed he only stopped experimenting and learning when he became too ill to be involved. Although a capitalist employer all his working life, there is no record of him ever falling out with his employees, only with fellow directors. Famed for his incendiary temperament, there is no record of his ever using his power as an employer over a worker. All his employees were union men and no Morris company had a labour dispute, for although he was the owner and had the money, his workers were masters of the crafts he loved and respected. It was an interesting face-off that deserves deeper analysis. He saw each work environment as a sort of Witenagemote (or meeting of wise men).

Elsewhere I describe Morris as a Renaissance man. Morris modelled himself on Leonardo Da Vinci in a number of ways and some have criticised him as they did Leonardo for allowing key works to be made by apprentices. Yet in the Renaissance world this was natural and important. The task of a master craftsmen then, (as later in the hands of Morris), was to be a master of his craft, not a master of men. Leonardo is considered a genius of his time not simply for his personal ability in any one art medium but because leading thinkers of his time were expected to become masters in all branches of knowledge. Morris did not want this just for himself, he thought it appropriate for all who had to work to live.

How could the man who said "apart from the desire to produce beautiful things, the leading passion of my life has been and is, hatred of modern civilisation," reconcile such opposites? Of civilisation he wrote, "What shall I say concerning its mastery of and its waste of mechanical power, its Commonwealth so poor, its enemies of Commonwealth so rich, its stupendous organisation – for the misery of life; its contempt of simple pleasure, which everyone could enjoy but for its folly; its eyeless vulgarity, which has destroyed art, the one certain solace of labour." His answer lies in a conception of art that these days has largely slipped from the popular mind. Civilisation set hand against brain, town against countryside, art against science, worker against worker and workers against themselves. Each opposite could be reconciled through the dispersion of the organisation of production that depended on division of labour, where, in Marx's words, "man was set against machine and against himself". It would be inadequate to exchange the rule of capitalist with that of workers, for people could only be truly empowered if the nature of the work was changed. Instead of having to make profit a priority they would need to aim for an artistry that focused on, the quality of the end product, a struggle for 'eight hours work, eight hours leisure or rest and eight hours for the pursuit of knowledge', and labour that was both collectivist and truly free from compulsion.

Morris's sweep was broad and radical. As he saw it, nineteenth century Britain was "living in the time of barbarism betwixt two periods of order, the order of the past and the order of the future."

He was one of those rare characters who managed to say something that would remain relevant beyond his time. The message of Victorian Britain was that things were as they were because God deemed it so, as if capitalism had been implicit in the Old Testament. Woe to any one who tried to change this. Respect was based on class rather than ability. This would never do for Morris. The aim he set himself was "to impress on the workers the fact that they are a class, whereas they ought to be society." His objective was "not the dissolution of society ... but it's reintegration."

Those who have chosen to look further and deeper into his work are many, indeed they form something of the kind of fellowship he spent his life working towards. In this fellowship, most things go – it is a model of democracy – bringing together theoreticians and practitioners of a whole host of crafts – from the professionals to the hobbyists, from park gardeners and professors to the ordinary, just plain interested. The Morris fellowship knows few boundaries and today, the work of Morris aficionados can be found active in every medium from fine art museums and decorators of church windows to the Internet and the electronic, from Australia to Iceland. Their enthusiasm is impressive and there are no superfluous hierarchies.

This book is one more contribution to understanding the work of one man with a big vision. But it could never be just a rehash of what has already been done by so many talented others. I wanted to add to the body of knowledge of Morris by approaching him from a slightly different angle. I hoped, by so doing, to raise issues in the mind of the reader about the nature of work and our working lives today.

"Manufactures ... prosper most where the mind is least consulted, and where the workshop may, without any great effort of imagination, be considered as an engine, the parts of which are men ...We make a nation of helots, and have no free citizens."

Adam Ferguson, *An Essay on the History of Civil Society* 1765

World in change

William Morris was born in London in 1834 and died in 1896. Throughout his life he was to experience, take part in and comment on the greatest changes that mankind had yet experienced. In *Capital*, Marx asks, "(the) subjection of nature's focus to man, machinery, application of chemistry to industry and agriculture ... clearing of whole continents for cultivation, canalisation of rivers, whole populations conjured out of the ground – what earlier century had even a presentiment that such productive forces slumbered in the lap of social labour?" As we have said, in some ways Morris was a man locked out of his time, but as the renaissance flame had long been extinguished he had no option to go back. However, he was not above reminiscing – he did so both in private and in public – but he knew that, in a century where profound change was constant, he could only look forward.

His life opened with the culmination of the ascendancy of capitalism as a result of the first of the Great Reform Acts (1832), and Charles Babbage's invention of an analytic machine – the forerunner of today's computer. It ended with the first applications of the internal combustion engine to travel and Becquerel's discovery of radioactivity in uranium. Five years prior to Morris's death Keir Hardie took a place in the Commons as MP for West Ham. During his life span the population of Britain doubled from just over 16 millions to 33 millions.

A numerically powerful working class, concentrated in larger production units emerged. This single development alone would change Britain forever. But the emergence of this force came against a backdrop of other changes. Science contributed to industry and to health. Education emerged to cope with the multiplicity of trades and occupations and to complement traditional ways of passing on knowledge. A look at the census returns for 1851, 1861 and 1871 illustrate the rapidly changing occupational structure of the population, for the first time more Britons lived in towns than in the countryside. The range of occupations did not breakdown a sense of 'the people' or the historic, 'commons', it strengthened it and, in addition to class consciousness a new kind of identity of nation emerged, bringing Scots, English and Welsh together.

Occupations: census returns for 1851, 1861 and 1871

Occupation	1851	1861	1871
Agricultural labourer, farm servant, shepherd	1,460,896	1,188,789	980,178
Domestic servant	1,103,791	1,106,974	1,237,149
Cotton, calico, manufacture, printing and dyeing	501,565	456,646	468,142
Labourer	376,551	309,883	516,605
Farmer, grazier	306,767	249,745	249,907
Boot and shoe maker	274,451	250,581	223,365
Milliner, dressmaker	267,791	287,101	301,109
Coal miner	219,015	246,613	268,091
Carpenter, joiner	182,696	177,969	205,833
Army and Navy	178,773	199,905	175,217
Tailor	152,672	136,390	149,864
Washerwomen, mangler, laundry keeper	146,091	167,607	170,598
Woollen cloth manufacture	137,814	130,034	128,464
Silk manufacture	114,570	101,678	75,180
Blacksmith	112,776	108,165	112,471
Worsted manufacture	104,061	79,242	94,766
Mason, paviour	101,442	84,434	95,243
Messenger, porter, errand boy	101,425	75,629	93,182
Linen, flax manufacture	98,860	22,050	17,993
Seaman (merchant service) on shore or in British ports	89,206	159,469	169,933
Grocer	85,913	93,483	111,094
Gardener	80,946	78,533	98,069
Iron manufacture, moulder, founder	80,032	125,771	180,207
Innkeeper, licensed victualler, beershop keeper	75,721	66,386	94,011
Seamstress, shirtmaker	73,068	76,493	80,730
Bricklayer	67,989	79,458	99,984
Butcher, meat salesman	67,691	68,114	75,847
Hose (stocking) manufacturer	65,499	45,869	42,038
Schoolmaster/mistress	65,376	56,139	58,152
Lace manufacture	63,660	53,987	49,370
Plumber, painter, glazier	62,808	74,619	103,912
Baker	62,472	54,140	59,066
Carman, carrier, carter, drayman	56,981	67,651	74,244

Charwoman	55,423	65,273	77,650
Draper (linen and woollen)	49,184	57,653	74,337
Engine and machine maker	48,082	60,862	106,680
Commercial clerk	43,760	55,931	91,042
Cabinet maker, upholsterer	40,897	41,037	56,945
Teacher (various) governess	40,575	49,743	68,595
Fisherman/woman	38,294	17,227	21,043
Boat, barge man/woman	37,683	31,428	29,864
Miller	37,268	32,103	30,060
Earthenware manufacture	36,512	38,072	45,122
Sawyer	35,443	31,637	27,965
Railway labourer	34,306	27,773	45,070
Straw-plait manufacture	32,062	29,867	48,863
Brick maker, dealer	31,168	39,620	38,779
Government Civil Service	30,963	31,346	28,644
Hawker, pedlar	30,553	21,792	44,617
Wheelwright	30,244	30,070	30,394
Glover	29,882	25,300	16,811
Shopkeeper (branch undefined)	29,800	14,580	39,991
Horsekeeper, groom (not domestic), jockey	29,408	36,600	42,682
Nail manufacture	28,533	26,130	23,231
Iron miner	28,088	20,626	20,931
Printer	26,024	30,590	44,814
Nurse (not domestic servant)	25,518	24,821	28,417
Shipwright, shipbuilder	25,201	31,294	40,626
Stone quarter	23,489	21,004	25,681
Lodging house keeper	23,089	20,700	25,932
Lead miner	22,530	18,552	14,563
Copper miner	22,386	17,727	–
Straw hat and bonnet maker	21,902	18,176	–
Cooper	20,245	17,821	19,300
Watch and clock maker	19,159	20,757	21,273
Brewer	18,620	20,352	25,831
Dock labourer, dock and harbour service	18,462	32,487	28,794
Clergyman of the Established (Anglican) Church	18,587	19,195	20,694
Protestant Dissenting Minister	9,644	7,840	–
Police	18,348	21,938	28,330

Plasterer	17,980	18,550	24,587
Warehouse man/woman	17,861	21,798	44,013
Saddler, harness maker	17,583	18,229	23,011
Hatter, hat manufacture	16,975	13,814	21,778
Coachman (not domestic servant) guard, postboy	16,836	17,251	39,999
Law clerk	16,626	16,605	18,886
Coachmaker	16,590	18,870	23,034
Cowkeeper, milkseller	16,526	17,694	20,558
Ropemaker	15,966	13,486	11,695
Surgeon, apothecary	15,163	12,030	14,692
Tin miner	15,050	14,314	10,617
Paper manufacture	14,501	13,357	16,772
Coalheaver, coal labourer	14,426	17,410	27,998
Greengrocer, fruiterer	14,320	18,045	25,819
Muslin manufacture	14,098	–	–
Confectioner	13,865	14,526	16,988
Tinman, tinker, pin plate worker	13,770	–	18,324
Staymaker	13,699	11,482	–
Solicitor, attorney, writer to the Signet	13,256	11,386	12,314
Dyer, scourer, calenderer	12,964	–	12,882
Currier	12,920	13,109	14,710
Builder	12,818	15,757	23,300
Farm bailiff	12,805	15,698	16,476
Hairdresser, wig maker	12,173	11,064	13,125
Coal merchant/dealer	12,092	12,266	16,250
Glass manufacture	12,005	15,046	20,081
Carpet and rug manufacture	11,457	–	11,568
Goldsmith, silversmith	11,242	15,893	22,031
Brass founder, moulder, manufacture	11,230	16,284	21,421
Maltster	11,150	10,677	10,356
Railway officer, clerk, station master	10,948	14,580	22,083
Book binder	10,953	11,920	15,474
Road labourer	10,923	–	–
Wine and spirit merchant	10,467	–	10,969
Fishmonger	10,439	11,305	14,880
Merchant	10,256	12,982	15,936
Ribbon manufacture	10,074	–	–

House proprietor	–	36,082	17,086
Land proprietor	–	30,766	22,964
Railway Company's servant, porter, attendant	–	26,846	49,102
Costermonger, general dealer, huckster	–	15,879	–
Beerseller	–	15,767	16,361
Dockyards (HM) artificers, labourers in	–	14,314	–
Boiler maker	–	13,020	–
Gunsmith, gun manufacturer	–	11,873	11,576
Manufacturer, mechanic	–	11,639	17,530
Chelsea Pensioner	–	11,342	–
Brush, broom maker, seller	–	11,178	11,708
Provision curer, dealer	–	11,052	13,236
Commercial traveller	–	10,779	17,922
Railway engine driver, stoker	–	10,414	13,715
Miner (branch undefined)	–	–	38,712
Engine driver, stoker (branch undefined)	–	–	31,026
Government messengers and workmen	–	–	24,582
Machinist, machine worker (branch undefined)	–	–	23,421
Agent, broker, factor	–	–	22,962
Musician, music maker	–	–	18,631
Cutler	–	–	17,903
Ironmonger, hardware dealer	–	–	17,368
Tobacco, cigar, snuff manufacture	–	–	14,367
Weaver (not otherwise described)	–	–	14,260
Gasworks service	–	–	13,570
Municipal, parish, union officer	–	–	13,423
Institution service	–	–	13,304
Wood, timber merchant/dealer	–	–	12,859
Corn, flour, seed merchant/dealer	–	–	12,765
Gamekeeper	–	–	12,431
Manufacturing chemist, labourer	–	–	11,328
Stationer (not law)	–	–	10,889
Bank service	–	–	10,887
Box and packing case maker	–	–	10,570
Coal mine service	–	–	10,346

Source: The Victorian Web. Compiled from Parliamentary Papers 1852-3, 1863 and 1873

To see where Morris was coming from and why he was to rebel in the way that he did, it is necessary for us to survey the exciting and dynamic changes that were taking place up to and throughout his life. Excitement is a word best reserved for the processes of industrial growth but it cannot be applied to the conditions of labour which only worsened, Morris observed this drama and concluded 'I despise this civilisation'. In 1880 he wrote, " Ancient civilisation was chained to slavery and exclusiveness, and it fell; the barbarism that took its place has delivered us from slavery and grown into modern civilisation." Capitalism however, came at a price, or what Morris termed 'the residuum': waste in quality, goods and people. "If this residuum were a necessary part of civilisation, as some people assume it is, then this civilisation carries with it the poison that shall one day destroy it." If civilisation "does not aim at getting rid of this misery and giving some share in the happiness and dignity of life to *all* the people that it has created, ... it is simply an organised injustice, a mere instrument for oppression, so much the worse than that which has gone before it, as its pretensions are higher."

Poverty in the city and in rural areas, crowded housing, insanitary conditions and rack vents. Many succumbed. Many more, organised, to press for better and more.

The nineteenth century saw irreversible breakthroughs in three developments that had been gathering pace for hundreds of years. Handicraft, usually based in the home or small workshop, was giving way to machine production based in factories. Raw materials once gained from animals gave way to mineral and man-made substances. Physical power became eclipsed by mechanical. The independent craftworker gave way to the proletarian worker who, having been stripped of his independence, toiled merely for his wage.

The impact of change in the nineteenth century was most felt with the coming together of science and industry and the application of new sources of power in industry. Materials used in manufacture changed, the diversity of goods available exploded and geographical shifts in the location of productive industry occurred. They were needed in increasing quantities. New names appeared, derivatives of related mineral and man-made products and processes. A chemical industry emerged. Amonia, nitric acid, artificial fertilisers for agriculture, and soda appeared. The heavy chemical industries became based in the North as so many were derived from carbon. The extent of their exchange burgeoned, with trade routes criss-crossing the globe and the machines by which they were furnished developed at a bewildering pace. The place of production shifted from the home to the factory – growing bigger and more concentrated. Britain, which had depended for so long on agriculture as a source of wealth, now saw it dwindle to a mere detail. For this was the century of textiles, of steam, the railway, steel and coal, then electricity, and the telegraph, but the biggest change came in the character of the workforce that laboured to sustain each development. Where once there had been a family unit working long hours from the home and owning their own tools and elementary machinery, there came a 'workforce', herded into towns and cities, working in increasing numbers in factories, for wages rather than for themselves and on machinery wholly owned by the employers. They were stripped of the independence of a thousand years in a single generation. As a result Morris devoted his whole life to the restoration of that precious independence.

It is commonly accepted that the industrial revolution took place in two distinct phases: the first – during which it gathered pace and power – extending up to 1815 and the second, roughly covering the years up to the end of Victoria's reign. A number of other major changes also took place. Wood gave way to metal and the time-honoured skills of the carpenter and stonemason were overtaken by the metalworking wrights. One characteristic of the industrial revolution is that it forever left agriculture in shadow. Henceforth whatever Britain was unable to grow she could pay for through traded goods. As industry grew it had a profound and revolutionising effect on the nature of agriculture. The population shift from the land to the cities created a sharp drop in the numbers available to work this labour-intensive area with the result that farmers turned to mechanisation and farms grew bigger to make this pay. Land prices increased as the owners discovered that industry could be lucrative, especially if one wanted to open a coalmine or run a railway track over land previously used for cultivation. All areas of life were drawn into the change. There was a revolution in habitat. The nature of city dwelling dominated literature and influenced Government commissions for a century.

There was, too, a revolution in the relationship between science and industry. For 150 years, the inventors of this relatively small island completely dominate the often better-resourced innovators from abroad. Britain was the place to trial and sell new ideas and British capitalists were swift to snap up these inventions and put them to practical use.

For years the Guilds had been able to delay the introduction of new machinery. There were two reasons that enabled them to do this. One was that science was then in the hands of an aristocracy which had intelligence and a culture of learning that enabled them to progress but who only saw science as a means to understand the world about them, rather than to change it. The second was that the law allowed the Guilds to physically limit the number of looms or furnaces that could be used. After the English revolution of the mid-seventeenth century much of this changed.

Alchemy, a natural inquisitiveness based on superstition and remnants of magic and non-mainstream religions sharply diminished in this period and rationalism and science as we now understand it began to emerge. The class from which scientists were drawn expanded hand in hand with the range of education available to such newcomers. Science began to attract the craftsmen who had a practical as well as theoretical knowledge and who sought new solutions to existing practical problems. As such, when breakthroughs were made, there was a ready audience to receive them and they were put into play very quickly. The Yorkshireman, John Harrison, who invented the longitude clock in 1713, was such a man. A carpenter by trade and deservedly well known, he represented a whole new class of working scientists. Watt, who invented the steam engine was a watchmaker, Arkwright who invented the throstle was a barber and Fulton who invented the steam engine was a jeweller.

Other revolutions centre on population growth and on the development of local government and a franchise that workers could influence to an increased degree. Many of these workers had lost their land and been moved into factories as they were dispossessed of the tools of their trade. Science intervened to produce massive machines either to supply power or to dramatically increase levels and rates of production. Thus, it became less and less likely that the dispossessed would, ever again, be able to generate sufficient capital to re-enter the market place as serious players.

Whereas in medieval times it was usual for a craftsman to serve an apprenticeship, journey for several years and then employ others, the structure of factory life and the rush to generate increasing amounts of capital meant that, even where a craftsman could retain his skill, he would, in all probability, only get work if he could find an employer. Wage labour and loss of ownership of the means of production was an essential feature of the accumulation process.

How did these workers perceive their condition? The greatest breakthroughs in the industrial revolution came in the development of the means of generating power: steam and the steam engine, the turbine, the internal combustion engine and electricity. Yet the craftsman saw the greatest change and challenge in smaller machines that he was compelled to operate and that deskilled and demeaned him. Basically they took his job. The pace and degree of industrial change was such that, for any of these things to happen he would not have to wait long or look very far. In his reaction to the first phase of the industrial revolution, the craftsman was concerned with how he might block, or at worst come to terms with, the introduction of such new machinery. By the second phase, he is reshaping his guilds into trade unions and working out how he can take his revenge. Of course this kind of accommodation is understandable in one attempting to survive an industrial tidal wave, but getting even is not the same as retrieving ownership of one's tools and it was this that galvanised Morris.

Morris was born into this fast lane, into a period in which change and economic growth reached previously unprecedented levels. He was born just as the first industrial revolution was making way for the second. By the time he died, Britain was already facing a challenge to her position as first amongst empires.

For centuries up until 1800, there had been a continual search for greater power sources to enable larger machines to dig deeper than ever, carry ever heavier loads and power even more machines. Prior to that, for 25,000 years civilising mankind had looked to the sun as its only source of original power. The sun it was that determined all life on earth, the movement of the seas, the flow of wind and the growth of all vegetation and from this source, man learned how to draw food, fuel, power and make shelter. Habitations were determined by purely the proximity to good agricultural land and the availability of water. During the industrial revolution, for the first time, man created a source of power that did not depend on the weather or the time of day. In addition, because the new source became increasingly flexible and portable, centres of living and working would change fundamentally too. In the metal-based industries from nailmaking to swordmaking, water-power was being used extensively, which both limited the amount of power generated and the geographical positioning of users who had to be situated close to a source of flowing water. So the search inevitably led from fixed sources to independent ones – to steam. The demand could only grow as industry ceased to be a junior partner to agriculture, which had hitherto played the dominant role in industrial and social life in Britain. It was not long before the sway of feudal lords and aristocrats and the rigid control they exercised over land and labour was broken.

For centuries, industry had consisted of small concentrations – often within a single extended family – of independent craftsmen who owned their own tools and workshops. As his worked progressed, a craftsman would take on apprentices and journeymen who were employed as itinerant artisans in training, working across and even beyond Britain. However, because of its limited size, this kind of operation found it impossible to generate enough capital to set new inventions, machinery and techniques into operation.

Power loom work – by removing the need for great physical strength and introducing machinery requiring different forms of manual dexterity, independently powered, women began to supplant men in textiles, a key industrial sector in early 19th century.

Where trades were concentrated, craftsmen banded together in guilds. Established over generations these provided standards for the craft, organised the supply and training of apprentices, protected prices and excluded the unqualified or insufficiently qualified from working at the trade. They were therefore able to regulate levels of pay by controlling the numbers entering the guild. Hereby also making membership desirable.

Underpinning them was their control over the quality of the product. Most trades, from printing to papermaking, to spinning and metalworking, were dominated by the guilds throughout the Middle Ages and well into the first stage of the industrial revolution.

Towards the end of the seventeenth century, new forms of power allowed the development of heavier machinery that required a greater number of workers to be concentrated together in 'manufactories'. This machinery was owned by individual capitalists, whose wealth enabled them to purchase land for building workplaces large enough to accommodate both it and their new workforce. Of course they also had the means to pay wages to those able enough to labour for them, but did not employ guild members, which diminished the power of many guilds. Capitalism in industry first gained ascendancy in those industries where machinery was necessary, in coal mining and in the potteries, in metalwork, printing and the all-important textiles. Guild members could not compete in those fields where simple repetition dramatically increased the volume of goods of a similar kind.

The fifty years leading up to the birth of Morris is a time of collapse for the skilled craft worker. The separation of those higher up the guild into a new and emerging capitalist class begun in the 1600s reached a mature phase. This took place in guild after guild, representing crafts as disparate as blacksmiths, goldsmiths, butchers, bakers, furriers, weavers, skinners and cordwainers, this last the (now archaic) guild for a shoemaker.

The craftworker was losing his independence and found access to work increasingly difficult. Nowadays it is fashionable to say "so what?" or, "it serves them right for trying to hold back history", supposedly the craftworker had stood in the way of capitalist enterprise in order to freeze-frame the world as it was. The 'Rebecca' and 'Swing Riots' and the 'Luddites' – now a term of abuse applied to those who question or reject change – did not in fact oppose change *per se*. Rather they struck out in a premeditated and systematic way only at those machines they deemed unfair and an immediate threat to their livelihood. Even then, mass, destructive action was only initiated after the employer had been given an opportunity to negotiate change. The craftworker suffered much more than generational change and dislocation. He lost ownership of the means of producing life and has yet to retrieve it. Some 'inventors' recognised the profound disruption caused by the machinery they had conjured up and would, in effect, 'mothball' them. Others pressed on, regardless. Over a prolonged period of time, stretching from before the English Revolution right up until the 1800s, the guilds sought to check the advance of 'progress'. Although, on the surface, they appear to have tried to check the factory system, it was the actual machines that they feared most. As early as 1552, the guilds tried to persuade Parliament to outlaw the use of the power driven gig-mill. It was only much later, after fruitless appeals to law and government that craftsmen, such as loom workers, resorted to force.

Industry and science meet

Throughout the 1700s science was being teased away from being the plaything of a well-meaning aristocracy and becoming allied to capital. After Lee invented a knitting machine in 1589, the first British mechanical invention of the industrial age, the number of innovations and scientific enquiries began to increase and change in character. An interest in astrology was giving way to questions of how to generate increased quantities of power and dovetail it into the development of industrial processes. Initially, what was unique about Britain was not the extent of her inventions, but the speed with which they were being applied to production.

In these early days of industrial change, production of coal increased tenfold in the century to 1680. The number of merchant ships weighing over 100 tons rose tenfold in the half century to 1629. Coal-fire powered production, ships supported the trade of goods. The growth of tonnage carried by inland canals and coastal shipping is testimony to the growth in the economy. Ocean-going ships took wares to markets abroad and brought back raw materials and goods to trade. In a general sense, the English revolution of 1640 stripped away those aspects of feudalism that prevented the rise of capitalism. Many of these structures, including, crucially, the power of the Crown to establish monopolies over certain trades, (thereby protecting themselves and the old order), were swept away.

Although the revolution weakened the aristocracy and forever tamed the monarchy, it brought pro capitalist elements such as bankers and merchants to power. The industrial or manufacturing capitalist was not to complete his ascendancy until the Great Reform Act in 1832, just before Morris's birth, but the revolution of 1640 gave Britain a 150-year head start over her nearest rivals-to-be, the French. Clearing the logjam in 1640 led to a growth, indeed a surge, of industrial activity. There was an influx of invention. Each one compounded the process whereby workers were separated from the tools of their craft and confirmed the shift towards the mechanisation of work.

Capitalism proved to be a much more aggressive mechanism than feudalism for accumulating capital and greatly accelerated industrial processes. This was especially true when it involved the kind and volume of capital needed to finance large-scale machinery. For example, in just half a century, the core transport system for Britain was put in place. An extraordinary feat! The following mainline stations were built: London Bridge (1836), Euston (1837), Fenchurch Street (1841), Waterloo (1848), King's Cross (1852), Paddington (1854), Victoria (1860), Charing Cross (1864), Broad Street (1865), Cannon Street (1866), St Pancras (1868), Liverpool Street (1874) and Marylebone (1899).

Creating a market with its own internally generated dynamism meant that less efficient producers, including those seeking collective security in the guilds, were ruthlessly cut down or transformed into agencies for the promotion of capital accumulation. At the same time it meant that the costs of entry into the market and, in particular into the markets used to generate capital that underpinned invention, became prohibitive. The separation between the craftsman producer and the capitalist was widened by the vast amounts of capital involved. One textile capitalist wrote in 1825 that he was operating twenty times more capital than the decade before.

This development takes place over the best part of two centuries. It begins in the period up to 1815 when capitalism expanded to create its own market in which commodities circulated close to home. In the second period up to 1870 that market expanded so that of the total goods traded worldwide, in that year, three-quarters passed through the London docks. After 1870, imperialism developed, (which meant that the world trade in commodities was complemented by the export of the means of production, which then competed with the home market), resulting in the dominance of capital in its finance form.

Capitalism was based around, but of course much bigger than, individual owners of capital. For the first time those aspiring to membership of the ruling class – in contrast to the monarchy, feudal lords and the aristocracy – involved themselves in production. This meant that the capitalist had of necessity to become competitive, not so much as a philosophy of life, but as a means of survival. Once competition became a permanent feature of life, it soon became dominant. Anything that gave one capitalist an advantage over another fired his interest, because without this edge, he was finished. As he intervened more in production to do things his way and fashion them to his choice, workers lost even more influence over their way of working.

This involvement by factory owners, which would have been entirely alien to an aristocracy which paid others to take part in production changed the nature of production for ever. Hitherto the ruling classes were quite unversed in the processes that underpinned their wealth. Indeed they were largely unconcerned by them, deeming them unworthy of their interest. To them, science was divorced from and superior to production; they saw it as a means of engaging with the world, indeed the universe. Where the aristocrat looked up through a telescope at remote galaxies, the capitalist wanted to look downwards into the world beneath his feet and find out what needed to be done to turn material reality into a saleable commodity. It changed for ever the role of thinker and doer. Thinking, henceforth, was measured by its ability to make profit, or to comprehend the world so that profit would become more likely. The capitalist was mainly concerned with work, so the man of science, who depended on capital for his patronage, turned to the craftworker for inspiration and insight. Inventors would employ whole teams of such men, thus creating a closer bond and interplay between the theoretical and the practical; yet each was at the same time becoming disengaged from the means of production.

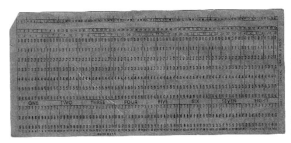

Card used in setting a carding machine which controlled patterns in woven cloth – often complex patterns. Carding controlled machines, de-skilled operators and opened the way for children to drive machines from an age of seven.

This process has influenced much of what we call science today, but it started as early as the fifteenth century and gathered speed from the eighteenth century onwards. In many cases craftsmen were seekers after knowledge: embryo scientists in a sense. JD Bernal, Hobson and Henry Slesser have all drawn this conclusion. Slesser wrote, "though great epoch making discoveries have, from time to time revolutionised the industrial world, by far the greater part of invention has not been done by the actual 'discoverers', who are but few and far between, but by the ordinary run of engineers, who, one inventor developing this, another modifying that, improve upon the original conception until a highly efficient machine, the product not of one man, but of many, is evolved." To prove the point, the cotton spinning machinery that dominated the spinning trade in the mid 1850s was a compound of 800 separate inventions. A carding machine alone comprised 80 individual patents.

The meeting of the minds of inventors and craftworkers was becoming a kind of democracy in ideas at a time when opportunities for individual responsibility of thought and action was being withdrawn. Practical science, in the service of profit, was a challenge to both church and aristocracy who wanted to hold the world as it was. Production was experiment. The speed of industrial development made it difficult for authorities such as Crown and Church to hold back new thinking. As each scientific breakthrough was applied to production, seekers after truth could see quickly what worked and what did not. Those seeking answers to what worked in industry and what did not turned away from God and sought authority in rationalism and materialism. The invention of telescopes and microscopes in the sixteenth and seventeenth centuries which allowed inquirers to look beyond what could be seen by the naked eye, gave great impetus to this materialism.

Science was finding a role in a range of fields: in scientific research and medicine. It forged ahead in manufacturing and extractive industries by its concentration through technology. Industry was struggling to keep up. An expansion of fine engineering and the precision industries such as clockmaking, instrument manufacture, machines for weighing and measuring and those employed to extend trade through sea travel, occurred.

Although it may not have felt like it to factory hands in the late 1700s, Watt's steam machine was a significant step forward. Thereafter, production no longer required water power to drive it.

Nowadays, all serious progress is based on a mass of accumulated scientific knowledge garnered from a broad range of sources; domestic and international and collectively from groups within and across separate nations. But in Morris's time we are describing a period when such knowledge simply either did not exist or was still being processed. It is true that the number of failures far outweighed the successes, but each tentative advance moved forward the general body of knowledge and made its mark, often in the least likely quarters and in ways not originally intended. Separate industrial or craft disciplines began to be more interwoven. The revolution in printing in the seventeenth century accelerated this with an explosion of book publishing that promoted and explained new scientific methods, processes and developments in machinery. The body of knowledge contained in these books was easily communicated throughout Europe and beyond.

It was said of the eighteenth century that if the French built a bridge, which subsequently fell down, they would build an *école technique* to try to find out why it had happened. The British, however, would build it again and again until it stayed up. The nineteenth century was a remarkable one. During this century many of the philosophical streams that we, today accept as normal, were established and took root. At the same time others that had existed for much longer were changed beyond recognition.

Power surge

The most dramatic breakthrough in technology came as a result of the search for and application of new sources of power to manufacturing processes, the effect of which was to be felt at its greatest in textiles. The development of the steam engine, a search that began with Galileo and Torricelli is a motif for the development of science and technology and its relationship with production. The driving forces for the creation of the steam engine were many. Principally, the aim was to use steam to create a vacuum that could raise water as old suction pumps could do this to only a limited level. Galileo discovered that water was not sucked up into the vacuum but raised by the force of atmospheric pressure on the water in the sump below. The task was to find a way that could raise water beyond the then optimum level of thirty feet. This was necessary because mine seams were being driven deeper and deeper into the ground. By the 1650s an air pump had been invented that could create a vacuum at will. The pump allowed a whole new area of knowledge to be developed around vacuum and atmospheric pressure – it proved to be a powerful force. By the 1750s some mines in Britain and Belgium were being driven as deep as 600 feet and the pump began to come into its own both for draining the mines and controlling the flow of water. In 1702 one mine owner is recorded as using 500 horses underground to power his pumps. The first

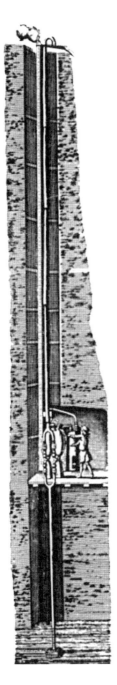

engine, unsuccessful as it happens, was patented by Savery in 1698 and was intended to drain water from mines. It was called the Miner's Friend (see left). Though unsuccessful it served to focus attention on the other requisites for making a steam engine viable – the development of pistons and cylinders. At about the same time Papin was able to use the expansion of steam to drive a piston upwards in a vertical cylinder and use its condensation to create a vacuum to draw it down again. Thus a weight could be raised by means of a rope passed over a pulley and attached to the engine. However, the boiler was integral rather than separate. By 1712 Thomas Newcomen, a Dartmouth ironmonger, had constructed an engine that had a separate boiler and could therefore be put into operation commercially. Hundreds of these were soon in the tin and copper mines of Cornwall.

The greatest transformation took place in textiles an area that captivated Morris as early as the 1850s. In the seventeenth and eighteenth centuries, silk became a luxury commodity amongst the wealthy. The production process whereby a lustrous yarn was made out of the cocoons of silk worms originated in China and was brought to Sicily, then Italy and later, France in the Middle Ages. An influx of refugee protestant Huguenots who gave great impetus to the use of linen, at the end of the 17th century, gave Britain an opportunity to end dependence on foreign supplies of silk. The industry took root in Spitalfields in east London. It was organised on a domestic system with weavers working in garrets which had long 'weaver's lights' – long windows on the upper floors. Many can still be seen today. By the nineteenth century new techniques for finishing cotton meant that the silk industry faced competition. It partly relocated to Coventry, Stockport and Macclesfield where it became allied to other processes such as stocking knitting and ribbon-making. It was always dependent on foreign supplies of raw materials, which were often disrupted, especially by war.

Silk produced the first modern factory – manufactory – based on the employment of many people working on a single complex process requiring machinery. The factory employed 300 people and was built on an island in the River Derwent in Derby by Sir Thomas Lombe. The machinery was driven by water power.

Work in progress in the home of a spinner (above). This kind of work involved entire families as an economic as well as social unit. It allowed protection for the elderly, young or infirm, especially in better times of trade. The factory (below) radically changed all of this and brought with it the overseer. In the past a chargehand or foreman would have been the most skilled worker. Overseers did just that; their purpose? Labour discipline.

Textiles had for centuries up until the 1750s been based on local craft and cottage work using their own distinct work patterns, cultures and disciplines.

Manufactory was a rude and rather crude awakening. The early system was based on 'putting out'. In areas such as Lancashire, spinners and weavers would buy their raw materials in and work them up in their own homes. The finished product was then sold back to the original raw materials providers. This model was the norm for textiles in this country and was the same for Burnley and Glasgow as it was for the silk weavers of Spitalfields in east London. In spinning, John Kay's Flying Shuttle, invented in 1733, and in general use within two decades, mechanised the movement of the shuttle through the web, dramatically speeding up the earlier method, and freeing up one hand to perform another task. Home spinners could not hope to compete with this rate of work. Other inventions came on stream that improved the quality of the thread and the speed with which fibres could be drawn out to make it. This allowed machines to run at even greater speeds whilst reducing breakage time. By 1738 this spinning was mechanised and in 1764 Hargreaves produced his 'Spinning Jenny', which allowed a single worker to control as many as 80 spindles at once.

James Hargreave was one of the classic innovator's of the nineteenth century. Uneducated, indeed illiterate, he worked as a spinner, carpenter, and inventor. He lived and worked in Blackburn in Lancashire where the Spinning Jenny was invented in 1764. Sadly this brilliant machine was designed to be worked by children and a single operator could work eight spools simultaneously. Hargreaves worked in secret but was once hunted down by local spinners and his machines smashed.

It takes no great leap of imagination to estimate the effect that such combinations of machinery would have on the industry – both on the putting out system (why put out to 80 workers when you can bring them in under one roof and get each of them to operate 80 spindles?) and on the numbers employed. Arkwright raised the stakes when, in the late 1760s, he developed a 'water frame' which used both animal and water-power to drive the spinning process. An industry that had, for as far back as one could imagine, operated on the brain and muscle of individual craftsmen, was now to operate on brain and mechanical means, powered independently. Muscle has a breaking point and has to be rested, while machines can be run all day, then replaced. Muscle forms part of the same body as the brain which sets it to work. Yet in the new way of doing things, brain and muscle are applied to run machinery that belongs to some one else: the factory owner.

When Crompton combined the best features of Arkwright's and Hargreave's work to create a 'Spinning Mule' there could be no going back and no amount of machine breaking could rescind the process that had been set in motion. By 1825, this 'mule' became fully self-acting and, in addition, could be power driven without the use of skilled labour. When steam power was added, productivity rose and cottage industries were crushed in a race to manufacture under a single factory roof. The reverberations were soon to be felt in weaving.

Textile factories were built on a grand scale dominating the skyscape of many a city such as Leeds or Newcastle, Bolton and Burnley. But, relative to homeworking, they required fewer workers.

The dream of a power-driven loom went back a long way. Leonardo Da Vinci had designed one and like many a good thing, it was impracticable at first and could not work. However, by the 1700s the mechanical elements described above began to converge. First, arrangement of the raw materials used in weaving had to be standardised, then production automated. Kay had achieved this by 1745. Many contributed, (most notably Reverend Cartwright), to developing machinery and processes that eventually resulted in a power-driven weaving machine. These machines were sophisticated and robust and were in wide use by the 1830s. The draw loom that allowed the weaving of patterns complemented the ordinary loom used for plain weaving. Carding machines, with punch holes arranged to produce complicated patterns, were in use by 1800. Most aspects of textiles were standardised, mechanised and automated by the 1830s. Increasingly production became continuous and power driven by the application of steam. In 1783, Bell produced a machine that used engraved cylinders to print cotton.

This application of machinery allied to the pool of knowledge and skilled labour accumulated over centuries, led to an 'explosion' of Britain's textile industries. By 1870 they had captured the world market. Whereas in 1701 the total value of textile exports was £23,253, by 1870 it was over £71 millions. By 1800 the demand for power was far outstripped by the potential growth of industry. This potential could be applied to ever broadening categories of industry: from the potteries in Staffordshire in need of power to crush sufficient quantities of flint and grind enamel colours, to the flour mills trying to keep pace with the demand for bread from a rapidly growing and concentrated urban population. So, machines increased in size and power and in range of application – to meet the needs of the multiplication of processes within industries, and in a growing number of industrial sectors.

Weaving was one of those ancient staple industries rudely interrupted by the industrial revolution. The logic of the textile capitalist was the pursuit of profit, if possible on a world-scale. Based on homeworking this aim could not be achieved. So homeworking had to go.

Power and technology meet

The development of textiles was mirrored in the other great industry that set Britain apart from others: engineering. The expansion of the domestic industrial infrastructure, that included shipbuilding, rail, road, bridge and tunnel building, the expansion of the canal system and of communications, all increased the pressure to develop the capacity of steam engines. There was a need for bigger everything: larger furnaces, heavier rolling mills for steel, boring machines and power hammers, each requiring increased inputs of power to operate to the full.

Windmills had existed for two millennia or more (Vitravius mentions them operating in Rome in 25BC) and proved a useful local source of power. Recent research estimates that there were up to 10,000 in operation by the early nineteenth century in Britain. Key to the growth of milling required to feed a burgeoning population, there were 275 operating in Essex alone in 1840.

Initially, inventors sought to power such developments by reaching into the existing cupboard, seeking to get more from wind power, water, animals and the use of the Newcomen steam engine (although this had not yet been modified to drive rotary machinery). Trial and error had taken each of these a long way. Now it would be the turn of a new breed of scientist like John Smeaton who used a laboratory to experiment with and measure deviations in the output of power. Smeaton increased the value of the power extracted from the waterwheel and later the windmill, but his greatest contribution came in calculating and thence assessing the various elements required to build bigger and more effective engines.

Water driven equipment obviously meant that centres of production had to be situated near water sources. The Newcomen engine was a partial solution to this limitation but it could only be used for driving pumps. The obvious answer, pioneered by Darby, another iron founder, was to install a Newcomen engine that would then pump water to waterwheels that could then drive the machinery. Along came James Watt, known as the father of the Industrial

Revolution. His special contribution was to enable production to proceed without water power. By 1769 he had solved the problems holding back the Newcomen engine, principally how to keep the cylinder permanently at a high temperature. He did this by enclosing it in a 'steam jacket' and creating a separate condenser, kept permanently cold. By 1776 he was working in Birmingham with Matthew Boulton who used his capital to build Watts first effective engine and before long his machines were being used to pump water from Cornish tin mines and power giant bellows for a blast furnace in Shropshire. Within ten years he had produced an engine that could power rotary machinery.

Although Watt merits his place among the principal achievers of the industrial age, it should borne in mind that he had much more capital behind him than his predecessors and was operating at a time when the urgency for the accumulation of capital was accelerating. He was fully equipped to do his job. His engines were soon being used to work winding machinery in coal and copper mines, drive a flour mill and power a forge hammer at Wedgwood's pottery. By 1850, steam had outstripped water as a source of power. Watt's engines were used extensively in industry. An engine based on high pressure rather than atmospheric pressure was still some way off, as it would require considerable development in metallurgy and ironwork.

The impact on people

What was the impact of this on the people? And what did the young William Morris make of it? It is natural to dwell on the more obvious aspects of such rapid change, concentrated as it was into relatively few years. Gareth Steadman Jones has referred to it as "capitalism's incessantly restless, compulsively innovatory character; its iconoclastic subversion of all cultures, practices and beliefs." Whilst the conditions of labour deteriorated, advances began to be made in nutrition, in medicine and education. From Morris's point of view it was not the steady decline in the conditions of labour (which he described as a return to serfdom), but the nature of the relationship of worker to production that concerned him most. A worker who no longer owned the means of production, could be neither master of his own life nor in his working community as a whole. He could now only enter the market as a seller of labour-power and, not owning his own means of production, he did so in an inferior position to the man who lived by hiring his labour. Between 1700 and 1815, group after group of workers, who previously did own their means of production, fell into the web of capitalism. The impact was felt both at home and abroad. The growth of the cotton industry brought the town of Manchester from a population of 17,000 in 1770 to 180,000 in 1830, a ten-fold increase in just 60 years. Marx wrote of capital, "cheap prices of commodities are the heavy artillery with which it batters down all Chinese walls, with which it forces the barbarians' intensely obstinate hatred of foreigners to capitulate. It compels all nations, on pain of extinction, to adopt the bourgeois mode of production ..."

In Morris's schema, the capitalist is the one who owns tools, but does no work with them. He takes away the old tools, be they trowels or saws from those skilled to operate them, but his only labour is the attempt to increase his profit at the expense of other owners of capital and workers alike. Other tools, newer ones, are invented. The worker, who henceforth could not afford to own capital and work, is moved under a factory roof and beneath a hierarchy of overseers totally removed from the situation existing when production was carried out in the home. The worker no longer has control over the length and pace of his working day – he is trapped.

It is doubtful that things could have developed differently. The dynamic and revolutionary force of capitalism – that part which Marx says, "broke down Chinese walls" – arrested the power of the aristocracy and both the major and petty restrictions of feudalism and was unstoppable. What might follow capitalism? For Morris, the answer seemed to be in feudalism. His early critique of the capitalist system draws on feudalism as a known and proven alternative. But it has to be said that, his ideas depended too heavily on Ruskin's and that he was in danger of idealising and misunderstanding what feudalism was all about. However, not for the reasons that the reader might first think. Today we are told that medieval times were hard and harsh and that the ordinary man was subject to arbitrary and unfair rule. While there is obviously some truth in this, it does not appear so bleak when compared with the living conditions of those, for example, who were cleared off the Scottish Highlands in the eighteenth century. Morris did much to change our view of the feudal period and give it some balance and clarity.

Writing in *Art and Labour* (1884) he insisted, against the strain of thinking then current, "I repeat that for the workers life was easier; though in general life was rougher than it is in our day; that there was more approach to real equality of condition ... as the distribution of wealth in general was more equal than now ... so in particular was that of art or the pleasure of life; all craftsmen had some share in it ... " He searched for art as an expression of joy in labour and finds it in gothic architecture, built at a time when the craftsman was king. Such architecture was an expression of freedom in work where

When Craftsmen was crowned King. Ruskin's own illustrations from the *Seven Lamps of Architecture* illustrate the brilliant skill of the stonemason for whom art and labour were as one. Yet in Victorian Britain such buildings were being destroyed and lost forever. In it he wrote "the buildings it describes with so much delight being now either knocked down, or scraped and patched up into smugness and smoothness more tragic than an uttermost ruin".

craftsmen designed, manufactured and laboured and in return were well remunerated and respected. For only they could carry out these tasks, because the feudal lords did not care to know how.

Why Morris is sometimes considered guilty of idealising feudalism is easy to explain. He saw a future based on plentiful production of beautiful products which were a pleasure to make and manufactured as a result of a harmonious consensus between producer and consumer. However, feudalism was never able to produce that abundance and indeed sought to hold on to the old ways even when new ones came along that could yield enough to satisfy Morris's dream. Morris sought two things in history: craft and community. In his analysis of the fourteenth century, romanticised or not, he certainly found the British artisan at a high point. He respected his capacity to produce, the quality of his work, and his ownership of the tools that sustained his life. Above all, under layers of regimentation and regulation, he found community in the form of fellowship.

Morris, of course, only came to recognise this when he was in his forties and engaged in design, manufacture and commerce with his company trading on a world scale. He came to see in capitalism a necessary, if unpalatable, phase in human development, in which much was produced but often of the wrong kind, of inferior quality and at a price most could not afford. So he began to consider not the power of industry, but how to interpret the power behind industry: the worker. Thinking of the millions of handworkers driven from employment by machinery, in the midst of urban growth and with depressed wages, and high food prices, Morris wondered what motivated them?

Marx, too, independently concluded that capitalism was one in a series of historical successions of different property forms. He also thought that the abundance of commodities capitalism created, allied to the disinheriting of the workers, pointed the way to the kind of historical form of property relations that might succeed capitalism. Property would be socialised to allow the producer access to the means of producing the commodities that his labour power creates in such abundance. Morris drew similar conclusions but from a different standpoint. Where Morris is light on capitalism as an economy and is happy to rely, first on Ricardo and Ruskin, then on Marx, he is more thoughtful when assessing the impact of capitalism on the mind, body and soul of human beings in their role as producers. But it was Ruskin who put the question most sharply. He stated "you must either make a tool of the creatures, or a man of him. You cannot make both".

Change across widely divergent industries was thorough and irreversible. It altered for ever the way people experienced industrial life and work. It shaped too the way they responded to the changes taking place. Where, for example, families had once worked as one unit in their own homes they were now drawn into factories. Where families had been able to protect their children, the less able, pregnant mothers or older, slower workers, because they worked in the home and set their own pace, the factory exposed them all. The working day, in some industries, was sixteen hours and the factory, with its army of overseers and foremen, imposed a new regime and discipline. Fines were exacted for minor infringements and workers were often cheated out of wages. This system of workplace repression was matched by one equally draconian in society at large.

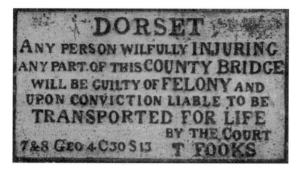

A sign attached to a bridge in Dorset. The legal code was still in operation when Morris was born.
(Reproduced courtesy of the TUC unionhistory.info)

Eric Hobsbawm, Edward Thompson and George Rude have researched doggedly in order to describe how workers and their families responded to this often traumatic episode. They have been diligent in uncovering the extent of the machine breaking and use of violence against those introducing new machinery to displace craft outworkers, and do a sterling job given that the organisation of 'Captain Swing' and 'Rebecca' were of necessity shrouded in secrecy. What is clear is that these acts were sustained over long periods. There were some notable and targeted attacks on inventors of new machinery and Crompton, for one, had to go into hiding and move around incognito. However, it is worth noting that in relation to the number of machines being introduced, the number of attacks was relatively small, and aimed at the machines because they were being used to depress wages. Some factories were set alight and direct attacks made on employers, but the British worker has never normally resorted to sabotage. Even at this early stage the wrath pitted against employers was not individual violence but collective organisation.

Between the development of the factory system and the 1832 Reform Bill hardly a month went by without a serious foot riot disturbance. In the absence, or rather the denial of historical rights, the people could express themselves in no other way. The hold of the state and the density of its presence in community and daily life was light. Organisation, in defiance of the law was secretive. Only rarely was the state able to prevail and when it did so, the hand of state sponsored agent provocateur could often be felt.

A scene of tranquility, a sense of light, space, fresh air and an assertion of life over production. Soon to be swept away.

In the same period prices rose, wages fell, and common land was appropriated with the support of Parliament. The introduction of machinery, with its consequent collapse of family life, left the working class in a spin. So it sometimes responded with a club.

Lancashire, early 1800s, was the world centre of cotton production. Between 1800 and 1840, 80 per cent of American cotton came directly to the area. The workers of Lancashire from shearers to spinners were in the front ranks of first Luddism, then Chartism and agitation for the vote.

As workers saw ownership of the means of production taken from them, they saw too, a growing monopoly in land and food. They may have been in a spin but they could exercise a collectivity and discipline too. Rioters dealt as harshly as any authority with those in its ranks who used the riot as an excuse to loot. Derbyshire colliers seized wheat on offer in a market at 8s 4d and sold it at 5s. In 1766, the Annual Register records fifty, "risings of the poor".

In August 1830, as the "Swing" riots shook the nation, labourers took control of Sussex for a short while. At Selbourne and Headley, the workhouses were burnt down. It is estimated that at one point, more troops were stationed against Luddites and 'Swing' than were deployed in the wars against Napoleon. In the one outbreak cited above, the government took 300 prisoners, hanged nine men and boys, transported 400 to Australia and imprisoned 400 more. The occasional break in discipline is understandable when we consider that this was a period when the order of the old guilds had broken down. Responses here were local and partial. That of the new trades unions had not yet been established. Some turned to Chartism.

As early as 1828, and only recently released from the oppression of the Combination Acts, unions, in this case weavers, were negotiating with employers over the introduction of power driven machinery and taking responsibility for the conduct of its members.

The new factory workforce was often shorn of the need to have a history of working at a particular trade, and deskilled – forced to put expertise to one side in order to earn a living operating machinery. These workers had been drawn from a number of occupations – such as agriculture – where they had a different way of expressing dissatisfaction and settling accounts.

Between the 1750s and 1820s, people were forced off the land by enclosure in increasing numbers and there was concern for their future. Generally, they followed family migration paths, flooding into already overcrowded cities. In the early part of the eighteenth century the Northern counties were sparsely populated; in 1724, Manchester was only the home of 2,400 families. This changed with the escalation of enclosure and the enlargement of factory work units. A good part of the population moved north. All across Britain, rural districts were depopulated as people drifted to the towns. The effect was so extreme that for nearly a century the 'labour' question became a question of the Poor Law. Landless labourers and dispossessed craftworkers did not automatically metamorphose into urban proletarians. Many became paupers first. Some of the machine breaking was more about the fear and anger of being reduced to poverty rather than an expression of organised, collective class-consciousness.

So it is surprising how workers seemed to recover so quickly from the shock of displacement and the new factory regime. They soon began to organise themselves collectively. First they wanted to keep prices down; boycotts and food riots were commonplace up until the 1840s. Secondly, they wanted good enough wages to afford some of the commodities that had become available on a large scale. In the sixty years to 1811 the population rose from 6.5 million to 10 millions. Those born into capitalism and the effects of the Industrial Revolution, had no memory of an age without employment as wage labourers. Only their grandparents could tell of these better times and it may be why for a century there remained a part of British folklore and culture within the working class that agreed with Morris about pre-capitalist times. Around the turn of the nineteenth century there was a marked fall in the death rate. Increases in the number of people working in healthcare, the improved quality of medicines and the consequent steady raise in the population meant that there were more grandparents around to tell such tales. The historian EC Fairchild has written, "when George III began to reign, wheaten bread was eaten by more than half the labouring population. With the money wage commanding a greater quantity of goods than at any time since the reign of Henry VI; the labourers standard of life in rural England, just before the industrial revolution, was far above that of his successor two generations after."

This was the capitalism that Morris was born into and from his twenties onwards, the pace of change accelerated. Other major changes began to kick in.

France had its bourgeois revolution in 1789. This unlocked similar forces to those unleashed by the English Civil War and through competition gave impetus to the creation of a domestic market in Britain. America gained her independence too and the struggle to unify both Germany and Italy, meant that Britain no longer strode the stage of world trade alone.

Capitalism – all-enveloping and irreversible?

There were still pockets in which the old ways remained. Indeed handicraft lingered for quite a while. As late as 1814 "love reaps" took place where all took part in harvesting in return for communal support in building cottages. In Soham, Cambridgeshire, as late as 1890, village and surrounding land was still unenclosed, and in the more mountainous districts of South Wales, Wilhelm Hasbach, a definitive historian of agricultural labour, found, "little farmers whose lives belonged to the patriarchal age when the division of labour was still unknown and when every family produced for itself whatever tools or utensils it needed, whether of iron, wood or leather." But in general, capitalist principles had embedded themselves so deeply into the national economy that the change quickly became irreversible.

After 1815 a mature phase of industrialisation began to emerge. Steam navigation pervaded the oceans and the rail network was firmly laid. In two bursts of 'railway mania', between 1820 and 1850 Britain opened six thousand miles of railway. Until then, no human being had moved faster than a few miles an hour. From clinging to a horse, people had, in a single generation graduated to, in the words of Hobsbawm, "The notion of a gigantic, nationwide, complex and exact interlocking routine symbolised by the railway timetable." It was the most dramatic expression of the novelty of industrial capitalism.

Offering cheaper and quicker methods of transporting, first goods, then people, the railways began to come into their own, redrawing the geography and demography of the nation. Journeys that had taken the best part of a week could now be made in a day or two. Morris himself, who did more than his fair share of travelling the country speaking and lecturing, regularly used the new steam passenger service to transport him from his home in Hammersmith to the East End of London. The original idea of applying steam to motion was to create a sort of locomotive for the road. Railways were initially about moving coal from pithead to dock, but later they were used commercially carrying people as well as cargo and commodities. Although networks were extensive, there was twenty miles of track at the Darby iron works in Coalbrookdale alone, that were horse-drawn. As a result of the work of Richard Trevithick it became possible to apply new steam-driven methods to locomotion. Along came another history-book-favourite, George Stephenson with his Rocket. Cotton manufacturers were quick to grasp the importance of steam train rail links. Word travelled fast, and that was good for business.

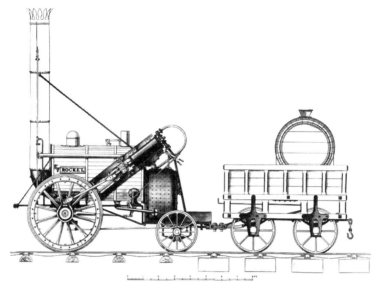

In many ways Stephenson's rocket (1829) has come to epitomise the industrial revolution. The original rocket, built to compete in trials that required it to pull three times its weight at over 10 miles per hour over a 90km course, can still be seen in the Science Museum.

Canals were having difficulty carrying the tonnage necessary and the presence of damp was not ideal. Despite the opposition of landowners, (who were soon to discover that they could join in the 'gold rush' too), a Stockton to Darlington line was endorsed by Parliament in 1826. In the five years to 1848, the length of track tripled and soon became the veins and arteries of industry. It also gave people freedom to travel to places that hitherto had merely been names on a map.

One of the most significant achievements of the nineteenth century was the harnessing of electricity and its audacious application across a broad range. The discovery of the voltaic cell in 1800 provided continuous electric current for the first time. In 1808, Humphrey Davy demonstrated his arc lamp; Faraday established the basic principles of electric motors in 1821 and ten years later, invented the electric dynamo.

As a result of the increasing complexity and internationalisation of commerce and finance, pressure grew to develop a telegraph. It was in industry that the telegraph first found use – introduced so that signalmen could be forewarned that trains were on their way. By 1851 a Dover to Calais cable was laid under the Channel and in 1866 a transatlantic service was established. The human voice soon followed the telegraphic signal. Electricity was proving at least as capable a source of power as steam and was soon to far outstrip the capacity of any other form of energy. It enabled industry to locate outside towns, and away from sources of water, severing the link with pithead and wharf. An important aim in the development of electricity was the possibility of electrification of street lighting but advanced experiments also existed in rail travel, power machine tools and even domestic appliances. Water and steam turbines and the internal combustion engine appeared, alongside electric power, the telegraph, the telephone and radio. Agriculture and the extractive industries became further mechanised. The engine gave a kick start to the extraction of oil which in turn underpinned the late emergence of plastics and man-made fibres.

Later, towards the end of Morris's life, steam turbines were built to generate power in factories and on ships. Their increasing reliability meant that they were also used to generate electricity. Although effective, much of the machinery was cumbersome, complex, and noisy and involved the use of overhead belts that were dangerous. What was required was something as powerful but more compact, efficient and flexible so that it could become part of – rather than an adjunct to – other production machinery, such as lathes and saws. Where steam engines had powered large-scale industry in the first half of the 1800s, by the second half, gas engines were being used to power light industry. By 1885, Gottlieb Daimler had adapted an engine to run on petrol; Karl Benz added an electrical ignition and Wilhelm Maybach a carburettor. Together they confidently set a course that would take nineteenth century industry into the twentieth. If the face of the earth and the seas could change so rapidly and fundamentally in Morris's lifetime, the sky could be used too. Gliders existed from 1857 on, alongside power-driven model aeroplanes and also airships; count Ferdinand von Zeppelin was working on his famous model in the last years of Morris's life.

Two other developments were to have a dramatic effect on Britain and each related to the sharp rise in agricultural productivity. The first was canning, allowing food to be sealed at or close to the point of production and shipped around the world. Trade in food thus expanded. Diets were supplemented by foodstuffs that could not have been grown in this country. Of course, canning fell easily in line with the great triumvirate of the Industrial Revolution: standardisation, mechanisation and automation. The second development was refrigeration. Britain began to import refrigerated meat from as far away as Australia and Argentina. Standardisation across industries took a big step forward with the establishment of a Patents Act (1852) and the unification of three patenting authorities in England and Wales, Scotland and Ireland.

In the sixty-two years of Morris's life machinery came to affect every aspect of the life of the worker. The machine played a role in all areas: from match manufacture, boot and shoemaking, bottle and can making and the production of cigarettes, at work, at home and in the community. They became as much a fixture as animals had been when man gradually ceased to be a nomadic hunter-gatherer and established a settled life on the land. Indeed it changed the world. By the middle of the nineteenth century, Britain's factories and mines were producing two-thirds of the world's coal, half of its iron, half of its cotton, and more than a third (in value) of its manufacturing machinery.

With the advent of the telegraph the later nineteenth century became an age of person to person communication. Typesetting and printing together with the telegraph would bring news into the community almost as it was happening. Or, in the case of the Rothschilds, before. Typewriters, the phonograph, cameras, films, calculating machines, sewing machines, locks for doors and the bicycle were all mass-produced, impacting deeply on people's lives. Small wonder so much thought was given as to how this new abundance could be shared.

So much had changed. The materials from which machines were made, the tools used to make them and the methods used to operate them were radically transformed. Until the end of the eighteenth century wood was the principal material used for making industrial machinery. Metal was only used to make bearing parts and cutting edges, where the relative softness of wood, would have been impractical and uneconomical. Even the boilers in early steam engines had been made of wood with metal harnesses. Iron smelting had not changed much since the middle ages, for the iron industry relied on a plentiful supply of charcoal and England was not rich in wood. Gradually, because this scarcity had pushed up the price of charcoal, the iron industry was forced to search for an alternative. The answer was coal. In England, Scotland and Wales, there was an abundance of coal and South Wales coalfields could provide anthracite coal of very high quality. Abraham Darby I (II and III were his son and grandson) was converting coal into coke for use in furnaces as early as 1709. Slowly, cautiously, the number of coal-fired furnaces crept up, the best of these using bellows powered by Watt's engines.

THE IRONFOUNDER.

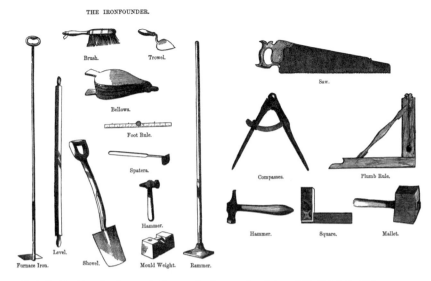

Tools that had barely changes in thousands of years of metal working. Yet they were transformed in a generation with the emergence of the industrial revolution. From the *Boys Book of Trades* (reproduced with permission).

Cast iron was too brittle for its role in the Industrial Revolution so wrought iron was developed. However, the level of expertise and the high grade of materials required limited the quantity that could be made. Pig iron was the answer and production rose from 68,300 tons in 1788 to 272,000 tons in 1806, an increase of 200 per cent. It was enough to make machines wholly out of metal.

The Lathe – shock trooper of industrial age

Metal swiftly colonised the construction of machines from printing presses to ships. Before 1800 an engineering industry was barely evident. By 1900 it thrived and employed 1,447,000 people.

As wood surrendered to metal, so the carpenter conceded to the mechanic. Industry began to furnish new types and grades of iron through hammering and rolling.

Henry Cort was dubbed by some the "father of the Iron Trade" because of his important innovations made by heating pig iron and striking it with a hammer to reduce the number of impurities; it was therefore "wrought" by hand. The new method was known as "puddling", whereby molten pig iron was stirred in a reverberatory furnace. Impurities were burned off and the resultant soft balls of metal were raked together to form a large lump. This was flattened by a powered forging hammer and fed directly into the grooved rollers of the rolling mill, to produce iron bars or sheets of uniform thickness. Cort patented his rollers in 1783 and his puddling process in 1784. John Wilkinson applied steam driven power to its processes a decade later.

In 1856 Henry Bessemer established a Bessemer converter which used air in a confined space to blast away impurities in metal. This turned iron into steel, allowing increased production at reduced costs. Bessemer was born in 1813 in Charlton, Hertfordshire, the son of an engineer and typefounder. Self-educated he took out nearly one hundred patents in metallurgy and his work was translated into many languages. Modern steel is still made using technology based on his processes. In the middle of the century Bessemer had devised a shell for the French army, then fighting in the Crimea, but it was too powerful for the cast iron cannons. He experimented by using blasts of cold air against molten iron which removed most of the carbon but allowed it to retain sufficient (about 2 per cent) to make it hard enough to work with. The impact was immediate. Suddenly, metal became cheap enough to use in building structures, as well as smaller machinery and armaments. Alloys followed which involved adding small quantities of different metals to create an alloy of steel that could be cut to greater accuracy and at higher speed. The demand for new, higher grades of steel arose because more of it was needed at cheaper production costs to fuel the building boom in homes, factories, railways and shipping.

There was also an increased demand for materials that could tolerate being fashioned to extreme accuracy. In 1830 a good craftsman was one who could work to a tolerance of one-sixteenth of an inch. In building an engine, or boring pipes used for the transportation of water, this is not good enough, and it would be totally inadequate for boring the barrel of a cannon or a rifle. It was not that the ability to work with accuracy did not exist, rather it could not be yet reproduced precisely enough for mass production. The new boring machines required higher quality materials that could be measured and cut with little or no tolerance. This was also true for the lathe. Up until the end of the seventeenth century, this versatile machine was used to cut soft materials, turn wood or may be the softer metals used in clock and measuring instrument manufacture. In the following century it was developed to apply more widely to metals but on finer work such as clock, weighing machines or the production of surgical instruments: what today we would call precision engineering.

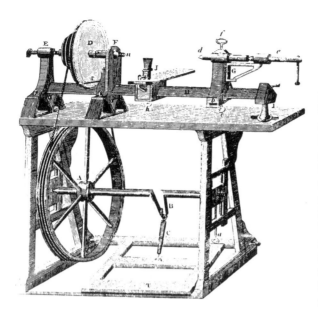

Lathes existed since the first days when humans needed to fashion wood, then metals. As invention after invention added independent power, accuracy and greater cutting ability at ever higher speeds, the lathe became the machine par excellence of engineering. It also greatly empowered the operator in a way Morris found difficult to envisage.

Henry Maudsley made a significant breakthrough in 1800 establishing many of the core mechanisms that shape lathe work, even today. He invented a workable slide rest, made a lathe entirely from metal and established accurate surfaces to guide tool movements. The use of all-metal machinery made the lathe rigid, heavy, trustworthy and reliable, regardless of climate change. He even brought gears into general use. The lathe was now fit to take on the harder metals at greater speed and accuracy.

For this reason the lathe is one of the machines that have come to epitomise the second stage of the Industrial Revolution. It had existed in the middle ages but was quite unsuited to use in the home – delivering quantities of raw metal through the back gate was quite impractical. It had become, a factory machine and as power was added and refinements made, it became the factory machine *par excellence*. Ironically, given the scepticism of William Morris, the lathe became a significant machine for the working class, requiring increased, not less skill, and relying on a knowledge of old skills and the development of new ones. At its height it was used by hundreds of thousands of craftsmen, and later, craftswomen. The toolmaker became the backbone of the engineering industry. The very nature of the machine – which required common skills but was used in many diversified settings and workplaces, lent itself to the formation of a unified engineering culture from which emerged (within half a century), the shop stewards' movement. This was not the effect that Morris had predicted. Because the lathe could so easily be positioned as a central feature in the production process, its operators also became central to production, a natural step to trade union organisation. The toolmaker was the single most important force in British industry right up until the 1970s, when control of the machine was taken off-line and onto computers and core workings were outsourced. Arguably, they are still the key, and would be again if and when Britain wakes up to the need to rebuild its manufacturing power.

The lathe became vital to mass production industries from around 1870 onwards. By reason of its speed and accuracy, it brought down the cost of constructing the huge number of machines needed to make a mass of goods. Where a product is based on a single form, like pins, nails, type fonts, or the assembly of a small number of standardised parts, mass production is relatively easy to arrange. Where there are many parts to be assembled to make a machine, with the assembly taking place in a different workplace or where there are a number of separate companies making parts of a machine, accuracy and standardised measurements and materials become very important.

The increasing accuracy of lathes and the establishment of strict industrial standards of weight, size and measurement, made possible the mass-production of complex machines, for these could now be made from the products of a range of suppliers. The system of mass production, reliant on inter-changeable, identical parts began to develop at speed. In Morris's early life such complex production was limited and at an early stage. The advanced forms as shown in Taylorism and Fordism, that in many ways came to characterise capitalism, only began to develop towards the end of his life. Mass production came naturally to capitalism and the lathe was crucial to its development.

Of course Morris's critique of capitalism was much more than one sceptic's view of the onward march of machinery. He did not want to end this progression, nor did he believe it possible: his fears concerned the effect such machinery had on craftsmen of the pre and early capitalist age. However, as we have seen, the lathe only became a force after the village and small-scale, often rural, craftsman had been absorbed into factory work. Morris's critique of capitalism was a gospel for the dispossessed. It also questioned the goods these machines turned out. He saw capitalists as masters of inferior products and needless waste. If standardisation did not lead to plenty for all then it could only mean poor quality and second-rate knockdowns. For this reason it has often, incorrectly, been assumed that Morris opposed machinery. When it was grudgingly accepted that he was, in fact, not opposed it was then asserted that he was against mass production. However, he was merely against production of inferior quality goods sold at too high a price to those who did not need them when what was required was the benefit of high quality goods at cheaper prices. So he was contesting, not the production process itself, but why such goods were produced in the first place.

One further development which had a major impact was the use of conveyor belts. A belt allowed a continuous and unhesitating flow of production. Raw material was introduced, passed through various stations with multiple operations to work it up into a finished product. Although not the antithesis of hand operation it does not lend itself to cottage industry. Indeed continuous operation shapes the factory system. Some trace the conveyor belt back to biscuit manufacture in the 1830s, with a tray passing between workers onto a continuous power-driven roller. Largely undeveloped in Britain until the 1870s, it was used extensively abroad, especially in newly expanding industrial nations such as Germany and the USA. In America it was but a short step from a continual process of dismembering animal carcasses in food production to assembling Model 'T' cars. Whilst the fruits of this system came after Morris had died, the seed was germinating before his eyes. And he did not like it. For Morris, the continuous assembly line reduced the worker to an appendage of the machine with each job separated down to a minimal function. Interaction with others was poor, the skill factor low and workers could be hired and fired at will to match the trade cycle. Morris's benchmark for industrial advance was based on how it increased interactivity, raised the skill factor, produced a versatile craft worker skilled in whole processes, while providing him with sufficient time away from the job to rest, increase his knowledge and improve himself and his family.

The very adaptability of an engine, driving in rotary fashion, meant that it's use spread quickly to all industrial processes from driving water wheels, on paddle steamers, or production belts, or the record-breaking crossing of the Atlantic by the steam ship, Savannah. No aspect of a worker's life was unaffected.

Lathe City

Machines had been developed that could grind, bore, forge, roll, hammer and polish. Each function called up machinery such as the milling machine, the cylindrical grinder or the Capstan lathe. These not only produced accurately and at high speed, but once set up by a craftworker, could be successfully operated by someone unskilled. Where success could be achieved with one lathe the operation could then be standardised and automated to execute the same function many times, simultaneously. The sewing machine became the first mass produced tool. When this was extended to agricultural machinery, the village blacksmith, in so many ways the archetypical metal worker, was doomed. He was the personification of Morris's ideal craftsman and through him industry was introduced to a fount of knowledge assembled over generations of smithery.

No guards and no safety clothing, conveyor belts at hazardous head and body heights. Children move in and out, dodging cogs. A picture portrait of a nineteenth century factory.

Machines changed people and the relationships between them. They also changed the geographical location, shape and size of towns and cities. They affected relationships both in agriculture and industry and between town and city. Birmingham, in Morris's lifetime, Britain's second city, is a good example.

Birmingham was an early driving force in the industrial revolution, its position reinforced as a result of the extent to which, its capitalists and workers, embraced metal working as an industry. The city thrived for three reasons: proximity to coal, proximity to iron ore, and the maturity of her engineering tradesmen, especially the mechanics.

In the early nineteenth century a system of canals was built, linking Birmingham to Liverpool, Hull and Oxford, the latter, bringing direct access to the lucrative Thames. This meant that at a stroke, the price of coal was halved, costs greatly reduced and the engineering base of the city, secured. Supplies of power and raw material were guaranteed and with supply time reduced, good quality could be maintained. Nowhere was the impact of this more keenly felt than in precision engineering. Birmingham became a centre for the minting of coins where the Janvier transfer-engraving machine could work to one-thousandth of an inch. There were factories that could produce millions of pen nibs to meet the demands of improved education and postal services. Factories in Birmingham produced a million square feet of glass in ten weeks for the

Crystal Palace in Hyde Park, an exhibition Morris felt both "stupid and empty" and "full of pretentious triviality."

Birmingham developed an advanced small armaments industry. With the invention of the flintlock rifle at the end of the eighteenth century and the war with Napoleon early in the nineteenth, Birmingham factories turned out five million musket rifles in a decade with the result that their engineering prowess had an impact as far away as India, China and Afghanistan.

In many ways, the city challenged Morris's concept of society. It brought together both the best in highly skilled workers, endeavour and innovation and the worst in the form of slums, dislocation and capitalism's ubiquitous residuum. Perhaps for this reason – this very clash of qualities – Morris became something of a mentor to Birmingham and found a ready audience there to whom he delivered some of his most notable lectures.

Spot the shoes! Child poverty ... Booth, Rowntree, Dickens all played an important role in changing attitudes to child labour and poverty. But it was pressure on Parliament and political action by trades unions, especially in making education compulsory, that turned things around.

Tale of two industries

How did machinery affect contrasting sectors of industry? Take two industries as divergent as agriculture and printing. In the former, the key question from 1800 onwards was how to feed the rapidly growing and urbanising population. One could not conjure up more land, except by reclamation, as in the east, and this would be a lengthy process. This terrain was a substantial size and potentially useful but the immediate answer lay in how land already in use could be made more productive. There were three main strategies: introduce new crops, organise existing crops differently through rotation and bring in mechanisation. Only the small size of Britain's farms and holdings precluded mechanisation from becoming the dominant approach.

Capitalism began in agriculture. As early as the 1830s, and certainly by the middle of the century, most of the land was owned by landlords who leased it out to tenant farmers: they in their turn, hired farm labourers.

A steam-driven agricultural threshing machine did not need feeding or paying.

Between 1630 and 1850 virtually all arable land was enclosed. Open fields had disappeared, private property rights were secure and the management of farms was left to individual farmers or their landlords. Common rights were now rare. By 1850, the proportion of owner-occupiers, was below 15 per cent, the increased use of machinery reinforcing the rural class divide. Around 1830, the Swing disturbances were aimed at threshing machines which were replacing the hand flail and within twenty years threshing was powered by steam. These machines brought savage cuts to a labour-intensive (though highly seasonal) process. The time required to thresh an acre of wheat was cut from five man days using a hand flail to 0.8 using a steam powered thresher.

From the decade of Morris's birth to that of his death, output per worker in British agriculture increased by 70 per cent.

Jethro Tull introduced a horse driven hoe and developed a seed drill which opened the furrow, inserted a seed and then covered it up when laid. This greatly reduced wastage and, by creating a uniform distance between the seeds, gave them a better chance to thrive. Metal came to an agricultural world long dominated by wood. In 1732 Menzies invented a water driven thresher, which was advertised rather tellingly as giving " more strokes in a day than forty men with as much strength". And it didn't stop for tea breaks.

The changes were so dramatic that in a single century to 1890, the share of agriculture in the gross national product fell from 45 per cent, employing 55 per cent of the working population, to single figures in both cases. At the same time output increased so much that in 1850, a population which had tripled in size in the past century, was still being fed without the need for significant imports.

From top left, clockwise, a tale of change. The Ascensius Press (1507), The Albion (1820), The Adams (1855) – there were thirty presses in Harpers many operated by women, and the Applegarth four-feeder cylinder machine built for *The Times* in 1828.

In 1800, a London printer adapted a hand press to be driven by steam. When in 1814 the Times introduced a power driven press, speeds increased tenfold to 1,100 sheets per hour. This alone heralded the beginnings of a mass media. Within two decades, Hoe produced a sheet fed rotary system producing 20,000 page impressions an hour. In 1846 the Times introduced a web press based on a continuous and uninterrupted supply of paper from a roll. This instigated a revolution in the way paper was manufactured. Printing now moved close to the paradigm underpinning the Industrial Revolution as a whole: standardisation, mechanisation, and automation. Standardise the product, make it by or with the aid of a machine and then adapt it so that the machine can run continuously, without skilled handwork.

The demand for reading grew during the Middle Ages and paper made from rag-pulp superseded animal hide or velum. By the 19th century papermaking underwent a mechanical revolution with Dickinson and Fourdrinier making machines that could produce continuous rather than single sheets. The demand for paper swiftly outdid the supply of rags but at about the same time, the lumber industries of Canada and Scandinavia began to supply pulp made from wood. China clay was added to some papers to produce a gloss finish. Board factories were built in Bristol. With paper in position and a machine to print on it all that remained was the application of power. Printing progressed more in the ten years that marked Morris's formative years than in the previous 300.

Critics of capitalism

Capitalism had many critics and few champions. The critics had divided opinions. There were those who wanted to turn the clock back, those who wanted to smooth down its rougher edges, and others who saw it as nothing but an aberration, to be swiftly superseded by something different and better. There was a good deal of overlap between them.

In stepping forward to state his case, Morris was joining some of the greatest critics of the age. Some, like Ruskin, he came to know personally. It is surprising that he never met Karl Marx, the sharpest of them all. John Ruskin was born in 1819 the son of a founder of the Domecq sherry empire. He wrote his first poem at eleven and his first prose at 14. He excelled at Christ Church College, Oxford but decided against serving in the church. In 1839 he defended Turner against his critics and wrote one of the most influential books of the century, *Modern Painters*. Ruskin toured widely and drew inspiration from the architecture he experienced in Venice and on the Rhône. He returned to teach at the Working Men's College, later becoming SLADE professor of Fine Art.

Another influential work was *The Nature of Gothic*. This had a great impact on Morris who, in his last years, produced a kind of tribute edition under the Kelmscott Press imprimatur. Ruskin drew his inspiration from the craftsmen of the Middle Ages and was among the first to assert that the quality of working life determined the quality of life as a whole.

In *Unto This Last*, he wrote, "Luxury is indeed possible in the future – innocent and exquisite; luxury for all, and by the help of all; but luxury at present can only be enjoyed by the ignorant; the cruelest man living could not sit at his feet, unless he sat blindfold. Raise the veil boldly; face the light."

Perhaps the deepest and most consistent critic in the early part of the century was Robert Owen. What impressed Morris most about him was that he was a man of action. He was the first to make co-operation work in the modern age. The extent and depth of his influence was extraordinary. Born in Montgomeryshire in 1771 and a successful industrialist in the first 'machine surge', Owen was a philanthropist in the truest sense. Morris applauded the cooperative community of New Lanark Mills describing Owen as having "unbounded generosity and magnanimity".

Owen was also indefatigable in stamina and new ideas. He petitioned Parliament to reduce working hours in cotton mills, drew up plans for communistic villages to offset famine in Ireland, bought land in the New World to export his ideas, and set up a labour exchange in the Gray's Inn Road where labour was equitably interchanged.

Through Owen we can observe that all three of the strands critical of capitalism were complex, substantial and rich in food for thought. Today they are often categorised too quickly and thus misunderstood. Although, presently, we think of Owen as a reformer, in his own time he was considered a threat.

For example, in 1857, his 86th year, he convened a Congress of Advanced Minds of the World. It was held in clubs that were synonymous with working class education and trades union organisation. Convening in St Martin's Hall in Long Acre in London's Covent Garden, and the John Street Institute in Fitzroy Square, the Congress met for two weeks. Each day had a different theme and audience – first the Press, then legislators, producers of wealth (both capital and labour), teachers, distributors of wealth, republicans, democrats, secularists and spiritualists. It had a huge audience and was a centre of lively and influential debate.

Despite his later flirtation with the metaphysical, Owen consistently called for and sought ways to "abandon competition in the production of the necessities of life. Using practical science, a rationalistic and educated populace would look upon the creation of wealth as a mere pastime. It would be conducted for enjoyment and as a means of exercising to maintain health. The immediate cause of your sufferings is the amount of productive power throughout society, and especially in Great Britain, opposed to the value of your labour ... It is this new power misunderstood, and most irrationally applied, that has caused your late and present suffering!"

Morris was not alone in having a 'big reach'. In 1845, Robert Owen was drafting a New Constitution of the State of New York, "no ordinary constitution, but a model one for the world!" Not bad for one who had only been in America for a year, but the President of the country and members of Congress met with him to analyse it!

A 'labour note' used as a medium of exchange in one of Robert Owen's Labour Exchanges. (Reproduced courtesy of the TUC unionhistory.info)

Owen wrote of three great objects to life, "useful character, desirable employment and superior associations for all."

He proposed that the government purchase land on which to establish townships that were each, "self-supporting, self-employing, self-educating and self-governing". These townships would then be federated and extended all over Europe, then, the world, uniting to all in one great republic, with one interest."

At one point during the Great Exhibition of 1851 Owen met with Giuseppe Mazzini, Louis Blanc and Francis Place to propose a demonstration to change the system without using violence. Later that year he addressed a meeting called to celebrate his 80th birthday. Marx was in the audience – he called on all 'to well-educate, well-employ, well-place and cordially unite, the human race.'

It was at this time of rapid change that Morris developed his own powerful critique of capitalism and explored different ways of working which naturally involved new goals for production. His attitude was shaped by the ugliness and aggressive nature of an early phase of capitalism, as it sought to take control of the domestic market. Capitalism was urban and mechanical and scarred a landscape which had remained unchanged for as long as the popular memory could stretch. It was noisy, dirty and dangerous. It depopulated some areas, while overpopulating others to a point where conditions became unsanitary. To atone for these 'blunders of civilisation' it could only offer, *more* civilisation.

Morris delivered his critique as one of Britain's foremost and influential designers, but he himself was a manufacturer: running a company with a thorough working knowledge of production processes. It is usual nowadays to believe that the machinery and production processes that have been bequeathed to us by the Industrial Revolution were the only way to proceed. What is more, this view is reinforced by a distortion of the Darwinian principle. If they survived they must have been right. If they triumphed over others they must have been the best. This, of course, is untrue for two reasons at least. First, machines and processes did not just appear from nowhere. They were the product of many breakthroughs from a range of often unrelated sources and developed as much from lessons learnt from failure as from success. Secondly, in the environment of nineteenth century Britain, a machine was most likely to triumph where it was the most likely method to increase the margin of profit and improve the speed at which the product was made. Morris felt that machinery was chosen where it was of most use to the capitalist and that little thought was given to the quality of life of the operator or worker. He began to elucidate this outlook in a series of lectures. He came to lecturing late in life and, although often nervous and likely to stick doggedly to his text, he was considered a very able and much sought after public speaker. Most of his speeches were delivered on street corners, or at public gatherings and were of a propagandist nature. But there was no ego or mere rhetoric. Morris's lectures are notable, first and foremost, for their quality of thought. Over time he developed a range of lectures that he wrote down and gave many times. When on his favourite themes he excelled and his ideas developed rapidly concentrated over the period between 1860 and 1890. The idea at the core was always the same – that art was the natural result of man's joy in labour, that art was for the many, not the few and where there was no art, there was no joy, and where there was no joy, something had gone wrong with labour.

Perhaps it is now not so difficult for the reader to grasp how and on what basis Morris drew his early conclusions about civilisation. To the capitalist, the

Industrial Revolution gave birth to modern civilisation. To Morris it was its undoing. Morris, in his early years observed through the eyes of Ruskin. He saw the worker becoming a cog in a machine, first becoming weary of the machine itself, then of those who own and direct production. Writing in Capital, Marx describes this process as one whereby "all means for the development of production, transform themselves into means of domination over, and exploitation of, the producers; they mutilate the labourer into a fragment of a man, degrade him to the level of an appendage of a machine, destroy every remnant of charm in his work and turn it into a hated toil". The similarity of view shared with Morris is remarkable, especially as Morris was not to read Capital until twenty years after it was published.

"*All countries and all individuals hang to the past, but seem hardly to think of the future. I suppose we should, like the Jewish prophets, get the habit of looking onwards...*"

William Morris, 1882.

Looking back to look onwards

Morris's preferred mode of expressing ideas became the spoken word. To his speeches he brought all the expression, formulation and skill that he used daily in his working life. Key lectures handed down to us, or selected by Morris himself for publication, were given many times over, and to widely varying audiences throughout the country. He did not enjoy public speaking and liked street speaking even less, but he developed a style that was very much his own and in his presence became an art form. He was open about his ideas and fearless to modify them. His work had no single publisher – some of his major works such as *Monopoly – Or How Labour is Robbed* were printed by ten different presses during his lifetime.

As a lecture, *Monopoly* was given many times. In this way he was able to expand, refine and take in new ideas. His diary records lecturing on *Monopoly* in Mitcham, Hackney, Chiswick, Haggerston, Edinburgh, Hammersmith, Mile End and Victoria Park, Hoxton, Salford, Paddington, Nottingham, Pentonville Hill, Thornton Heath, St Pancras, Kilmarnock, Aberdeen, Norwich, Manchester, Hendon, Rochdale, Southwark, Lambeth, Bethnal Green, Yarmouth, Liverpool, Chesterfield and also the Northern Radical Club.

In 1887, Morris wrote notes for a lecture and pamphlet entitled *Feudal England* which was an opportunity to outline where he thought capitalism was going. In particular, he wanted to show how it had broken with historical continuity. Feudalism was a controversial topic in nineteenth century England.

Morris shared a fascination with the Middle Ages along with many others of his time. Called the Middle Ages because they formed the bridge between the primitive and the 'modern' world, the former rested on a form of chattel slavery, the second on the peasantry – half free to work their own land but paying rent in money and services to a landowner. Slavery gave way to serfdom.

With the break up of Roman rule in romanised lands, feudalism changed into hierarchy where all paid service of one kind or another. A lord might owe the King occasional military service; the peasant paid with productive labour. The Corporations came to dominate.

109

Morris estimated that despite the several versions of Christianity, and the fractious and uneasy relationship between people, religion and state, there existed a massive driving force. This was a "tendency to association". All men belonged to the greatest Corporation of all, the Church. The upper classes belonged to fraternities of knighthood and other ranks of the nobility. Production and exchange were in the hands of those great associations of traders and craftsmen, the guilds and the merchant guilds which dealt in commerce. The guilds – the most important early one, that of the ploughmen – were legal and had the power to enforce their own rules, peculiar to their own craft. They came to be represented at the Corporations which had, by Royal Charter, been given jurisdiction over towns. Morris documents some instances where the guilds took over whole towns, kicking out the aristocrats of the Corporations. The hierarchies in town and industrial life were strictly and, by law, closely regulated.

It is true that in our eyes, such Middle Age life appears rigid or somehow lacked comfort, but how could a mediaeval tiler or thatcher miss comfort or 'freedom' which society had yet to invent and make widely or cheaply available? Our picture of the Middle Ages has been built up by writers of the Victorian period. It is ironic that these writers saw only the darker side of the mediaeval period, whilst tens of thousands of children worked in mills and mines on their very doorsteps. The totality of the people's aspirations and considerable achievements became obscured by tales about a few Knights sitting around a table. Of course the apologists for capitalism had a vested interest in showing how the new capitalist system had rescued the world from the strictures of the 'Dark Ages'.

To Morris the Middle Ages was the epoch of Popular Art – art was amongst the people and in every home, he contended, so how could the 'Dark Ages' produce such art while modern Victorian 'civilisation' produced very little? He did not apologise for the Middle Ages but did defend them in comparison to modern times.

It was a time of broadening horizons. It was a period too, he reasoned, that gave rise to the rapid and international development of printing, called the 'black art' by the church, not because of the colour of the ink, but because the intellectual monopoly of the priest was now permanently ended. Before 1500, Constantinople had been taken by the Turks and both the Cape passage, which ended the dominance of the overland silk route, and America had been discovered.

To some it appeared a depressing time, where all that had changed between the 'dark ages' that followed after Roman domination and up until 1066, was the nationality of the rulers. For some it was a time of romanticism and chivalry, while to others, it was a time of servitude, rigid social hierarchies and ignorance, yet Ruskin, William Blake and Morris saw something else. Stripping away the arbitrary nature of rule they discovered stability and a sense of freedom, where the craftworker had considerable power.

It is certainly true that in comparison with other European countries slavery came late to Britain, never affected more than ten per cent of the population and was relatively quickly banished. The concepts of freedom and the common good that so intrigued Morris, were strongly exemplified by the large group of people who had been colonised by the Normans, but had never really accepted such rule, except in the formal sense. They had not allowed themselves to become enslaved in the cultural and intellectual sense. They remained themselves.

Writing about such people, especially craftworkers, Morris said, "there exists, and has always existed, a tradition, obscure and uncertain, but deeply seated, that there was a time when his lot was happier, his means more ample, his prospects more cheerful than they have been in more modern experience."

In these times, the struggle over taxation was constant: so were uprisings whenever the popular idea of what constituted freedom seemed under threat. King John had been forced to sign the Magna Carta while other monarchs abroad considered themselves omnipotent. The people had their own champions. Captain Pouch, predecessor of Luddism and Captain Swing, for example, co-ordinated attacks on those enclosing land in Northamptonshire, Leicestershire and Warwickshire. Such actions involved tearing down hedgerows, filling ditches and returning common land to tillage.

There had been constant friction over the rights accorded to freeborn Englishmen, which continued, and at times dominated, the period between the 1300s and the onset of the first Industrial Revolution. In this process, the English revolution, the first of its kind anywhere in the world, was pivotal. Morris was alert to this and had, as we have seen, studied history in great detail. In some ways this Revolution was repeating the same popular theme, which had been dominant in the Middle Ages. This was well illustrated by veteran republican, Colonel Rumbold, executed following a state trial in 1685, who said in his defence, "I am sure there was no man born marked of God above another; for none come into the world with a saddle on his back, neither any booted or spurred to ride him." The similarity with Morris's book, *A Dream of John Ball*, is striking.

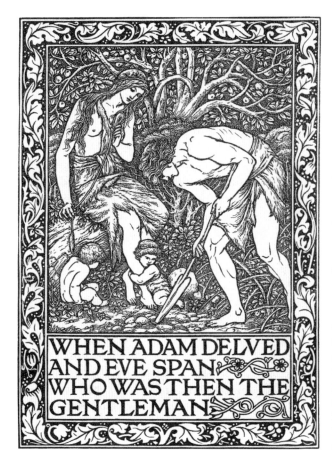

WHEN ADAM DELVED
AND EVE SPAN
WHO WAS THEN THE
GENTLEMAN

Variation on a theme. This Kelmscott illustration popularises a common view of mankind's lot. As Colonel Rumbold said previously: none born saddled. Used as an illustration for Morris's *John Ball*. Little is really known about Ball, one of two leaders of the Peasant's Revolt, the greatest pre-industrial uprising of the British people. John Ball was excommunicated in 1376 for preaching "ecclesiastical poverty and social equality".

Having read Ruskin Morris began to develop a theory of feudal England that formed the basis of his socialism. A core feature of this socialism became, from 1870 onwards, a fusion of the histories and legacies of two unique islands, Britain and Iceland. His first trip to Iceland in 1871 was a revelation, for there he found that the communalism he thought lay only at the centre of feudal England, still survived. Iceland taught him that communalism worked, albeit at what most Victorians would have considered a very low level of social improvement. In Iceland, class had not developed and man's struggle with nature was paramount. He was fascinated and remained in Iceland for a full year.

His second visit in 1873 confirmed this view. Iceland's system convinced him that communalism could be progressive and his embrace of modern socialism taught him that through the class struggle, workers could rediscover and reassert their critical role in production and society. His eager acceptance of Marxism revealed the inner workings of capitalism and confirmed conclusions he had reached alone. Even this was not enough for Morris who would only be satisfied when he could demonstrate practically that life could be different. Society as it existed in England could not be adapted. It would have to be radically altered.

Feudalism then, is the key to understanding what Morris believed was wrong with the industrialisation process and how it could be put right. It enabled him to draw on an enormous range of knowledge and ideas to form a unique analysis of a system that reached its greatest degree of maturity in his own country.

The Norman invasion introduced a fully feudal system, breaking ancient tribal bonds with the Scandinavian countries. The Normans forced a form of separation of both class and nationality on the native Briton by helping themselves to most of the land and speaking a different language.

Mediaevalism is associated with the fourteenth century and it is here that Morris sets out his stall. This was a special time, in which Edward III enacted the Statute of Labourers, and the peasants' rebellion went against Edward's successor, Richard II. Duke William brought an army from Normandy to England which was quartered on the people and gradually seized their land. The English, hitherto linked as a Teutonic people with a Celtic fringe, were usurped and forced to labour under a romanised feudal system imported lock, stock and personnel from William's fiefdom in France. It was a baronial system. Although it was the barons who secured the Magna Carta from King John and provided the social basis for Simon De Montfort's rebellion against Henry III, monarchy and barony soon found common quarter against the people. The crown struggled against the church for ascendancy but no great principle separated any of the ruling class. God's kingdom in heaven moved to earth and became, to quote Morris, "much vexed by politics and power". The Conqueror's successors had to co-opt the English and come to an uneasy compromise with them. Under Henry I the trading and industrial classes began to increase in size and influence and the merchant guilds developed into corporations in the towns. These were promoting their own freedom and exemption from a punitive and centralised tax regime. As one writer put it, "the relative position of the workman was one of far more hope and far more plenty in the days of the Plantagenets than it has been in those of the House of Hanover."

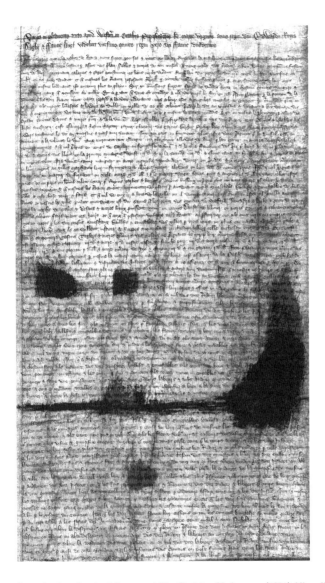

A much misunderstood document. The Statute of Labourers (1351). Like all laws, it became a ceiling in bad times and a baseline in good. But it offered some protection from the aggressive acts of the new industrialists seeking to break the guilds. The Black Death led to such a shortage of labour that, if employers did not pay enough, workers voted with their feet. The legislation also reflects Royal fear of a people who, during the same period, secured victory at Crécy, Poitiers (1356) and Agincourt (1415).

The Magna Carta spelled liberty for the barons and the completion of the feudal project. Edward I's centralising tendencies needed increasing and greater funds, so, in 1295, Parliament was put on some permanent and representational footing. During this period the struggle began to weaken between the monarch and the barons and sharpened between them and a new burgeoning industrial class. Although by the accession of Edward III, feudalism is virtually over, society is not fully stable, nor quite independent. The age of the Teutons and Celts had long faded from popular memory, though it continued still in ritual and some aspects of culture and law, and that of the Roman Empire had not been much more than superficially embraced. What actually gripped the imagination of the people, according to Morris, was "the strange mysticism and dreamy beauty of the East". This was reinforced by trade and British participation in the crusades. England was reaching a kind of cultural and artistic highpoint. This was the time where Chaucer spoke for the court (despite this Morris was a big fan) whilst alongside him ran another culture, expressed in the ballads of the people "true to the backbone, instinct with indignation against wrong, thereby expressing the hope that was in it." This was the time of the Lollard poetry of William Langland and his 'A Vision of Piers Plowman'. Langland was the popular sage of the age. He wrote, "I counsel you, says Conscience, come with me, ye fool, Into the Fort of Unity, and hold we us there, Cry we to Nature to come and defend us From the hurts of the fiend for love of Piers Plowman, Cry we to all the commons to come into Unity, And there abide and fight 'gainst Belial's children." Morris considered this period both brilliant and progressive and that the life of the worker of the time was better than it had ever been.

Morris observed in the Middle Ages not only the complex interrelationship and struggle between classes, but the full potency of social change, for "it could not last, but must change into something else." This struggle was recorded in a Mayor's Court Rolls of the City in 1298. It complains, "There was held a 'parliament of carpenters at Milehende, where they bound themselves by corporal oath not to observe a certain ordinance or provision made by the Mayor and Alderman touching their craft.' And in March, a parliament of Smiths was formed with a common chest."

According to Morris the last war that England had engaged in, in which race figured, had been the Crusades. Thereafter, the wars with the Scots and the French were neither national, racial or tribal: they were the "private business of the lord of the manor". Feudalism could not enable expansion in production. Slavery was incompatible with real exploitation because it tied one individual to another and even lay down geographical boundaries beyond which a serf could not travel. What was required was freedom of the individual, the better to exploit his flexibility, in the form of hired labour. The craft class grew and made demands on a feudalism with which it could not cope. And the spectre of commercialism overshadowed them.

When issues like enclosure and manufacturing produced men who were neither slaves nor noblemen, with feudalism unable to accommodate them in its social framework they began to develop a sense of freedom and station and to organise themselves to get 'a place at the table'.

The occasional outbreaks of the plague, greatly reducing the numbers of able-bodied men who could be employed, accentuated the process and made the new 'free' labourers more powerful. Shortages of labour increased the leverage of such workers allowing them to change their role in society – securing the freedom to sell their own labour power as a commodity – and to change the way they related to others. Labour evolved as a separate class. As with all new classes before them, they first demanded to be players and then proceeded to impose a contract on society that forced it to recognise their specific interests and aspirations.

In his tragic play Coriolanus, William Shakespeare illustrates how a separation between classes feels when a citizen cries, "Care for us! True, Indeed! They ne'er cared for us yet – suffer us to famish, and their storehouses cramm'd with grain; make edicts for usury, to support usurers; repeal daily any wholesome act established against the rich; and provide more piercing statutes daily, to chain up and restrain the poor. If the wars eat us not up, they will; and there's all the love they bear us ..." This class divide has continued from the late Middle Ages until the present day. It is given formal expression in the Statute of Labourers that no monarch, for a full 400 years felt strong enough to seek to undo.

To Morris, the driving force that brought down feudalism was the assimilation of craft guilds into town corporations. In seeking to throw off the rigidities and controls of feudalism – many of them petty, but some which cut to the bone – they liberated the whole country from a system of governance that had outlived any usefulness. Morris refers to guilds seeking "definition and differentiation of rights." At the close of fourteenth century, England was battered by a long war with the French and depopulation resulting from the Black Death, a particularly serious outbreak of plague. The uprisings of Wat Tyler and John Ball, although strictly a failure, sealed the fate of the feudal system. The majority of people simply would not be ruled in the old way.

A guild for every trade. Remarkably successful and durable, the guilds fought off nearly every external attack on their activities, only succumbing as a result of internal class divisions. Active throughout Europe, from Italy to England, some Guilds lasted 500 years.

It was in the early days of the fifteenth century that workmen began to form a distinct class and brought in their wake a body of labourers who had never been serfs. In England, capitalism had set in very early and with each growth spurt of commercialism, trade and industry, this labouring class grew. It became so numerous that it began to develop outside the guilds. Labourers moved into towns where the increase in numbers allowed them the anonymity they needed to successfully evade feudal restrictions. Its size increased further when landlords uprooted whole rural populations throwing tenants off the land and turning it over to pasture. Sheep momentarily had their day. Thomas More

117

captured the moment brilliantly in his *Utopia* of 1516, which was translated from the Latin in 1551, "Forsooth, my Lord (quote I), your sheep that were wont to be so meek and tame, and so small eaters, now, as I hearsay, become so great devourers and so wild, that they eat up and swallow down the very men themselves."

J. Thorold Rogers, one of the most accomplished researchers and economic historians wrote in 1884, "... the fifteenth century and the first quarter of the sixteenth were the golden age of the English labourer, if we are to interpret the wages which he earned by the cost of the necessaries of life. At no time were wages, relatively speaking, so high, and at no time was food so cheap".

Payment was high and rising. There was little regional variation in rates and the differential between the pay of a labourer and an artisan was much narrower than we would expect. Nor did it vary greatly across trades, for a master carpenter skilled in joinery, earned the same as a mason or plumber. Only in London, where the guilds all but ruled industrial life and were able to keep labour scarce, were wages significantly higher, but prices were 15 per cent higher too.

Women's work at harvest time was paid at only slightly lower rates than men's. Eight hours were worked and there was no work on Sundays or on the principal holidays. Sometimes there were as many as 90 such holidays to celebrate Saints' days and various popular festivals and this was only half the number of holidays enjoyed during Roman times. With food so cheap it was often provided by the master. Craftsmen and labourer were paid a *viaticum* for travelling to and from work at a set mileage. A sort of certainty had stepped into industrial affairs. It may seem incredible to us now, but the price per quarter for the wheat food staple between 1260 and 1400 was set at 5s $10^3/_4$d. It simply did not vary. From 1401 to 1540 it was 5s $11^3/_4$d. In the sixteenth century nearly every basic grain food dropped in price to below that of the twelfth and thirteenth century. More meat was eaten by the poor of the fifteenth than the early nineteenth century.

The average cost of board was rarely more than a shilling a week, so the average worker earned between two and three times the cost of his subsistence. In addition, where poverty struck, the Church stepped in. Contribution of the tithe was enforced so that a third went to relief of the poor. It was a kind of insurance fund.

In the fourteenth and fifteenth centuries the worker secured increased wages whilst prices decreased. In the sixteenth century this at first began to unravel and was then sharply reversed as the enclosure of common fields and arable land accelerated depopulation and the development of a capitalist artisan. A growth in sheep farming was the result of a rise in the price of wool and it became more lucrative than employing men in food production. In 1533 some farmers were recorded as keeping 24,000 sheep. Money was so greatly debased by the crown that the silver penny of Edward IV weighed half that of Edward I. This led to a rise in prices. The cost of meat rose threefold, while corn and dairy increased two and a half times. The wage rise of one and a half times could not keep pace.

Having not changed much in the two previous centuries, prices doubled in the sixty years between the reign of Elizabeth I and the English Civil War. In the decade between 1641 and 1650 the workers' purchasing power was a quarter that of their grandfathers and great grandfathers. In general, in 1495 a labourer could provide for his family's annual needs with 15 weeks of normal work, an artisan with 10, but by 1610 an artisan needed to work for 43 weeks to make similar provision and a peasant had no chance of making ends meet.

Perhaps even more significantly, Henry VII was a serial overspender. He squandered the funds raised from the monasteries and the debasement of the currency. He drew up a bill for the dissolution of all colleges, chantries, hospitals and free chapels, and sought a net prize in the funds held by guilds. A kind of windfall tax. The guilds ran schools, almshouses and hospitals and had a fund set aside for widows, orphans and hard times but their land was confiscated and their funds effectively sequestrated by this act. Only the London guilds prevailed.

Rogers wrote of this time, "I contend that from 1563 to 1824, a conspiracy, concocted by the law and carried out by parties interested in its success, was entered into, to cheat the English workman of his wages, to tie him to the soil, to deprive him of hope, and to degrade him into irremediable poverty." The lowest point for working conditions was reached about the time when the King and Parliament joined in Civil War.

In the midst of this, Morris wrote of the nineteenth century craftworker, "the workman of today, if he could recognise the position of the forerunner, has some reason to envy." For under feudalism, the workman owned his own tools, hired out his own labour, worked to his own time scale and schedule and often worked close to his family where they could be protected, and children raised with security. Wages and prices were relatively stable and any dramatic rise could be offset by popular intervention. He had great autonomy in production too. Those who commissioned work did not participate in it because aristocrats did not get their hands dirty, so the craftworker was able to impose control over the labour process using his skills and knowledge to determine how a job would be done.

The craftsman, unencumbered by the kind of division of labour that began to appear with capitalism, was a master of all related trades therefore skilled in whole processes. Design, and manufacture were as one. What is more he could pass his wisdom on, usually to his son, within the guild, thereby ensuring protection and continuity for his offspring and a constantly growing pool of knowledge and experience that only he and his own could access. When times were hard he could 'journey' or 'tramp' thereby sharing work round with fellow guild members. In this, he would be sustained by the guild as a 'travelling brother'. The journeying could take him far beyond the shores of England and thus he could increase his value by securing work on any of the big projects then under construction in Europe. These were usually the cathedrals later much admired by Ruskin and Morris. In times of peaceful trade he could work on ports or roadways, even universities, and in times of friction and war on fortifications. With this degree of control he could concentrate on the function and form of his product not just on speed and its finished wealth. So labour became synonymous with art – each contributed to the other – and each product reflected the unique contribution of the craftworker.

The new England that was emerging was well placed to exploit new opportunities. The Hammonds claim, "the world was learning to pay to wealth the homage it had paid to magic, to religion, to courage, to authority, or to the blood of heroes and the Kings". Capital was the new god.

In the new society the guiding principle of mutual obligation, a source of greatness in the 500 years to 1800, is subverted by a distortion of individual liberty, not of the uniqueness of each individual to contribute to the good of all, but to accumulate capital. Many factors contributed to the dramatic breakout from feudalism. There was the emancipation of the villeins, the emergence of capitalist class in embryo, the mobility of labour, the reformation, the discovery of the Atlantic routes and gold, slavery, land enclosure, the coming together of science and industrialisation, and bountiful and well placed raw materials. Critically there was too, a replacement of the Church centre stage by a state, with national structures and an army. By comparison with her nearest competitors it didn't hurt that German economic life was destroyed by war and France was convulsed by religious dislocation.

In its first phase capitalism made fabulous profits, legal and illegal as in the East, but the profit was used to fund expansion in home markets rather than more foreign speculation. There was a willingness to learn, especially about banking, from the Dutch. Britain, uniting England, Scotland and Wales was, unlike Germany or Italy, or the failed marriage of Holland to Belgium where internal cohesion remained elusive, able to establish an enormous free trade area within her own borders. Internal controls on the movement of goods had been done away with by the end of the Middle Ages. It also had a single system of taxation. Adam Smith thought this the principal reason why Britain emerged first and was more able to exploit industrial revolution. At the same time France had 101 internal customs barriers.

A significant role was played by Henry VIII who in dispossessing the Church, gave amply to the projects of commerce and bolstered the new type of 'money man'. In Britain, the monarchy danced to the tune, first of the aristocracy and then of the capitalists. Elsewhere monarchy eschewed commerce and held industry back.

Break-up of village life

The shift away from feudalism to capitalism is well illustrated in the break-up of both the village and the guild. The factory and urban centre drew from the village and countryside, but the village was already dissolving. In the peasant village of the Middle Ages, custom was strong: elementary freedom and restrictions were adjudicated by manor courts and culture was communal as each village battled with nature to feed herself from land worked in common. Only relatively light duties were performed on behalf of the Lord. There was little room for capitalism. So the progressive breakdown of these structures made space for capitalism to move in and take root. Indeed, in Britain, capitalism got its first foothold in agriculture, with the village at its heart.

The growth of larger towns gave anonymity to many seeking to avoid the controls over the feudal restrictions described elsewhere. The growth of textiles fragmented the villages and reinforced the towns. Outbreaks of the plague resulted in a shortage of men to work the land and many thousands reinvented themselves from village peasant to hired hand. In other words, they became wage workers.

Village life was irrevocably diminished with the movement to enclose land. This process began in early 1500 and accelerated as the Industrial Revolution gathered pace. Under George III, 5,686,400 acres had been enclosed, whereas in the preceding fifty years the number had been only 337,000 acres, ninety per cent of this took place during the reign of George II. The need for wool to feed the textile industry was so great that tenants were turned off land so that it could be used for the grazing of sheep. For capitalism to take hold, that which was customary and held in common had to go and the owner of the land given a free hand. This was done by Acts of Parliament piece by piece. During the Napoleonic Wars alone, 2,000 associated Acts were passed.

The peasant disappeared along with the mediaeval village, a change which came to England long before her continental rivals. It allowed swifter exploitation and introduction of new production techniques and a rapid rise in productivity to meet the needs of a growing population. By the beginning of the Industrial Revolution, no country in the world was as urbanised as Britain. In 1800 the urban population in France was 9 per cent, in Germany 5 per cent, in Britain 20 per cent. By 1850, the figures were 14 per cent, 11 per cent and 41 per cent respectively.

Break-up of the Guilds

In many ways the Guilds represented in industry the same way of doing things – through custom and community – as the villages. The Guilds, to all intents and purposes, controlled both industry and commerce. The individual trades were known as mystères or "mysteries" – known only to those initiated into the guild. The Guilds began as associations of producers bringing masters, journeymen and apprentices under one umbrella. Class struggle was rife within the Guilds which tried to reconcile the irreconcilable. Increasingly, the masters fell under the sway of the commercial Guildsmen. The rules were changed to make entrance to the Guild more and more difficult for all but the most wealthy. Guilds were based on control, but the Industrial Revolution needed freedom from control. Guilds set wages and conditions, oversaw quality of product and arranged apprenticeships and access to markets. As commerce expanded, the richer Guildsmen, many of whom no longer had any skills in the craft of their Guild, needed to break out. When the Guilds began, craft skills were relatively less complex and undifferentiated. Three hundred years to 1800, progress was based precisely on differentiation and division of labour. Where a mediaeval craftsman was a manager of journeymen and apprentices, supplying food and lodging, buying in raw materials and selling finished goods, by 1800 five different people would be required to perform these functions. Jobs were bigger, faster, more complex and involved sourcing and selling outside the district or even the country, far outside the narrow geographical reach of the village or borough system.

As the Guilds broke up the state stepped in to secure some rights for journeymen and apprentices. The rich Guildsmen were allowed to form companies, giving them control of all the saddlers, or upholsterers, or tanners in their district. These were then allowed to unite across different trades to form joint stock companies.

So, in mediaeval times both agriculture and industry had been regulated to a greater or lesser degree by associations of producers. Each was eroded from the inside and transformed by external factors. Their very parochialism in a swiftly expanding market sealed their doom. The struggle over the enclosure of common land and the loss of ancient rights, can be likened to the strife of the Luddites who sought only to maintain the status quo, though holding back the inevitable. It was just their way of trying to retain a protection that would once have been supplied by the Guilds and which, with the breaking up of the Elizabethan labour laws, they were unable to get from Parliament. The groups of Yorkshiremen who attacked the mechanically powered shears, the Nottingham framework knitters who destroyed knitting frames and the Lancashire Luddites who rebelled against the power loom had all energetically lobbied Parliament to act on their behalf. Occasionally it had responded, with Prime Minister William Pitt the Younger establishing a Cotton Arbitration Act in 1800. They were unprotected by Guilds which had been usurped and transformed by its wealthiest members and did not yet have trade unions. However, they had their champions. In his maiden speech in the Lords in 1812, Lord Byron memorably spoke out against making machine-breaking an automatic capital offence. "Will the famished wretch who has braved your bayonets be appalled by your gibbets? ... when a proposal is made to emancipate or relieve, you hesitate, you deliberate for years, you temporise and tamper with the minds of men; but a death-bill must be passed off hand, without a thought of the consequences." So it will be of little surprise that all three of these groups of workers were amongst the first Chartists and their children the first trades unionists.

We have a partial record of the life of the Guilds because Richard II gave an order that these bodies should give account of their activities. It is interesting that some Guilds were founded by women, who wielded much more civic power than their descendants in the 1800s. The Guilds of Clothworkers, Drapers, Brewers, Fishmongers and Weavers all admitted women on an equal basis to men. Records exist from the reign of Edward IV which mention a women-only Guild of 'Silkwomen and Throwsters'. These were mighty organisations that survived centuries of upheaval and change.

Even today, 500 years on, many of the places we are drawn to visit either at home or abroad are those built by the craftsmen and women of this age. A few examples are the Tower and Basilica of Pisa, the cathedrals of Notre Dame and

Santiago de Compostela – the latter on the mason's journeying route to Palestine – York Cathedral and Caernarfon Castle: all formed a tangible testament to a time Morris considered the high point of unity of craft and art and freedom for the worker. His was not then, the common view of feudal England, although it is more readily accepted now. Art in history was important in one other respect concerning imagination and the collective memory. Morris asked "Who can say how little we should know of many periods, but for their art? History, so called, has remembered Kings and warriors, because they destroyed; Art has remembered the people because they created."

We can see that there is much more we have all yet to learn about such times for misconceptions abound. Few are aware that by the mid seventeenth century the population of England and Wales totalled four millions and that a good half of them earned their keep as a result of weekly wages. "Though it is a foolish dream to think that everything was better in the past," observed Morris, "it is arrogant presumption to conclude that all progress is a modern acquisition, and that we can complacently despise the wisdom of our ancestors."

Morris refused to see the worker as victim. His vivid knowledge of the role of craftsmen in the fourteenth century meant that he saw in him the potential to lead and to be strong, knowledgeable and self sufficient. He used these core qualities as a benchmark when making a detailed analysis of the development of the Industrial Revolution, machinery and patterns of ownership that emerged under capitalism. He wrote, "Would that we could unite the opulence of the fifteenth century to the civilisation of the nineteenth, and diffuse or distribute both."

"Labour being as proper for the bodies' health as eating is for its living ...
labour adds oil to the lamp of life, when thinking inflames it..."

John Bellars
Proposals for Raising a College of Industry of All Useful Trades and
Husbandry (London 1696)

Useful Work

In 1884, Morris wrote, *How We Live and How We Might Live*. He was now fifty.
He was emerging from a period of consolidation in his life. Morris could have
spent these middle years in honing his skills in some of the crafts to which he
usually lent considerable energy, but by reason of his temperament alone this
proved impossible. Events conspired to end this quiet period and bring him out
of his easy chair firing in all directions. His work now brought him into daily
contact with workmen of diverse trades, views and ages as he travelled the
length and breadth of Britain helping them establish socialist groups. He
lectured and listened, learning all the time by dialogue and reading. But
essentially he was a journalist, first on *Justice*, then, editor of *The Commonweal* one
of the two best-known working class journals of the industrial age. As such he
had to think on his feet and put pen to paper, without the fixed certainty of
consulting the scriptures or Sadducees.

Therefore, from necessity Morris became an original thinker, shaping the
outlook of others. In his articles, first in *Justice*, then, in *The Commonweal*, which
constitute two sizeable volumes, he attempted to answer the ubiquitous
question. What would socialism be like? – the subtext being: could it be better
than capitalism? He returned to the theme again, later in the decade with, "*How
Shall we Live Then*".

In grappling with this question Morris had a number of strings to his bow.
He was a historian, an educator, a craftsman and a manufacturer. He was also
foremost amongst Britain's writers of poetry and prose, and an original thinker
who revelled in working things out for himself. When he met an obstacle, he
preferred to work his way through rather than round it, and as a designer, he
simply went to the shop floor to remedy any shortfalls in his understanding. If
he could not do something he would ask those who could. He would watch
and learn and then go away and try things for himself. In that way he developed
an enormous body of knowledge about industrial processes in crafts like
stained glass manufacture, weaving and printing. His influence was immense
spreading as far away as Chicago and Sydney. He was, of course, aware of this,

127

so when he took on the editorship of *Commonweal* he did not treat it as an ordinary calling but one in which his pen could be applied, his ideas elucidated and influence gained for the new world he wanted to help create. 'Thinking aloud', which today is often considered a nuisance, was, in his hands, a revelation.

"I won't submit to be dressed up in red and marched off to shoot at my French or German or Arab friend in a quarrel that I don't understand; I will rebel sooner than do that. Nor will I submit to waste my time and energies in making some trifling toy which I know only a fool can desire; I will rebel sooner than do that."

Many of his finest works, including *Socialism From the Root Up* (1886), the first attempt to systematise socialist thinking in Britain, and pamphlets such as *True and False Society* (1888), were first serialised in the *Commonweal*. Serialisation was a Victorian device and many of our most famous writers such as Dickens and George Gissing wrote for the 'serialised' audience. At this special moment in his life Morris used it as an opportunity to outline how he thought socialism would develop in the series later bound as the *Dawn of a New Epoch* (1888).

In *The Dawn of a New Epoch* he moved into more difficult and controversial territory and was certain that some of the audience that he had drawn by his pleas for Art, would be lost. In this work he draws together aspects of his writing found in *Useful Work versus Useless Toil, Monopoly – Or How Labour is Robbed* and *A Factory As It Might Be*. Nowhere in any of these did he fall into the trap of asserting that socialism was inevitable. Equally, it is in this series of pamphlets and articles that labour is brought into sharp focus. "Nature yields her abundance to labour only". Mankind therefore must work to live. Hence as soon as work forces division into classes it promotes a struggle to ascertain which one will survive to appropriate the fruits of this labour.

Instead of pressing the issue, he invites his audience to consider the difference between historical moments where change is unconscious and times when all around know change is coming and see themselves as players in it. The time of which he was writing was indeed one of enormous change, both materially, and more importantly, as we have seen in preceding chapters, in terms of ideas. Morris saw in socialism a completely new society and way of organising industry. Those with whom he conversed agreed, but the majority he engaged with only saw a variation of the New Jerusalem, which was a legacy of Ruskin and Blake. Of course, this can be thought of as an enduring testament to their continuing influence in working class circles, but in Morris's mind it was not enough. Although they shared certain elements, the New Jerusalem and socialism could never be the same thing.

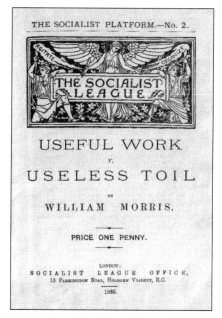

"Once more I say, that for a man to be the whole of his life hopelessly engaged in performing one repulsive and never-ending task, is an arrangement fit enough for the hell imagined by theologians."

In the Dawn, he asks whether the great clash of ideas that form a backdrop for the industrial age is still one between Absolutism and Democracy? He argues that the French Revolution a century before had largely settled this issue. The two great ideas now are 'Mastership and Fellowship'. Both feudalism and capitalism were based on the unequal distribution of labour amongst different classes of society and the unequal distribution of the results of that labour. What varies between these two systems is how that labour is organised. "Now as then there are people who have much work and little wealth living beside other people who have much wealth and little work? The richest are still the idlest, and those who work hardest and perform the most painful tasks are the worst rewarded for their labour."

The difference is that capitalism simplifies the class system of feudalism by leaving only two contenders: capitalist and worker. However this serves to sharpen the antagonism of interests that separate them. "There are those," he wrote, "who exist through their monopoly of all the means of production of wealth except one: and those who possess nothing except that one, the Power of Labour." The latter can only exist by petitioning the monopolisers of land and machinery to set them to work. This they are allowed to do only in return for sufficient money to allow them to survive and multiply.

This is how it stands with unskilled labour – each a mere missed wage packet away from destitution. Through supply and demand and through organisation or association, some, usually the more skilled, are sometimes able to extract a little more in wages or have more regular employment, yet the tendency is normally towards subsistence. We need only look at a picture of working class areas of Salford, Manchester, or the Old Kent Road in Victorian London to see why Morris had a ready audience. The masters maintain themselves by extracting the surplus value created by that labour power in full. Publicly, they appear to compete for advantage by cutting prices, while in reality they try constantly to hold down or cut wages and also introduced machinery. This has a threefold effect.

First it sheds labour to reduce the wage 'burden'. Secondly it lowers the quality of labour required thereby reducing the necessity to employ more expensive skilled labour. Lastly, it increases the exploitation of labour. In the early part of Morris's life a man could often only work if he took his wife and children with him. Then, the women and children would work whilst the men were made idle. Later in his life the men and some women worked. However, there was no stability to build a new society and rarely enough work to go round to all those who needed it and who were of sufficient age and health to carry it out.

Morris never subscribed to the notion of an 'iron law of wages' that many Victorian socialists thought had emanated from Marx, yet in reality came from Ferdinand Lassalle. In the 'iron law' the way of setting the level of wages is not affected by class association, therefore unions are deemed useless, as they cannot influence rates of pay. Strikes are counter-productive because the worker forfeits more in lost pay than he can gain in increased wages. It seemed that only a new political settlement could release the worker from wage slavery. However, Morris observed that workers were increasingly influencing their environmental, social and economic conditions. What is more, the highpoint of his consideration of these issues coincided with the greatest outbreak of labour militancy of the century with strikes by the gas workers, followed by the match girls, and then by the dock workers in search of their tanner. The fact that they emerged victorious nipped any thoughts of implementing the 'iron law', in the bud in Britain, though it rumbled round socialist circles on the continent for years.

According to Morris, under capitalism, man was set against man, rather than, as it should be, men united to find their place and peace with nature. Human beings could only hope to advance through association. Where there is competition, the opportunities for association are fundamentally weakened. When he first began to think in terms of a formal socialism towards the end of the 1870s amongst his influences Morris listed the work of Fourier, the French utopian socialist, and our own Robert Owen, a pivotal figure who has been forgotten too quickly. By 1886 Morris had cleared his lines. Owen was a great man and a pioneer, but there was to be no mixed economy of associations living and working as co-operators alongside capitalists. "Labour," he said, "had to be free from all compulsion except the compulsion of nature." He reasoned, "a rich man accumulates property, not for his own use, but in order that he may evade with impunity the law of nature which bids man to labour for his livelihood."

Divisions of labour

The division of labour took centuries to emerge but occurred across all industries, old and new, and in every craft that survived as far as the Industrial Revolution. This development was based on a range of factors: the unique nature of the Industrial Revolution in Britain, the break-up of the guilds, the introduction of new machinery and forms of power and the shift of production from the home into the factory. However, it goes much deeper, impacting as much on work in agriculture and on the high seas, as it did at the furnace face. The division of labour was about the essence of capitalism. No other issue so dominated the political economy of the nineteenth century for it was the most profound change in industrial production in 500 years.

On the surface, according to Morris, the division of labour emerged when; "the artist came out from the handicraftsmen, and left them without hope of elevation." In the Middle Ages, production had largely had been for use rather than exchange. Capitalism was about exchange rather than use because the aim of production was profit, and demand was based, not on need but on available income. To survive, capital had to multiply itself to make more and more capital. What made capital productive? The division of labour.

Adam Smith was the first to perceive the impact that an increased division of labour would have on production. In *Wealth of Nations* (1776) he makes two bold projections that shook up British economics for centuries. We are grappling with them still. First, he asserted that wealth was produced directly that the division of labour is applied and secondly that as an island nation, dependent on external sources for the supply of raw materials used in much of manufacture and food consumption, Britain could only advance under a system of free trade. The first assertion destroyed the contention of the physiocrats that agriculture was the source of all wealth. The second destroyed the corporation control over cities such as Newcastle and Liverpool, finished off the guild control over craft, and was embraced as a creed by the new factory owners. Smith had shown that the secret of wealth production lay in the manner in which labour was associated, brought to the market place, and applied to production. So the power of production lay in the cooperation of workers. They needed to be brought to the market place as free agents, able to sell their ability to labour to an employer, and each job must be broken down into narrow isolated silos of production. Where in the past all stages of production of a screw or a saw were undertaken by one person, the division of labour required that the job be broken down into many parts and, where possible, mechanised.

Smith has become a sort of talisman for those advocating capitalism as the only way, but he had a streak of radicalism in him that cannot be ignored. For example, he recognised early on that as each job – previously performed by a skilled worker who understood a whole process – was broken down into partial and minor detailed work, the impact on the human intellect would be seriously destructive. He could see that, to divide and sub-divide organic processes, would strip the worker of his innate sense of himself and his rightful place in the world and inhibit his formerly inherent natural curiosity of the art in his chosen craft. In a daring move to offset this negative tendency, he proposed that, as the division of labour deprived the worker of opportunity to train their minds and as the apprenticeship system declined, the state should step in to fill the gap with a national system of centrally funded education.

Given that, fifty years after his death in 1839, one district of Lancashire with a population of 100,000 had no state school, it was a radical proposal indeed. Yet what would happen once these workers, having passed through an education process, sought to utilise their newly acquired knowledge?

Marx and Morris never met. They came from distinctly different backgrounds, cultures and countries. Yet the conclusion they drew was remarkably similar. In 1844, in his *Economic and Philosophic Manuscripts*, Marx wrote "…the worker feels himself only when he is not working; when he is working, he does not feel himself. He is at home when he is not working, and not at home when he is working. His labour is, therefore, not voluntary but forced. Its alien character is clearly demonstrated by the fact that as soon as no physical or other compulsion exists, it is shunned like the plague."
(Photo from Illustrierte Zeitung, Leipzig 1895)

In volume one of *Capital* Marx described how the division of labour raises production. To paraphrase: one worker cannot shift a concrete block. Ten can drag it. One hundred can move it using a single finger. If one hundred are set to dragging the blocks, then some might be employed in preparing tools, clearing up, preparing the next move, gathering raw materials and rearranging the blocks to greater, more precise plans. So the power of production is increased and costs reduced. This kind of labour intensity and organisation of workers is how we picture the Industrial Revolution.

Morris saw a kind of dehumanisation in this process. Elsewhere in *Capital*, Marx shows how at one time a needlemaker in the Nuremburg Guilds would carry through all twenty of the operations required to make a pin. When production was established in Britain, employers took twenty needlemakers and set them to work side by side, each performing only one of the twenty operations. Time was saved, costs reduced, production was speeded up and profit rose. It sounds logical, even sensible, but just imagine being one of those men making needle parts twelve hours a day, six days a week, year in year out with no completed product he could call his own work.

Division of labour emerged and gathered momentum between the middle of the sixteenth and late eighteenth centuries. It happened because the guilds were trying to hold on to old ways of production, which, with the intervention of science, had become quite untenable. However, as profit was the new driving force of production, no-one was free to consider, let alone mitigate, the effects the division of labour would have on people. By the time it had become irreversible by way of factory production, (to quote Marx), "its final form is invariably the same – a productive mechanism whose parts are human beings." Workers became dehumanised, crafts lost their uniqueness and allure. Art was driven out of production. The worker, dispossessed of the tools of production, could only operate when employed to do so on someone else's behalf – the someone else being the owner of capital.

Initially, certainly up until the time of the birth of Morris, work was still conducted largely by hand and relied on the pace, ingenuity, level of skill and accuracy of the craftsman. Later though, machinery put in place in all crafts, introduced a certainty and uniformity that human labour cannot have. Machinery can be worked non-stop, even on Saints' days, consumes raw materials, but not wages. Far more expensive than a simple hand tool, the introduction of machinery raises the stakes for those wishing to become capitalists and widens the gap between workers and any hope of owning the means of production.

What is more, it greatly increases the kinds of tool on which a craftsman must be trained. When blacksmiths ruled the metal world they would operate a few types of hammer, used in a skilled way. By the mid eighteenth century, division of labour had increased the number of different hammers in operation to over 500, each used for a particular and individual function, within a detailed operation. It would be impossible to train on even a small proportion of the hammers available.

It is easy to see why Morris was so enthusiastic about *Capital*. The similarity in outlook can be summed up as follows. Any single worker will have strengths and weaknesses: some prefer one type of work to another. Some may be more physical, some more cerebral. Some prefer to work indoors, others out. Some enjoy routine tasks, others prefer to use bursts of intense intellectual concentration. Some people are more or less creative at different things. All these factors are present when a craftsman is responsible for seeing a whole production process through to completion. The finished product will reflect all those, but when labour is divided, and sub divided again, and is task rather than process based, the worker is selected for his aptitude for one particular task. On one hand production is more economical and serves to make profit. On the other hand all pleasure in the work is lost and the worker becomes dehumanised and alienated.

Such division introduced hierarchies that simply did not exist in the Middle Ages when craft skills determined production. Then, there was little division. The plasterer would make the plaster as well as apply it. Most unskilled work would have been performed by an apprentice. When processes are divided and reduced to unskilled repetitive work, the need for apprentices disappears. Workers became frozen into a sort of time warp whereby they were unable to break out of their 'skilled', 'unskilled' or 'semi-skilled' cul de sac. In the workshop, the guilds had been able to check this development and a merchant could not purchase both raw materials and hire labour. However, the factory was a different story, being a space where the capitalist could operate outside the control of the guilds.

Morris bitterly regretted this illustration of art being driven out of work. He wrote "for that beauty, which is what is meant by art, using the word in its widest sense, is, I contend, no mere accident to human life, which people can take or leave as they choose, but a positive necessity of life if we are to live as nature meant us to; that is, unless we are to be content to be less than men." To him art was history, as it depicted the visible expression of change through the ages, but it was also about why we make things too. Morris wrote, "Nothing can be a work of art which is not useful" in an age when the dominant economic force would have said that, nothing can be art which does not bring in a sizeable profit.

Morris was not fazed by this, as he knew that art and a love of beauty had existed long before commerce and capitalism, "Men have at all times more or less striven to beautify the familiar matters of everyday life." He knew they would again, for, without art, "our rest would be vacant and uninteresting, our labour mere endurance, mere wearing away of body and mind." Never one to mince his words, Marx wrote that the division of labour "converts the labourer into a crippled monstrosity, by forcing his detailed dexterity at the expense of a world of productive capabilities and instincts."

Where once the worker was respected for his skill and knowledge painstakingly gathered as a result of much travelling between a range of projects, he was now tied to monotonous work in a soulless factory. Worse, he came to be seen as an appendage to his machine, only respected if he worked harder, or longer, or more quickly, all to the detriment of his workmate. Morris said that all he could do was, "go on increasing his speed of hand under the spur of competition with his fellows."

To this day few have been able to challenge either the concept, notion or practice of division of labour. The positive gains are obvious, but they are only successfully constructive when making a profit is the chief aim. To challenge division of labour, it is necessary, as Morris did, to seek out a rationale for production which centres on use, not profit.

The restoration of 'Hope'

So what would socialism put in place of competition? Morris outlines a concept that few have dared to pick up – then or since. Man should find reward in *labour*. When he excels at production, his reward is to receive more of what motivates him – space to think and time to develop his special talents and skills and to enjoy his family and community. He works because he is fit for it. He chooses this job, the job does not select him. To Morris, socialism meant the free and full access for all to the means of life. The unravelling of the many good things about the Middle Ages and their collapse in the nightmare drive to industrialisation was epitomised in the separation of the craft worker from the means of production. Morris considered that the first act of socialism would be to begin to restore the link – officially at first and enshrined in a new form of property relations – then in practice, the actuality of producing the means of life.

He expressed the view that society was made up of two groups of dishonest people, "slaves submitting to be slaves yet for ever trying to cheat their masters" and "masters who eat of the common stock without adding to it." When he described much of the work performed in Victorian Britain as 'useless' it was the equivalent of dropping a bomb. It was made all the more potent as he was acknowledged as one of England's greatest craftsmen ever and one who possessed the strongest of work ethics. Instead of 'useless toil' he countered with 'Useful Work', the tension between these two concepts even today remaining unresolved. In the age to come he had thought the contest would be less about working conditions and more about the nature of the work itself. In the struggle between capital and labour, trade unions have ensured that the working conditions will never deteriorate absolutely, which was a worthy achievement. However, it is a small change compared to the project that Morris had in mind.

Capitalism made work the dominant feature in most people's lives: the search for work, the regularity of it, and the level of remuneration, all governed the way people lived. It came increasingly to sideline and alter family and social relationships. Even in Morris's lifetime, trade unions came to have a pivotal role in establishing and maintaining the price of labour, shoring it up as best they could when times were bad and pushing it that bit further forward when good times returned. However, a routine repetitive and artless job based on unsocial hours, no matter how well paid it is, is just that. If human beings are to really reach their full potential – or in Morris's view, return to the potential they had once rejoiced in before capitalism had evolved, they would have to begin to consider what it is they produce and why, as well as how, then, and in what conditions. The early socialist movement had thought about these questions, but ironically, as the strength of organised labour grew, such considerations were pushed aside.

According to Morris in his talks based on 'Useful Work versus Useless Toil' (1885), the wealthy assume that all work is useful and desirable. Even if the work is pointless, it must be useful if by dint of it, a man receives a wage, which he can use to feed his family. Of course for the best part of the century, and just to make sure, the-well-to do put the wage earner's whole family to work too, for the more hours worked, the more 'useful' and 'industrious' the worker. He was not, of course, industrious enough to run industry, and, Morris jibes, if he does not use up his holiday entitlement he is better still. How brilliantly values are turned upside down, but through logic and understanding, Morris succeeded in standing them the right way up again.

By 'useless' he mean four things. There was work performed on commodities that do not enhance the quality of life for all, work that does not enhance the life of the producer and the producing class, work on useful commodities but performed only for the enrichment of those who survive by appropriating the labour of others; and, finally, the many tasks performed such as the manufacture of armaments that exist as a requirement of the society as it stands. But what if society changes?

In socialism as in capitalism, work is central to society. It is one of life's unavoidables, so, the "race of man must either labour or perish. Nature gives us absolutely nothing gratis; we must win it by toil of some sort or degree." This last quote gives us a clue as to how Morris thought socialism might work. In other words, human beings work because they have no choice, so why not make a virtue out of necessity? Human beings are separate from other living species because, to survive, they cannot just let nature take its own course. They are both a part of nature and a conscious agent acting from sources within themselves to change it.

To Morris, remuneration is an object of the wages system. It does not describe the relative usefulness or importance of the work performed but merely represents the value placed on labour power or the workers' capacity to work. Even if the system is changed to one not based on wages, he asserted, we are still left with the question of whether work is useful or not.

We already argue constantly over whether a job is useful or not. Reflect on this. If the job does not meet the four criteria set by Morris or appear to be moving towards them, most workers would consider moving on. Turnover of labour is a constant of industrial life under capitalism. When did we last stop to consider why? Where workers stay in a job there is a constant quandry as to its nature: how quickly should the wall be built? how long does one stay behind to stack those shelves? the job can be done better and more safely but are workers inclined to say so when they are never listened to? All these points reflect a desire to improve the character of a task and display an understanding that it is possible for changes to be made, even where employers refuse to implement them.

However, an interest in new ways of working, greater on and off the job training, different work patterns, team working and greater flexibility to accommodate parental or carer needs, all serve to illustrate a shift of interest from the conditions of labour to content. The two are inextricably linked. Where workers establish a consciousness and confidence by advancing in one sphere, the other is naturally reinforced.

Morris was amongst the first to show just how interrelated aspects of life had become, for with the coming of industry, the interdependence between people grew. Yet at the same time as Samuel Smiles was urging self-help, entrepreneurs were being lauded as the exemplars of individualism and endeavour. However, it was not like that in places like Merthyr Tydfil, Stepney, or Byker, for here it was not unusual for the worker to live in a company dwelling and shop 'on the never never' at the company 'Tommy' shop. Attendance at the church school was a brief time of independence from the Company. Crammed together in such a way it was not difficult to see that a man's workspace was also his social area, for each person's actions impinged on the quality of life of his neighbours, workmates and friends.

To Morris, one of the key things that separated useful work from useless toil was 'hope' a difficult concept for us to construe. He defined 'hope' in three ways, "hope of rest, hope of product, hope of pleasure in the work itself". Rest, because all work is arduous and exacting, both mentally and physically. These days we have labelled this in a negative way by calling it 'stress'. We define the issue not by how we want to improve and change it – by making enough time for relaxation and leisure – but as a problem that appears too big to ever resolve. So the amount of workplace stress just increases. Of course 'rest because work is arduous' applies whether work is deemed useless or useful. Alongside all the other complications of life, the greater the amount of effort involved in work, the greater the amount of rest that is required.

It looks like a medal for those who built the bridge. In fact, it was a token paid on 'wages' and which could only be exchanged at the retail outlets owned by the recipients' employer.

Morris did not think of rest as simply sleeping off exertion, rather as a complete social scheme. In this way rest is not just recovery in order to simply return to the work at the same pace and level of effort that caused the need for rest in the first place. Rest is a factor in its own right so that energy is restored partially for more work, but also, to enjoy the new quality of life that can arise when a worker has more time to spare. In Morris's hands, 'hope' is much more than a dream: it is not idle thought but deed, a practical plan for looking ahead beyond the current malaise to 'what might be'.

It will come as no surprise to find that he expended much energy writing and campaigning on the issue of working hours. In the 1870s and 1880s this became the issue, as workers struck to secure the nine-hour day, and fought for the eight-hour day. Nowadays it is common to refer to a campaign for a 35-hour week. Yet a century ago the vision was much greater than this and Morris played his full part in developing the theory for those times. You will not find reference to the campaign for an eight hour day – it was always a campaign for eight hours work, eight hours rest and eight hours leisure. The leisure hours were tied strictly to the ideas of building family and community life and of self-improvement through education. It is often said that the securing of the nine-hour day in engineering after the great strike of 1871, was a huge boost to technical education, with engineers using their leisure time to study. To the unskilled it was even more crucial. Will Thorne, member of the SDF and leader of the gasworkers relates in his memoirs how he would get men out on strike by proposing a reduction of work to eight hours, "shorten the hours and prolong your lives."

Hope is 'expectation' – agreed upon through dialogue and the struggle between conflicting ideas, resulting in a consensus and change in public outlook. We should heartily thank those who changed the Victorian view that child labour was acceptable, or that women should work up to and immediately upon giving birth. They fought for eight hours work, eight hours rest and eight hours leisure, and raised 'expectation' at a time when conditions were so bleak, that people could scarcely think beyond their next meal.

Morris's concept of hope was inevitably a historically determined condition agreed upon and secured through struggle, prior to becoming the conventional wisdom handed down from one generation to another. In fourteenth century England it was generally assumed that each generation would fare no worse than the previous one and could even expect an improvement. The Industrial Revolution constituted such a major dislocation in community life that this received wisdom was called into question. Hope was never surrendered and came to prominence once more as soon as labour was organised into trade unions on a more permanent footing. However, it was not until the twentieth century that hope or the expectation that each generation would build upon the endeavour of their predecessors and live better than their parents became a fact. The generation that suffered setback as a result of the 1979 government was, no matter how bad things looked at the time, the victim of a temporary move away from what had previously been a substantial upward curve. So, today, although there are more people in work than ever before and with greater disposable income, they have fewer hours to spend either in the community or in self-improvement. The simple reason is that they work excessive hours.

The gap between expectation or 'hope' and reality is wide and complex. To Morris, industry represented hope through productive labour because that is what human beings do. It is what our existence has always been about – but it is hope in mind and body – hope for work of sufficient quality raised to the level of art. This he called 'hope of product'. If achieved it would represent a new, higher stage of liberty for the working class.

Morris rails against the inequalities inherent in work. On the one side there are those who are only "toiling to live, that we may live to toil" and those who carry out the most arduous of tasks. They work without hope of rest. 'Hope', 'fears', 'expectation'. The producers, work "not only to sustain themselves but all non producers too". 'Pleasure in work', 'rest' and 'fulfilment' are, today, phrases used by advertisers to make us work even harder, and toe the line more smartly and more quickly. Pleasure comes in the form of Bountys and Mars bars. But in the hands of Morris, such terms had a quite different meaning. Capitalism has hijacked the terms to encourage us to work harder whereas Morris, the original user of such terms, saw in them, the possibility of working class liberation. Work without hope, was, to him, work without end – a life sentence rather than a calling. On the other side were those who lived off the toil of others.

The meaning of words have become turned into their opposite. Take wealth. What is it? We usually see it as possessing those things beyond our financial reach. Some people become obsessed by wealth but most do not give it counternance. In Morris's day the docks of London, Liverpool, Manchester, Glasgow, Portsmouth and Swansea contained warehouses full of items that denoted wealth. They were stocked high with ivory and animal pelts such as snake, crocodile, and tiger skins, 'essential' items for which whole species of animals were destroyed and ecologies set in unnatural imbalance. Few thoughts were given to how these stocks would be replenished, and, by the time they were, it was too late. What was 'essential' to the wealthy of Victorian Britain was a threat to the habitat of others. The average citizen managed to go a whole lifetime without touching a snakeskin or sporting an ostrich plume, so they were obviously not that essential. Yet the goods that were basic needs like pencils, vaccines, maybe a second suit were beyond the reach of many. 'Need' was defined by the wealthy and this Morris sought to put right. He did so both in his practical work and in the thoughts he committed to paper. To him capitalism was no more than the consumption of an unproductive class at the expense of a productive one. Wealth should mean well-being for all and a healthy sense of achievement at a hard job well done. Indeed it can be judged in every conceivable way *except* in terms of money.

Something had clearly gone wrong when we were importing ivory, snakeskin and ostrich feathers and yet exporting people. Between 1881 and 1890, 3,259,000 people emigrated from the shores of Great Britain and Ireland fully 9.3 per cent of the population. If you check the timeline at the front of this book, this period of mass flight came nearly fifty years after the famine in Ireland which has been called 'genocide' and an 'exodus'.

According to Morris there is something worse than the production of wares that no one wants, or needs, (save the least productive members of the community). Workers had to make necessary goods for themselves and their own families, but were forced to keep them of inferior quality. They had to content themselves with "miserable makeshifts ... with coarse food that does not nourish, with rotten raiment which does not shelter, with wretched houses which may well make a town dweller in civilisation look back with regret to the tent of the nomadic tribe. Nay the workers must even lend a hand to the great industrial invention of the age – adulteration, and by its help produce for their own use shams and mockeries of the luxury of the rich". 'Bargain' has replaced the word 'cheap' but the meaning is much the same. An inferior product is just that, whatever it is called. Morris saw this as a waste of precious resources. It was a denial of the rationale which had once made 'work', in 'production' such a great vocation.

Morris thought that the position of the producer was made worse because civilisation was rich and abundant. Primeval man could expect nothing more than savagery because he was a prisoner of nature and beholden to its whims and ways. It took him thousands of years to progress to the most elementary stage beyond mere survival, which was the invention of tools and thousands more before the domestication of animals. Yet in the two hundred years since 1800, civilisation, especially in science and manufacturing, has accelerated, and offered modern man a life potential previously undreamt of. In 1885, Morris sensed this and expressed the view that the "struggle with nature seems nearly over, and the victory of the human race over her, near complete."

Yet at the same time, conditions were in danger of worsening and the chances for progress appeared to be drifting away. Whilst in that time conditions had barely changed, the difference between pre capitalist and latter day industrial society was one of choice, or rather, lack of it. "Compulsion by nature to labour in hope of rest, gain and pleasure " Morris wrote, " has been turned into compulsion by man to labour in hope – of living to labour."

Morris's view of socialism was that it would abolish the unproductive class by allowing all citizens to work, according to their ability. They would be expected to produce at least as much as they consume and in this way a true society would be established where, "no man would be tormented for the benefit of another – no one man would be tormented for the benefit of society."

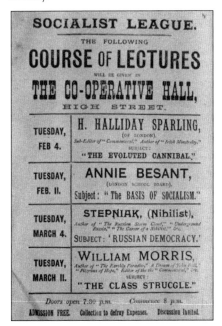

SOCIALIST LEAGUE.

THE FOLLOWING

COURSE OF LECTURES

WILL BE GIVEN IN

THE CO-OPERATIVE HALL,

HIGH STREET.

TUESDAY, FEB 4.	H. HALLIDAY SPARLING, (OF LONDON). Sub-Editor of "Commonweal," Author of "Irish Minstrelsy." SUBJECT: "THE EVOLUTED CANNIBAL."
TUESDAY, FEB. 11.	ANNIE BESANT, (LONDON SCHOOL BOARD). Subject: "The BASIS OF SOCIALISM."
TUESDAY, MARCH 4.	STEPNIAK, (Nihilist), Author of "The Russian Storm Cloud," "Underground Russia," "The Career of a Nihilist," &c. SUBJECT: 'RUSSIAN DEMOCRACY.'
TUESDAY, MARCH 11.	WILLIAM MORRIS, Author of "The Earthly Paradise," "A Dream of John Ball," "Pilgrims of Hope," Editor of the "Commonweal," &c. SUBJECT: "THE CLASS STRUGGLE."

Doors open 7.30 p.m.   Commence 8 p.m.

ADMISSION FREE.   Collection to defray Expenses.   Discussion Invited.

A handbill advertising a series of meetings convened by the Socialist League. What Sparling's lecture on "The Evoluted Cannibal" was about beggars imagination.

What would happen, Morris asked, if society were to be based on work that was completely productive with no waste? What kind of abundance would that bring and how would society change to cope with it? He believed that the surplus value created in production could be transformed into a fund to allow greater leisure time, the pursuit of knowledge and improved living conditions. By the late 1880s Britain produced more in a month than she could consume in a year, at a time when so much of the world could not produce enough in a year to keep it for a month. Little has changed in that respect. But Morris would not let the issue go. He asserted that the shift away from capitalism would afford greater abundance and greater rest if the worker only produced sufficient to meet the needs of consumption. "As long as the work is repulsive, it will still be a burden". He wrote, "Nature will not be finally conquered till our work becomes a part of the pleasure of our lives."

Capitalism boldly proclaimed its superiority over feudalism with the assertion that it called up a much greater force of production – true – that it put that force to work with greater resolve – also true – and that it organised

143

the most efficient use of that productive force – very doubtful. The first two claims centre on the effects of a system based on competition, yet both premises began to falter on the third claim. By 1882 it became increasingly apparent that competition was resulting in the mass production of goods that were inferior in quality and inflated in price. Commodities were being produced to meet the demands of the market rather than the needs of the people and the growth of the economies of foreign competitors, especially Germany, Italy and the USA hammered the point home.

Under feudalism, society was consolidated by personal rights, personal duties and the graduations of rank that everyone understood. As Morris showed, "To buy goods cheap that you might sell them dear was a legal offence (forestalling); to buy goods in the market in the morning and to sell them in the afternoon in the same place ... was forbidden and called regrating; usury was considered wrong." Strangely under capitalism all these aforementioned acts were rewarded by high office in the state. And then to top it all there was boom and slump.

The waste was not a by-product of the system, it was a result of its inner rationale. According to the Hammonds, "production had taken a form that was intensely isolating. The successful man kept his secrets, tried to find his neighbours secrets, strove for personal gain, took personal risks, made his way by personal initiative and personal enterprise." The industrial capitalist thought that what was good for him might be good for everyone. But if it was not, what was good for him prevailed nevertheless.

Morris could see the obvious and very public waste of labour power in unemployment that flared up and died off, according to season and trade flow. This was most conspicuous in the mid 1880s. However, he also claimed that there was underemployment in employment, meaning that far too much labour power was expended in the production of useless goods or goods for the useless. Worst of all, was the production of goods that were inferior in quality for the largest and most important class in society, the wealth producers.

Currently it is not a heresy to talk of "full employment". Indeed all governments of whatever persuasion since 1945, save that of the unhappy Margaret Thatcher, subscribed at least technically to the notion. But 'full employment' says little to those in employment or out of it and really means 'as many backsides on seats as possible given the prevailing conditions'. This would never suffice for Morris whose aim was not 'full employment' but employment to the fullest. It was hardly a question of how many were in work, rather one of what those in work were doing.

If they were doing what Morris envisaged, like working shorter hours, constantly improving themselves, their community, and their end product, working to constantly raise their level of skill until it became an art, then by definition more people would be in real work. They would not be working themselves into an early grave, and the obvious quality of the items they made would so change society that once again art could belong to all. He believed that at this point, man would have rediscovered pleasure in his work and the hateful form of 'civilisation' would fizzle out.

To underpin his analysis of capitalism – to unravel its workings – and then give substance to his construction of an inner core for socialism, Morris turned to the labour theory of value.

When discussing this most turn first to Marx who described labour power thus:

"By labour power or capacity for Labour is to be understood the aggregate of those mental and physical capabilities existing in a human being, which he exercises whenever he produces a use-value of any description."

The Labour theory of value had a pedigree that predates Marx. Adam Smith began to formalise a Labour Theory of Value – but elements of it already existed. William Godwin in his *Enquiry Concerning Political Justice* (1793) advanced a doctrine that Labour could alone claim the right to enjoy the produce of his productive efforts. There were echoes of this in Charles Hall who wrote *Effects of Civilisation* and in William Thompson in *Distribution of Wealth* (1824) later in Thomas Hodgkins. Under Smith, ownership of private property was inviolable. To the individual with capital accrued rights to be protected in law. But this was very quickly contested territory.

Smith and David Ricardo had shown that interest, rent and profit were a layer withdrawn from the total product. They liked the sound of that and it made them household names in manufacturing capitalist households. Godwin saw the same thing but drew the opposite conclusion. He saw capitalism as a system where some had the power "of disposing of the produce of another man's industry".

So we can see that although Morris seems to have accepted the theory in the late 1870s and ever more decisively by the early 1880s, it already had an established history in two different circles: those interested in the Labour question on behalf of workers and those who saw workers as a threat to the current order. Elements of it are in Adam Smith, Ricardo, and, of course, Marx. This was at the level of theoretical political economy, but it also existed in a popular form amongst workers and especially amongst those who applied themselves to the 'social' question. Amongst these was Thomas Hodgkins, a mechanic by trade, and a founder of the Birkbeck College (now part of the University of London), and a founder-writer of the *Economist*.

As early as the 1820s, Hodgkins was lecturing on the Labour Theory of Value and, as he lived nearby, Marx would often attend these lectures. Morris grasped the principles with both hands and transformed them into a theory of 'attractive labour'. His revolution was about opening up access to capital so that, in his words, "true manufacture" could take place, 'manufacture' here meaning, the making of a product by hand by workers employing cooperation. Capital, which could be no more than the accumulated labour of past generations, was used to produce goods for the rich who had more money than they could reasonably spend and who would, therefore, buy sham wealth. The poor had to buy shoddy goods because they had too little money to allow them to purchase products that are worth making. For Morris, the 'demand' which capital 'supplies' is false because it is based on a value of exchange (i.e. what is the optimum price at which the product can be sold), rather than on its true value and potential use to the consumer or to society.

Where there is no waste or misdirection of labour power, the other terrible twins, taxation and rent would wither. Communal services would be funded not out of tax but out of the surplus revenue previously called profit. This is not 'pie in the sky'. In China, for example, between 1949 and 1990, the largest ever health and education programmes were paid for without any personal taxation. They were entirely funded from the surplus values produced by industry. Rent, based on the private ownership of land and dwellings would disappear too. Morris gradually drew together a range of ideas that were strong meat in mid and late Victorian England. Though he was in favour, of land nationalisation and a republic, he always saw the labour question as paramount, indeed pivotal. Other major aspects of working class life would follow suit. He thought that lack of money due to old age, or the inability to work through illness, or infirmity, could be ameliorated by accumulated wage funds set up by company, industry, or occupation. Today, we call these occupational pensions and they constitute a quarter of all the capital in Britain. To attract savings, some banks would become building societies and would invest solely in building.

If life was to be so sweet, asked his critics – and the letters columns of *The Times* were often full of epistles about Morris's latest comments or observations – why would anyone want to work? Political economists alone have difficulty in finding answers, because here we enter the realms of consciousness, public service, motivation, and innovation. To speak of rewards in money terms alone, or even greater leisure time, would not suffice. Morris was in his element when answering such questions. He turned the questions around and in doing so rendered them more incisive. When asked why someone would want to work in a society where there was no compulsion to so do, he responded by enquiring why would someone not want to? And further, if there is no compulsion, what must be done to make work attractive, other than that which is based on narrow self-interest?

To this he replies, and in his lectures of the period he repeatedly returns to the subject: human beings will work willingly if they believe that their work is directed to a useful end. Even more willingly if the days worked are few and the number of hours worked are also reduced. Work is part of our daily life and becomes a positive driving force in it only to the extent that it is linked with other concerns like raising families or improving levels of knowledge. In enhancing life for the individual, what of life for the community? Work must not be seen as a means for chasing the elusive dragon of more money for the sake of accumulating even more money in Morris's view. The effect of this when applied to society as a whole, is that there is less to spend the money on and the quality of all goods and people are diminished.

He asserted that work should be varied and an ordinary worker might easily learn and practice numerous, quite unrelated crafts, in his working lifetime. Morris thought that individuals should seek after a broad knowledge of processes and practices in each chosen field, rather than a narrow range of competencies.

By this method the knowledge gained in one craft will serve to reinforce a worker's mastery of the others and assist him to broaden his outlook, the better to progress. Morris reasoned that contrasts should be sought in chosen crafts – one might involve working indoors whilst another is mainly practised outdoors. One might involve more mental application than physical. These crafts could be practised at different times of or seasons in the year. Today the more radical thinkers about work – even those promoting capitalism, as opposed to alternatives, subscribe to similar views. And it seems that, regardless of what one might prefer, capitalism no longer means working for the same employer and collecting a gold watch after many years of service. Nowadays there are likely to be a series of breaks in employment resulting from forced redundancy, travel, retraining or adaptation, if not physical relocation and separation from one's community roots, known as 'geographical mobility'.

Morris asked why, if the twenty per cent of our economy which is wealth producing, sustains the other eighty per cent, we do not share the work around? In that way we could each spend part of our working lives in the direct wealth-producing sector and our remaining years acquiring new skills and utilising the knowledge garnished from other sectors which all make their contribution.

When quality circles and teamwork were first introduced, into the car industry and light manufacturing in the 1980s, many viewed them as a 'capitalist plot' to undermine workers' organisations. Trade unionists and socialists were aghast, yet these ideas originated with earlier socialists like Morris. These ideas were really a recognition that capitalism had reached a stage where it could not function successfully unless the brains and collective instinct of workers were fully engaged and co-opted. The workers sensed this and welcomed it as they had long wanted to play a decision making role in industrial production processes. They colonised quality circles and team working, and used them to build their own strength and supplement that of their unions rather than, as the employers hoped, supplant them. According to Morris, the only alternative to this is to increase the compulsion to work. Taken on a world scale his prediction has become the most prevalent means of directing labour. In the more industrialised economies, workers are beginning, often through their unions, or despite them where they are slow to respond, to demand that their input in wealth creation and industry is recognised and matched with responsibility to direct it. The issue now is how that demand fits into company power structures. It constitutes a major challenge that will see unions either expand their potential, or fossilise. In this, we hear echoes of the guilds.

Morris thought that the wish to acquire a craft or skill was latent in all workers, and once that craft was mastered there was a strong desire within them to use their prowess in their ordinary day-to-day work, raised to the level of art. He contended that this process, which had once been the norm amongst medieval craftsmen, had been destroyed by capitalism in the rush to produce whatever would sell in the shortest time. Socialism would restore the possibility of 'art by and for all rather than the few'. William Lethaby, a leader of the Arts and Crafts Movement who was strongly influenced by Morris, thought that "much current exposition of the place and purpose of art only widens the gap between it and common lives." Morris contended that when people produced because they wanted to, it would become very difficult to establish where utilitarianism ended and art began, as each was a heartfelt and interlocking process. What is more, this 'natural', or what today we would call 'seamless' process, meant that art became an expression of the special characteristics

Morris referred to above. According to Lethaby, "a work of art is a well-made thing, that is all." It is the "well-doing of what needs doing".

Shorter hours, fewer days at labour, variety in the work, the learning of many different skills, a holistic approach to the craft, all contributed, in Morris's mind, to the restoration of art at work. It would be practiced by many rather than a few, and as the norm rather than as an exception. Each hour of the day liberated from 'compulsion to labour' meant an extra hour of worker freedom and space for improvement. Lethaby supported this view when he later wrote in *The Imprint*, "art is the humanity put into workmanship, the rest is slavery".

What would be required for the true expression of skill?

- Time
- Space
- An appreciation of nature
- A sense of history, combination and purpose
- A culture of seeking after knowledge
- An embrace of initiative
- A love of freedom
- Fearlessness of undue suppression and control
- Each worker a master of craft not a controller of people

The hierarchies of capitalism could not handle any of these.

To Morris the key was variety of work, though, this may have been a personal preference. He thought that the effect of the profit motive was at its most pernicious when it sought to subdue the worker's natural interest in a range of skills and reduce him to an operative working as an appendage to a machine within a strictly regimented division of labour. People were being fitted to the work, rather than the work adapted to their particular skills. On the division of labour, Ruskin had noted that, "if labour is divided, how much more so is the worker divided within himself?" He hated the fact that, in order to cope with the mind numbing effect of this division, the worker had to effectively 'switch off' in order to remain sane. Working in this way, suppresses all natural creative instincts as any reader who has worked a blue or white-collar assembly line will instantly be aware.

Morris saw art and work as one and the same thing, the complete opposite of a division of labour. Under capitalism the ornament or ornamental decorative item was more costly to produce, and therefore had to be reduced to a minimum. It had to be used, not as a beautifying feature of the product, but a ploy for a further price hike. Morris argued, that ornamentation should be life enhancing for the user, rather than a way of making extra money.

In asserting a notion of Useful Work, Morris provided us with a countervailing force to the seemingly all pervasive and soul destroying division of labour, which only resulted in 'useless toil'. The division of labour was devised solely for the acquisition of profit. The concept of 'useful work' could only function if its purpose was something other than for profit: namely, for the reason of use. 'Use' would be an art form. Time will surely tell how significant his outlook was. His ideas were way ahead of their time for when he did most of his writing, capitalism was still some way from reaching the mass production stage. Yet his words have a fervent ring to them, "As to the bricklayer, the mason, and the like – these would be artists, and doing not only necessary, but beautiful, and therefore happy work, if art were anything like what it should be. No, it is not such labour as this which we need to do away with, but the toil which makes the thousand and one things which nobody wants, which are used merely as the counters for the competitive buying and selling, falsely called commerce..."

Nowadays the average level of education and ability in terms of skill, is higher; workers are more confident and organised into class associations that are permanent. Yet the division of labour continues to underpin capitalism and production for profit. On one hand workers today have a greater technical capacity than Morris could have dreamt of, yet on the other, they remain banned from the corridors of industrial decision making and divided within and amongst themselves.

"...it is the allowing machines to be our masters and not our servants that so injures the beauty of life nowadays..."

From the speech *How We live and How we Might Live*, 1884

On Machines and Monopolists

Why did Morris concern himself with the machinery and monopoly questions? There are a few straightforward and relatively easy answers. As a manufacturer and craftsman he could scarcely avoid it. In Victorian Britain, machines became ubiquitous and at first, largely associated with factory life. Factory conditions, child labour, machine safety and the impact of factory buildings on the landscape, became an important concern, indeed a central theme, for writers like Thomas Hardy, Elizabeth Gaskell and Gissing, campaigners such as Booth and John Bright, Beatrice and Sidney Webb and legislators as far as the House of Lords.

Only a few of the social critics associated with the machine question actually experienced working on them. Morris did and saw them as both an opportunity and a threat. To his mind, all the intelligence and excellence of workmanship was levelled by the introduction of machinery, yet they had the advantage of reducing the drudgery present in all labour. He believed that workers did recognise this fact but still saw machines first and foremost as a threat to their livelihood. Marx referred to the duality of machines as the power of knowledge, objectified. Writing in *Capital* he stated, "Nature builds no machines, no locomotives, railways, electric telegraphs, self-acting mules. These are products of human industry; natural material transformed into organs of the human will over nature, or of human participation in nature. They are organs of the human brain, created by the human hand ..." So they heralded a terrible life for the worker at the same time as they illustrated, "to what degree general social knowledge has become a *direct force of production...*"

Morris was concerned that the machine would do away with hand craftwork, coming between the hand that made and the brain that directed that hand. He viewed machines as simply tools. In his eyes what was new was not necessarily good, and what was old was not necessarily bad. The trowel and the hammer were once the technological innovations of their time and had been used effectively, and with few modifications, for countless generations. He saw in the application of machinery a gravedigger of art.

Today, when there is such a deep rift between the craftsman and the artist Morris's claims for art seem almost quaint. The queue of ordinary workers and retired people enrolling on a myriad of adult education and part-time art classes shows that the natural instinct Morris referred to is still present. In most cases art cannot be practised at work, but it is not machinery that has come between man and art it is the character of the work that drives a wedge between the two. Machinery only widens the cleft that is already in place. In *Art under Plutocracy*, Morris wrote, "Art is man's expression of his joy in labour." This thinking was not unique. It was Carlyle who wrote "work alone is noble." Machinery laid waste the treasures of the past and more. It destroyed the old way of doing things. The growing use of machinery gave impetus to the development of the division of labour and in the process destroyed a good deal of the historically rich pool of knowledge. However, it did not destroy everything and did construct much that was new.

What conditions would allow man to express his joy in labour? In *Art and Socialism*, published in 1884, Morris wrote, "Every man willing to work should be so ensured: first, Honourable and Fitting work; second, a healthy and beautiful house; third, full leisure for rest of mind and body."

Even reading the terminology, let alone the views expressed, makes us uncomfortable now. Maybe subconsciously we see how much of the vision for a better life has been lost and surrendered. In fact, 'toil' is now taken for granted and the machine has become dominant in workplace and at home. It is almost as if we seek our joy at home, or at least outside of work, and expect work to be toil: nothing more, nothing less. Yet technology is undermining this development. In many trades the separation between life in work and outside is eroding. Expect the expectation that toil becomes work to be enjoyed, to gather pace. There is a great opportunity for trade unions here. Morris could see the potential for machinery "Our epoch ... has invented machines which would have appeared wild dreams to men of past ages, and of those machines we have as yet, made no use." Of the future, he wrote, "But then, what will people think drudgery in these days, and what pleasant work? Again, I don't know. I have a kind of idea that the time will come when people will rather overdo their hatred of machinery, as perhaps I do now?"

For him, socialism would save machines in the same way as it would rescue people and set each in balance with each other. Instead of being used to speed production and raise the numbers of unemployed, it could be used for "an honourable role of saving human labour." Displaced labour would become an opportunity for training and advance. Indeed the displacement of such labour would be an aim against which the success of industrial investment could be judged.

Morris came to recognise early on, that machinery would have a revolutionary impact. He saw that it shook up power relations and nothing could hold it still. Whilst the moralists and legislators discussed the social implications of one or other technological change, the change went on disgorging fresh problems and challenges. Sometimes, a relatively minor or incidental improvement in a piece of machinery, such as an increase in its accuracy or turnover, could have a profound impact across whole industries and affect thousands of workers.

In the light of this, Morris took three novel and more positive approaches to machinery. First, it would help keep labour to a minimum in the 'unattractive' and dangerous industries such as coal mining, fishing and construction. Secondly, it would accelerate productivity and create the material basis for the 'equalisation' of labour as applied to the necessities of life. In a lecture, *Art and Beauty of the Earth*, given in 1881, he said of machines, "I myself have boundless faith in their capacity. I believe machines can do everything, except make works of art". He felt that if something was made mechanically, then it should be done, "with a vengeance". He asked simply "Don't try ... to make a printed plate look like a hand-painted one: make it something which no-one would try to do if he were painting by hand." Thirdly and finally, machines would create a space that would "leave open to men the higher field of intellectual effort."

He could see that this free space might be filled in one of two ways, either it could increase exploitation, where a machine facilitates a single person doing the job of two or more – as occurred in the textile industry – or it could allow a worker the time and space to contemplate work and life itself. The latter is not a commonly expressed view today, but it was once the aim of all trade unionised workers and progressive politicians. The operation of the machine has come to resemble the working life of its operator with neither given rest or time, even for maintenance, until complete breakdown occurs. Morris once wrote, that to their employers, workers are, "so far as they are workmen, a part of the machinery of the workshop or the factory; to themselves they are proletarians, human beings working to live that they may live to work; their part of craftsmen, of makers of things by their own free will, is played out".

It is true and it is a very good thing, that whole families of machines have been developed, such as forklift trucks and power lifting tools, that have replaced the back-breaking work of unskilled and semi-skilled workers. In so

155

doing they have also led to a considerable decline in the numbers of such workers and the proportion of more highly skilled workers within the manufacturing environment has changed. What was the impetus to introduce machinery? Morris came up with five principal reasons.

A power driven riveting machine operated on the construction of the Forth Bridge. Built between 1883 and 1890, the bridge stretched 2,529 metres, weighed 11,571 tons, used 6,500,000 rivets and resulted in the loss of 51 men. This picture shows, in a nutshell, both the achievement and the danger of industry in the 1880s.

Firstly, under capitalism wherever the efficiency of labour depended chiefly on the output of muscular force in motive power, or precision in the regularisation of that force, humans would inevitably give way to machines. Secondly, machinery was given a boost in cases where restrictions were placed on the use of certain kinds of labour. Legislation against child labour in the tobacco trades led to the hasty introduction of steam powered spinning machines. Thirdly, in some industries such as print, paper and envelope manufacture, machinery was introduced as a means of offsetting worker restriction on overtime and unsocial working. John Stuart Mill observed, "Man moves a seed into the ground; he moves an axe through a tree; he moves a spark to fuel; he moves water into a boiler over a fire; the properties of matter do the rest." Further, "This one operation of putting things into fit places for being acted upon by each other, by their own internal forces, is all that man does, or can do, with matter." Morris improved our understanding of this relationship and moved us on. How does man combine to multiply that power of motion?

So, fourthly, if man is restricted to using only his own physical power he is fairly limited. Man is weak and ponderous in relation to the size of physical challenges he has set himself. At first glance his superiority lies in the quickness of his brain and the flexibility of his hands, so well suited to the control of mechanical devices. The machine makes up for what he lacks in strength, stamina and accuracy of repetitive motion over sustained periods as the optimum point at which the individual can produce or consume without mechanical devices is soon reached. Fifth and finally, production quickly becomes collective. The benefit of machinery is in the cooperative and social dimension.

Every tool, like every form of knowledge, represents a social growth which requires the cooperation of successive generations. This is true of both the lathe and the trowel. The chain that links Archimedes to Sir Joseph Bazalgette, the great engineer who established London's system of sewers in the mid nineteenth century, is an unbroken, continuous and cooperative thread of observation, experimentation, discovery, breakthrough and consolidation of knowledge, tool and technique. But Morris's concern was along these lines. Under capitalism the familiarisation of machinery expands and deepens, yet the ownership of those tools or means of producing, narrows.

Morris's sense of historical sweep brought him early to the conclusion that the machine would only find a harmonious role when owned by those who had no interest in exploiting it or themselves. This was no new discovery. Morris believed that these were the conditions that had actually existed and had worked so effectively before capitalism had hijacked industry – and that the stable relationship between man and tool had been usurped by the private urge for profits.

He extended this framework to the factory. The factory would become a "centre of intellectual activity", although he still saw many flaws and much unfulfilled potential in the system. Morris felt that it could offer too little scope to meet human satisfaction as it was, so he opted to supplement it with enhanced teamwork and by developing ways of structuring the labour process other than through the division of labour. He thought that this could be partially achieved by expanding the variety of work available. Some would be arduous and some not. There would be some machine tending, and some concept work, and there would be scope for everyone to work towards the improvement of quality.

The test of course is whether Morris's concept could be applied not in one workplace, but across a whole industry. He sought out machinery that lightened loads rather than reduced labour and machinery that could be used to increase productivity in goods that were useful. The creation of space to develop higher levels of knowledge and skill amongst the workforce was high on his list of priorities.

He maintained that in the phase of development that followed capitalism, the factory would become a centre of enlightenment and renaissance. Even repetitive labour would be made acceptable by the worker's consciousness of its potential usefulness. Morris drew three key conclusions. First, labour had to be emancipated and free from compulsion in order to advance. Second, the development of industry and machinery would erode the difference between town and countryside, and finally, that the separation of 'intellectual' and 'manual' labour would end. By 1883 he was not just convinced about the first point, but had made it an overriding concern that would stay with him always.

To meet his second conclusion, Morris redesigned the factory, surrounding it with gardens and linking it to farms to provide cheap and regular supplies of quality food for the workforce and their families, who would live nearby. In this factory there would be a new atmosphere for the worker where "no new process, no detail of improvements in machinery would be hidden from the first enquirer". The improvement in technical knowledge "would foster general interest in work and in the realities of life, which would surely tend to elevate labour and create a standard of excellence in manufacture." As we have learned, Morris was personally suspicious of mass production, preferring his notion of handicraft, so it is impressive that he had the insight to acknowledge its importance. At first the shift from handcraft tool to machine appears to favour quantity rather than quality. Machines mimicked the function of tools, sometimes of a number of tools at once, yet while all handtools require human power, ingenuity and dexterity to use them, machines increasingly worked by themselves. In 1735 John Wyatt described his revolutionary spinning machine as one "to spin without fingers".

All machine tools have built into their structure an element of the skill once performed manually with a hand tool. Take the lathe as an example: a work piece is rotated while a cutting edge is applied to it. Later Henry Maudsley added a slide rest which could hold the cutting edge more rigidly, which resulted in greater accuracy.

The steam hammer was invented by James Nasmyth, a pupil of Maudsley. Used extensively in heavy engineering, a piston would be raised by steam in a cylinder then allowed to drop back down. Different hammer heads could be applied. It ruined the blacksmith who had been at the centre of the handicraft industry for centuries. Where in a lathe, the workpiece is turned and cutting edges applied, in a drilling machine, the workpiece is held stationery and the cutting screw or drill rotates.

John Wilkinson invented the boring machine in the search to improve the bore of a cannon. This family of machines carried a cutting tool on a rotating bar into and through the workpiece: but its most important application was in the production of cylinders.

A grinding machine was based on an ancient machine used to refine the edge of knives. It was later adapted to smooth surfaces. The milling machine works to similar principles as a grinding machine but has rapidly rotating cutters. A planing machine operates a laterally moving cutting edge. All these machines are mimicking actions previously made by hand and tools. With the addition of unlimited power, these machines soon became capable of being set to repeat tasks without the constant intervention of the machine-minder: they became automated.

Henry Maudsley's invention of the slide rest which held the cutting edge in place for accurate metalworking was effectively a substitute of the human hand. The precision of this allowed machines to be used to make other machines. Their only organised way of being effective was to follow the path of the association of Labour, so we got the association of machines.

What characterises a machine over a tool is that it operates many times the number of needles, or cutters, or spindles and this overrides the natural restrictions of a tool operated by one person.

Gradually it became possible to drive machinery independent of geographical consideration. First horsepower – not much good in a factory – then, to a much lesser extent wind power. Then water – which was also partly subject to the seasons – gave way to Watt's coal-fired double-acting steam engine. Watt was certain from the outset that his machine would have an almost universal application including, (undreamt of at the time), sufficient power to drive a steam vessel on the high seas. As simple cooperation between human beings serves as a basis for capitalism, so does it similarly apply to the simultaneous operation of a number of machines. This had a considerable effect on production.

Handicraft could never keep up with such developments and inevitably gave way to machine manufacture. Once in place there could be no going back. Morris recognised this but thought that the principle of handicraft, whereby a skilled worker operated or controlled a whole branch of a production process, could be adapted to modern industry. If we look at current technique used in Japanese or Scandinavian auto manufacture, he is probably about to be proved right.

The prime motive for introducing machinery was to increase the productiveness of labour by shortening the amount of time required to produce a commodity, but because a machine does not rely on human physical power, the machine ended up lengthening the machine-minder's working day.

It also led to mass production. In 1831, The Society for the Diffusion of Useful Machinery produced the *Results of Machinery* which illustrated the impact of machinery on production. It showed that, "Two centuries ago, not one person in a thousand wore stockings; one century ago not one person in five hundred wore them; now not one person in a thousand is without them." The possibilities for production grew at a bewildering pace. Capitalism was at its most potent when applied to production for mass markets.

Looking ahead to the role of machinery in the future Morris saw an increased role indicating to, not "the lessening of men's energy by the reduction of labour to a minimum, but rather to the reduction of pain in labour to a minimum." He thought that early socialism would lead to a surge of utilitarianism, which would in turn lead to an abundance, if not an oversupply, but that, as society would no longer be driven by profit it would soon turn its back on excess and concentrate more on quality.

This would end the competition between town and countryside, which we shall discuss in more detail later in this book.

Morris's third conclusion is more interesting. How would the differences between 'intellectual' and 'manual' labour be dispelled? Marx saw part of this as a process whereby the professions would 'slip' and be absorbed into the proletariat, "the bourgeoisie has stripped of its halo every occupation hitherto honoured and looked up to with reverent awe. It has converted the physician, the lawyer, the priest, the poet, the man of science, into its paid wage labourers". Morris drew a similar conclusion, but went further and envisaged how workers would be able to raise themselves to a higher level through the acquisition of advanced learning and skill and the acquisition of a number of crafts. However, he did not see that many would do this by using and mastering the machinery that employers had brought in to supplant labour.

He may have hoped, though he nowhere makes it clear, that the space created by the introduction of machinery, would be filled by workers resorting to increased use of handicraft skills. He contested that the return to handicraft, where the worker was closer to actual production, with no interruption from a machine, provided the best chance of an early return of art as a desirable feature of the production process. In at least one respect, his personal attitude to machinery got the better of him. To Morris, machinery somehow was divorced from nature and served to reinforce the separation of human beings from their environment. He thought that the struggle of human beings as workers against nature was a noble one and that the use of machines gave them an unfair advantage. He also thought that by turning away from production by mechanical means people could re-establish a more balanced relationship with nature.

When machines were introduced in the first phase of the Industrial Revolution and first grouped together in factories, they almost destroyed the existing workforce. Over decades they reshaped this workforce, which would never again work from home. By the mid-Victorian period, those operating machinery were a new generation who had never known the old cottage-based, handicraft way of making things and had no expectation of working from home. Some historians have been able to show that handicraft work continued for much longer than was previously assumed, indeed up to 1914, but the dynamic force was the machine in the factory environment. The new generation, knowing only machinery, set about colonising it and wherever possible using it to strengthen the hand of labour. For example, lathes were much the same in London, Birmingham or Glasgow. This very similarity, along with a uniform way of organising production, brought about a shared outlook and culture between lathe operators across the country. So began a struggle for common wage rates, hours of labour and employment conditions for apprentices.

A brief overview of developments in the engineering industry illustrates this process of change and the impact it had on workers. In the first phase, invention mostly emanated from millwrights, blacksmiths, painters and masons. These trades, whose roots went back to Saxon times, together with those who worked with brass and iron, combined to form a new kind of military engineer and the civil engineers of the nineteenth century.

In our Industrial Revolution the engineer has a special place. Until the eighteenth century, most engineers worked on their own in small towns and villages fixing agricultural machinery. It was the increased size and scope of projects like cutting canals and building bridges and water courses that brought them together in greater numbers and new combinations. The former mutual societies of the engineers just could not cope, for what was really required was a "trade-wide" policy. Thus unions began to emerge. Should they petition Parliament to rejig the Elizabethan Labour code? Instead they chose to use their combined force to negotiate directly with the employer, and in so doing shaped the unique character of the British Labour Movement over the last 200 years.

By 1810, the Association of Engineers was so powerful that workers on the Waterloo Bridge were told "No Mechanics' Society ticket – no work!" The development of industry brought forth a new class of engineer – one who had not been indentured and the removal of Elizabeth's laws meant that the new engineer could practice this trade in any corner of Britain. Engineers began to replace the millwright in large numbers. And, as machine minders, working on machines that became increasingly self-acting, became mere machine attendants. The fact that in some parts of Britain they were employed at less than half the pay of a millwright, meant that they were likely to emerge the stronger. However, in order to fulfil the challenge of the newer larger jobs requiring greater accuracy and speed in the handling of intricate processes, the engineer soon began to master new skills that the millwrights did not have.

During the great lockout of 1852, the engineer's union put forward William Newton, who was the first trade unionist to stand for parliament, in the Tower Hamlets seat. His platform is interesting to note and worthy of a minor digression. It included the six points of the Chartist Charter including universal suffrage, parliamentary reform, the legalising of trade unions, universal education, the equalisation of the poor relief rate (and making it a right), state insurance against unemployment and a revision of the patent laws to allow poorer inventors into production. In a later contest in Ipswich he narrowly missed entering Parliament nearly two decades ahead of Keir Hardie.

In 1841, 31,566 were employed as engineers. By 1891, this had risen to over a quarter of a million in a metal industry employing over a million. In roughly the same period the total volume of machinery produced for export increased fifteen fold. In 1850 only 9% of ships were made of iron, and the rest of wood, but by the 1890s the position was completely reversed. In 1892 over 80% of the mercantile tonnage built in the world was built in British yards. Up until 1850 engineering was practiced in 'general shops'. Even George Stephenson in Newcastle – famed for making locomotives, also made iron bridges, and undertook marine and dock work. Increasingly work became specialised and there emerged a new layer of smaller companies.

After 1850 the pace of innovation reached a plateau, and made time for the refinement of existing machinery. Many more machines were utilised under factory conditions, and the key machines fathered a family of related equipment. In addition to the engine lathe, came the duplex lathe, a gap lathe for swinging heavy castings, a double railway wheel lathe and a lathe with a traversing cross-slide. Power was increased to drive bigger, heavier equipment. Where production could take place under one roof, specialism resulted in the establishment of 'shops' some of which remained unchanged for 100 years: the turnery or machine shop, the tilting and erecting shop, the pattern makers' shop, the smithy and the press shop. However, alongside specialisation came an even greater division of labour. Where in 1840 one lathe was used, twenty years later any one of five different lathes could be used in a single company. The engineers specialised to meet this challenge and it tested their union too as it sought to emphasise what bound engineers together rather than what separated them. Differentiation actually increased dependency on the whole as when problems like depression, skill shortage and machine breakdown occurred in one area it affected them all.

Morris was not alone in drawing detrimental conclusions about machinery in his early and middle years and it is not difficult to understand why. The factory, with its smoke stacks and battery conditions was a relatively new and very aggressive imposition on the community. This was a time when the first machines were used to change raw materials into manufactured commodities, or what Morris usually called wares. The use of machines today has changed entirely and in a qualitative way. Where once machines were an external agent working from the outside, engineering can now take place at the level of moving around atoms, that is, from the inside. Machines, themselves products of the work of other machines, have become a part of life. How else could one describe a dam or a milking machine or a pacemaker? Machines are now smaller, more portable, so much so that some factory work can be done outside, to suit the needs of workers. Given a choice they invariably opt to work the majority of their working week from home. Though this may not necessarily be as great a compliment to homeworking as some suspect! It may be more condemnation of our limited approach to factories and factory labour.

Morris embraced socialism in order to save the arts and crafts, which he believed were being killed by capitalism. He saw that the machine reduced the worker to a mere operative, an appendage to the machine, to be worked, like the latter until he dropped. His hatred of civilisation arose as a result of his condemnation of the effect capitalism had on workers. He wrote, "Through squalid life they laboured, in sordid grief they died, those sons of a mighty mother, those props of England's pride."

His attitude to machines changed over the decades even and although he personally opted to use handicraft in place of machinery wherever he could, but this did not stop him installing the most modern machines in his plants. After the 1850s, attacking machinery had become a blunt instrument, as it failed to differentiate between machines that destroyed skill and working practices and those that enhanced lives and created new more highly skilled work, the better to shape the human landscape. After the age of fifty, Morris explicitly differentiated between industrialism and the form of slavery brought about by industrialists. Of machines he said "we have as yet made *no use.*" This is not the usual criticism of machines that we have come to associate with Morris. In fact, his position on machinery and mass production is so consistent and transparent in its development, that it is difficult to see how he has become associated with 'small', 'quaint' 'premature anti-industrialism'. This was the man who used a lantern slide to illustrate a lecture he gave in 1894. That must have been some 'powerpoint' presentation. He had no fear of the new, for example, in designing for linoleum – he was the first person ever to print a floor covering.

Before the Royal Commission on Technical Education Morris stated in evidence, "Undoubtedly everybody ought to be taught to draw just as much as everybody ought to be taught to read and write." Morris sought to end the division between theory and practice. In his factories, the workers were multiskilled and whoever was nearest and available performed the task at hand.`

If machines were meant to be labour-saving Morris reasoned, why did they so often save on the labourer rather than the labour of the producer? He refers to machines as 'miracles of ingenuity', and the genesis of machinery such as the lathe, makes it hard to disagree. To the generation born in the 1840s, machinery and factories were relatively new and an object for suspicion, but machines were as much an objectification of human ingenuity as any Wren or Hawksmoor church or hospital by John Soames. Only the centuries had changed.

Morris saw a special role for machinery in his new way of thinking. He was among the first to incorporate new machines into his manufacturing establishments and was constantly on the lookout for new ones or experimenting with those he had. But the role was to be clearly defined and circumscribed and that meant a form of social contract between machine and operator. Machines, he asserted, should be used only where they restricted the amount of unattractive labour. He was being quite unrealistic. For what he could not yet perceive was that machines can raise and enhanced skill and be used, not just to alleviate unattractive labour, but to make ordinary labour attractive too.

Morris taught himself many trades including weaving with a loom. Was not the loom a machine? Did it not enhance the pride involved in mastering this ancient process? Likewise in printing, where he used machines to produce some of the most beautifully designed and printed works in the English language. Consider the Kelmscott Chaucer. Was the shift from wood blocks to movable type not a massive step forward?

It is worthwhile exploring this contradictory approach to machinery a little further. It seems as if Morris, deplored machinery, when it physically separated the worker from the act of production.

Where power that generated production and control of the physical process had been transferred from hand to machine, he resented it. However, was this not simply a different way of bringing hand and brainwork together? Morris mastered a range of processes of print, type and ink production and the working of the printing press itself. Surely the mastery of new machines that powered the process was an opportunity to extend skill to greater levels rather than reduce them? Once machines were introduced that were substitutes for intensive labour, the general impact was to raise both productivity and the level of skill required of those remaining in production.

There was a further flaw in Morris's outlook and one, which increasingly worried him. What would happen if he sought to partially implement his approach to machinery while everyone else – including direct competitors – took a different approach? The only result would be that costs of production in his establishments would be higher and therefore less competitive and the only way he could survive, given that he was also committed to paying his workers a skilled rate, would be to raise the price of his products. Ironically, in seeking to work in a progressive way in his own company he would only be able to produce goods that the rich could afford. For a while, Morris toyed with the idea of re-establishing his company as a workers' cooperative along the lines set down by Owen. Indeed, he came under some pressure to make this change as a result of newspaper jibes and criticism, but he chose not to pursue this path. His reasoning is interesting, for neither economic power nor personal aggrandisement played a role. He feared only the loss of artistic independence.

Doubtless Morris would have welcomed the x-ray imaging used by surgeons and would have looked with awe at 'Sharon and Tracy' the two largest boring machines in the world which were used to dig under the Thames to create the new Jubilee line extension. The first was the kind of machine that he dreamt of, and the other two saved men from doing backbreaking and immensely dangerous work. Today, where machines, or new ways of operating them, are seen as cynical substitutes for labour, they are barely tolerated. However, the printers of West Ferry would not want to go back to a time when paper bales weighing more than a tonne had to be manhandled with many a hand or foot injury as a result. The robots that move them round the plant now may be clunky metal copies of workers, but at least they do not crush fingers and limbs. Today we can also regard machines as opportunities to enhance skill, enabling us to concert diverse production functions and processes. In the last twenty years the advance of technology has had to be introduced to deal with the increased diversity and complexity of production, while greatly reducing the amount of unskilled and semi-skilled work required.

The issues Morris raised regarding machinery bear an uncanny resemblance to the current public debate over the industrialisation of agriculture. It seems here too, that people are looking to mix the positive benefits of intensive, industrial farming with organic farming. At the same time they express great reservation about the influence of multinational chemical companies and agro-industrial interests, including lobbyists, that appear beyond popular influence or control.

Morris was right to point out the dangers inherent in machine production where monopolists rule. The accuracy of his observation is today, all too clear. Hours continue to be far too long, labour is intensively exploited and the struggle for quality is constantly undermined. It is tragi-comedy to watch those employed on a production line being exhorted to aim at quality, while the work is speeded up, and mind-numbingly repetitive. It is a tribute to those thus employed that anything of quality emerges at all. Work is to be less enjoyable and therefore less productive than it could be. Even work in new sectors, using and producing the newest technology, is no guarantee that a company will continue to lead – one need only look at the case of Fujitsu and the precipitous fall in the price of semiconductors to the point where it is barely above the cost of production. This fall is not the result of too little machinery in production but from too much. Morris may have thought that "those who did the roughest work, work the shortest spells" but in all fields and in all trades, many people now work longer and harder than they did a generation ago – and that in a country which already works longer hours than most of its European competitors.

Throughout the 1880s, in lectures and meetings, Morris turned his mind to manufacture. What had gone wrong and what needed to be done to put it right? In grappling with these issues he produced some of his most incisive works. These followed a pattern of investigation, preparation, lecture, amendment, and publication. *Monopoly – Or How Labour is Robbed* has become one of his best-known contributions to the new way of looking at the 'labour question'. It emerged as one of the core texts of the new socialist movement.

Nowadays, the word monopoly is applied to a company that establishes a dominant, if not near exclusive, hold over an industrial process or product. To Morris, it referred not to a company but a class and one which had established a monopoly over the employment of labour. To live one had to work. To work one had to be employed by those who owned capital and thereby had a monopoly over who was employed, when and why.

Monopoly or How Labour is Robbed is important for a number of reasons, but for Morris personally, it is important for one very special reason. It represents a full step forward and away from Owen and Ruskin and he becomes his own man. Previously he had addressed the class into which he was born and the bourgeois whose views appeared to dominate society. He was no less scathing in his criticism of capitalism but did appeal to them to change before it was too late. He even offered fellow artists the chance of "throwing in their lot with the rising class." This formula is repeated in *Monopoly or How Labour is Robbed*, but less convincingly and without any enthusiasm. From here on, the emphasis is about 'how' labour is robbed and the appeal is to those workers who feel the lash, but have not yet considered why their lot was so bad.

It is not possible to fully comprehend Morris's views on the machine question without simultaneously grasping his view of monopoly. The essence of machinery was that it came to dominate the operator. Yet, as we have seen, machines could be both opportunity and a threat. Under 'civilisation' the threat would always overpower opportunity because one class, the owners of capital, had a monopoly over ownership of machinery and what direction it was used for. If they insisted that the main use was to make profit, then the needs of the operator could only come a poor second, where they were considered at all.

Morris asked: "Why do workers not understand their malaise even when they recognise it?" He concludes that workers will grow to understand it and that their maturity in relation to the question will be "proportionate to its freedom from prejudice and its knowledge". A mature working class is the one that rises above prejudice and difference to create a unity. It is knowledgeable in the sense that it understands both why it is in the condition it is and how it will rise above it. Morris warns, "Before they set out to seek a remedy they must add to this knowledge of their position and discontent with it, a knowledge of the means whereby they are kept in that position in their own despite; and that knowledge is for us socialists to give them … "

This phrase has caused all sorts of problems for and misinterpretations of Morris. On the surface he appears to imply that socialism and the 'knowledge' are a gift bestowed on workers from without, of middle class politics being injected into a working class incapable of thinking things through for themselves. It is safe to say that this is not what he meant at all. Indeed he meant something quite different, not least because, he was already familiar with the young workers being recruited to socialism. He saw in them the possibility of building something without contracting out the thinking to the middle class – a body that Morris had left behind decades before.

Morris refers to 'us socialists' as a party of socialists made up of working class members. He here rides a paradigm that has long beset socialist and workers' parties. Elsewhere he is precise and emphatic: that advanced and progressive working class thinking comes from within that working class and is a distillation of their experience and ideas. "It is they (the workers) who have to sweep away the monopoly." Again, "the recognition of the duty of the working man to raise his class, apart from his own individual advancement, is spreading wider and wider amongst workers."

How could workers break the monopoly? Why not simply stay away from work, work more slowly, work less, play work-shy or even, as occurred in the USA and in France, engage in a bit of sabotage? Some influential socialists such as Paul Lafargue called for a 'right to be lazy'. Morris had such a strong work ethic such that he could never countenance this ploy. This work ethic flavoured his socialism and drove his desire for the deconstruction of capitalism. He thought that what was wrong with capitalism was not that workers were idle but that the owners of capital were. They simply hid behind the notion – popular in nineteenth century England – that the owners brought a special category to the market place, 'entrepreneurship'. This would not wash with Morris, because through his company, he too was active and entrepreneurial in the marketplace, and saw straight through such claims. Indeed one of the problems of capitalism, Morris argued forcefully, was that it kept workers idle, when they wanted to work.

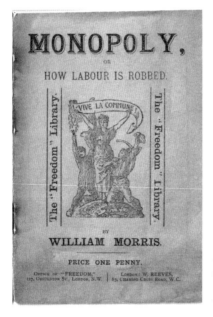

Monopoly was not a question of seeking to exclude competitors to gain control of an industry. To Morris, monopoly was *the* question. Employers could only exist by monopolising the means of production. This gave them a monopoly over labour and the means of life.

Morris reasoned that the owner of capital employed managers and foremen to do his work, so that they could themselves be idle. It was the capitalist class that was kept in its non-labour by the labour of the many. If one doubted that, asked Morris, "why does not the worker try to live on the usefulness of the capitalist and vice versa and see who lasted longest?" He contended that society would quickly fall into a state of disrepair. Elsewhere he states, "in the case of the labour process, the capitalist is truly a sleeping partner".

A monopolist is one who "was privileged to compel us to pay for imaginary services." His ownership of the power of monopoly is privately secured, excluding all others from entering the field let alone seeking a level one to play on. As everyone who wants to live must labour, monopoly over labour, the means of life, is power indeed. It is a power too far.

To exercise labour requires two things on the part of workers. Firstly, "bodily and mental powers … developed by training, habit and tradition." Second, "raw materials on which to exercise those powers and wherewith to aid them." The two must be fused before any commodity can be produced. If a worker cannot access the instruments of production, he becomes a dependant. Indeed in Morris's mind they can no longer be called means of production as this implies that they are put to productive use. In fact, they become "means of profit, of squeezing rent, interest and profit out of the producers." The aim of each company becomes, not to produce the greatest amount of wealth, but the greatest extent and maximisation of profit.

"When the masters fall short in getting what they consider the due amount of profit produced by this said machinery, they say times are bad; even though the warehouses and granaries are full, and the power of producing wealth with decreasing labour is every day growing. It is the classes which are necessary to what of real society still hangs together behind the monstrous machinery of monopoly, it is the workers themselves that must bring about the change". What is more, it is change "brought about or at least guided by the conscious intelligence of the workers." Monopoly, whilst being a near 'natural' tendency of capitalism is, according to Morris, an entirely 'artificial restriction' on true production.

"Is Fourier wrong when he calls factories, 'tempered bagnos*'?"
Marx on factory labour in Capital.

*A favourite of the Inquisition, a bagno is similar to a thumbscrew and could be applied to both wrists and ankles.

Transforming factory labour

To workers, factories could be either 'satanic mills' or 'palaces of industry'. It was logical that Morris would turn his mind to the factory question, for it exercised so many of the big social and reform thinkers of the nineteenth century. He began his analysis with a description of the new ways of working that were fostered by the first Industrial Revolution and then extended it to cover the physical environment in which work took place. In so doing he influenced the study and practice of architecture and others concerned with the design of living space and the natural environment.

Hastily erected, ill lit or ventilated, a place to work oneself into an early grave. Factories were built often with complete disregard for health or safety or welfare of both workers and the immediate community. Seen here, a factory overshadowing local tenements.
(Reproduced courtesy of the TUC unionhistory.info)

The factory was simply machinery organised into a system, but it changed everything. It altered the relationship between worker and employer and set them at each other's throats, and the rapport workers had with each other and within their families. In his novel *Sybil*, Disraeli wrote, "It is that the capitalist has found a slave that has supplanted the labour and ingenuity of man. Once he was an artisan: at best, he now only watches machines; and even that occupation slips from his grasp, to the woman and child."

Marx put it in similar terms, "in handicrafts and manufacture, the workman makes use of the tool, in the factory, the machine makes use of him".

He believed that the old slave-driver's code had been replaced by the foremen's arbitrary schedule of deductions for lateness, sickness and slacking –

demeanours which were more than likely the result of exhaustion. According to a report regarding conditions in a single mill, one spinner was fined for being dirty, another for washing: another man was fined for whistling and yet another for working with the window open in 84 degree temperatures. For capitalism to appear vibrant and energetic factory owners only had to make an end product and a profit: they were not obliged to forge a community. Very few did. The experiments of Bourneville, New Lanark and Saltaire stand out because there were so few of them.

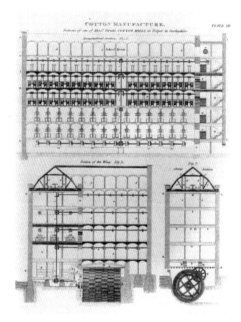

Herded from home into factories, workers discovered a whole new culture of tyrannies. They started with the clock. Clock in, clock out. Fines for lateness, fines for not being able to keep up. This architect's plan displays a capitalist sense of structure, good order and control. The reality for workers was quite different.

Where the 'animal' revolution appeared to enhance the productive power of workers, machinery tended to compete. Marx illustrated this in *Capital*, "the self expansion of capital by means of machinery is ... directly proportional to the number of workpeople, whose means of livelihood have been destroyed by that machinery ..." In the early stages of the Industrial Revolution, the impact of machinery on domestic and foreign markets was immediate. Up until the 1830s the gradual redundancy of English hand loom weavers resulted in many dying of starvation, while others survived on two and a half pennies in Poor Law or parish relief. At the same time the Governor General famously wrote, "The bones of the cotton weavers are bleaching the plains of India."

By the mid-century, factories were beginning to dominate industrial life even though they were still relatively few in number – 2,887 of them existed in 1861 – and the numbers employed did not at that time overwhelm handiwork. Indeed there is some evidence that as productivity rose in textiles, some factories were closed down. In general, however, the introduction of concentrations of powered machinery working on a core function, such as the weaving of cotton, under one factory roof, soon had an impact on supporting handicrafts.

These skills were mechanised in their turn in order to keep pace. For example, machines were invented that revolutionised tailoring, like needle making and buttonhole stitching.

The factory system had two immediate effects. Firstly it accelerated the output of various instruments of labour, and secondly, to sustain that progress, it was organised in a way that fragmented the work, further increasing the division of labour. The system drew workers away from homeworking, undermining familial care, especially for children, the elderly and the infirm and weakening the home and community-based framework of social welfare and insurance that had hitherto served to keep them strong.

In the census of 1861 fewer people worked in textile, mining and the metal working industries than were employed as domestic servants, yet the dynamism of the factory environment affected everything from legislation and science to literature. Capitalism and factory production produced deeper changes in economic fortune than had previously been the norm and with greater social consequences. The boom and slump described earlier in this book brought with it both economic and social instability. It was a time of insecurity for all.

Marx made a major contribution to describing how demand was perceived: first, production stepped up to fever pitch, resulting in overproduction, then a contraction of world scale markets leading to diminishing production.

Yet the logic of factories was relentless. The rationale was based on the limitations of human muscle power, when pitched against mechanised production. Elements like steam, water-power and a concentration of capital seem like almost supernatural forces in comparison to human frailty. By concentrating machines and people, factories could raise productivity, and profitability too, for costs were much reduced. In *Capital*, Marx shows how steel pins produced within the handicraft system could cost on average £7/4 shillings a gross, by manufacture this fell to 8 shillings a gross and by factory production to 2 shillings and sixpence a gross.

Early on, attempts were made, especially in the West Midlands, to sustain handicraft and homeworking based around a central source of power, but it could never work and was soon superseded by factory production.

The conditions in factories were often truly awful. At a Royal Commission into Employment in 1866 it was noted that so much child and female labour was employed in such dire and dangerous conditions in the London book and newspaper print houses that they were popularly known as the "slaughterhouses".

In those days paper was made out of cloth and rag-sorters had to wade through huge piles of fabric scraps which were imported from as far away as Russia and Turkey. The workers regularly fell victim to smallpox and other infectious diseases. In brickmaking and tile manufacture, children as young as four were employed on shifts lasting from 5am to 7pm. Instruction in straw-plaiting began between the third and fourth year of life – if it can be called that. The public health reports at the time make sombre reading and the death rates in agriculture, mining, fishing and printing are even more depressing.

Dr Thomas Percival of Manchester, whose work on conditions in industrial life marked the beginning of the movement for factory legislation, recorded the death rate for newborn babies in the area. In Manchester itself it was 1 in 25, in Liverpool it was 1 in 27, in Monton, just a few miles from Manchester, the ratio was 1 in 68 and at Horwich, between Bolton and Chorley, it was 1 in 67. However, rather than the obviously superior conditions of Horwich and Monton being emulated by Manchester industrialists, the opposite occurred.

The poverty was observed by Godolphin Osbourne who wrote reports for the Poor Law Commissioners. "Much is done to relieve distresses by many, and is done with judgement and discrimination; but when all is done, I could never make out how they can live with their present earnings."

By 1870 there were few domestic industries that had not been profoundly changed by the growth of factory production. Machinery grew to meet the needs of this new way of making things, accelerating the process even more. Social concern grew at the use of child labour and legislation was eventually passed to limit the number of hours a child could work in a day. It should be noted, however, that most Acts came into force when the worst of the exploitation was over and, of course, the result of these laws was even more pressure to develop labour-saving machinery.

The introduction of machinery into industries like packaging, which involved lighter loads led to the wholescale employment of women in lieu of men. Children were gradually eased out of the system due to a series of Factory Acts from 1833 onwards and after 1878 no child under ten years old could be employed as there was compulsory education for all under this age. Children from ten to fourteen could only work half days and greater care of their safety, including meal breaks and adequate ventilation were implemented. The importance of a childhood for the young was recognised as well as the benefits they would gain from learning. In many respects it was from the factory system that the education system grew.

In the Communist Manifesto of 1848, Marx and Engels showed how, up until the growth of the factory system, all trades sought to preserve the status quo with the state intervening to break up any machinery that disturbed the social balance. However, capitalism was naturally competitive with each advance over a rival a crucial step towards survival, therefore all attempts to check the introduction of machines and factories, from whatever source were ultimately doomed. They wrote, "All fixed and fast frozen relations, with their train of ancient and venerable prejudices and opinions, are swept away, all new formed ones become antiquated before they can ossify. All that is solid melts into air ... "

In the same way as the factory revolutionises production, it also fundamentally changes relationships between producers. The introduction of a division of labour within the factory takes the ancient crafts and strips the process down into any number of separate steps – each a detail that can be mechanised, and constantly repeated, preferably by machine. It also results in a reserve army of labour.

In this, Marx and Morris draw similar conclusions. Marx wrote "Modern industry ... through its catastrophes imposes the necessity of recognising as a fundamental law of production, variation of work, consequently fitness of the labourer for varied work, consequently the greatest possible development of his varied aptitudes". Workers would no longer be wrights or carpenters but flexible and interchangeable cogs in a production process, reduced to bit parts.

'Satanic Mills'

By the Treaty of Utrecht (1713), Britain became the principal slave trading nation in the world. The Government subcontracted operation of the external slave system to the South Seas Company, while, at home it was left to the employers. Many have wondered why it was that working class opinion in Britain was so strongly in favour of the Northern states and so strongly opposed to the Southern slave-owning confederacy during the American civil war. It could be that to them, the system that sustained slavery abroad was very like the one they had at home. Abroad it existed on plantations, while at home, it was in factories. The slave trade educated the slave owner to look on people as mere objects and taught him to believe that an object had no emotions and would not be concerned with rights. Where the skilled artisan had once been a pillar of the community, indeed the nation, under the factory system he became an underdog, and when we examine the employment of child labour and the workhouse, the situation is even worse.

When Richard Oastler, launched his famous attacks on slavery in 1830, he was referring to the slavery of the worsted mills of Bradford, "thousands of little children, both male and female, but principally female, from seven to fourteen years are daily compelled to labour from six o'clock to seven in the evening with only – Britons blush while you read this – with only thirty minutes allowed for eating and recreation."

"We respect our masters, and are willing to work for our support, and that of our parents, but we want time for more rest, a little play, and to learn to read and write. We do not think it right that we should know nothing but work and suffering, from Monday morning to Saturday night, to make others rich. Do, good gentlemen, inquire carefully into our concern."

This was written by Manchester's Factory Children Committee and sent to the House of Commons in 1836.

When a parish in London provided indoor relief, it gained the right to dispose of the children of the recipient. Children so 'released' were, by arrangement, sent to work in the Lancashire cotton mills. As one Parliamentarian described it, "The children, who are sent off by wagonloads at a time, are as much lost forever to their parents as if they were shipped off to the West Indies."

The struggle of Wilberforce to end slavery resembles Shaftsbury's efforts to promote legislation against child labour in Britain, often against the same or related vested interests. The Hammonds wrote in their seminal study of village labouring, "a traveller in 1830 who visited the mills of Lancashire … would have seen under the same roof a mechanical genius that was inconceivable to the mind of a crusader, and men and women still as much the slaves of dire necessity as the men and women of the mills of Antioch and Tyre." William Cobbett sarcastically claimed that the opponents of the Ten Hours Bill, which sought to restrict the number of hours that youngsters could be forced to work, discovered that Britain's manufacturing success rested on 30,000 girls. Likewise, champions of slavery – and there were some, in high places – argued that it kept Britain's navy in business! Some even argued the case of last refuge: if we didn't do it someone else would. The fact that whole cities came to rely on slavery did not make it right. In 1793, over forty per cent of the European slave trade passed through just one port: Liverpool. Yet when the slave trade was outlawed the port of Liverpool still prospered. When the children were removed from the Lancashire cotton mills did Britain lose out on the world market? With each decisive action to outlaw and abolish African and child slavery in Britain, the affected cities and industries progressed.

Five factors combined to change the character of early factory production. Machinery was one. Others included the Factory and Mines Acts, Education Acts, the Gangs Act which took children out of agricultural labour, and the combination of labour to advance its fortunes.

Palaces of Industry or Satanic Mills?

What was the answer to all this? We have shown how Morris developed the concept of Useful Work, counterposed against what he thought of as useless toil. Marx dealt with the same question and in the process came close to defining what constituted socialism. "It compels society, under penalty of death, to replace the detail worker of today, crippled by lifelong repetition of one and the same trivial operation, and thus reduced to a mere fragment of a man, by the fully developed individual, fit for a variety of labours, ready to face any change of production, and to whom the different social function he performs, are but so many modes of giving free scope to his own natural and acquired powers."

Morris wanted pleasant surroundings for the worker at a time when most lived in company shacks or rack-rent tenements. He thus became a prime influence among those who wanted to combine production with healthy living areas, later epitomised by Ebenezer Howard's garden city movement. He argued that in the past people had often worked in their own homes, which were mostly rented, often squalid and in need of the most basic amenities. Factory conditions were equally bad.

Nowadays, companies create prefabricated factories for their staff to work in while the boardroom is adorned with fine works of art stretching between the lift and the CEO's office. With very few exceptions this has been the case since the factory came into existence. Yet why, asked Morris, if we spent so much time and such an important part of our lives working in them, was there no attempt to make the factory itself the work of art? It was often possible, just by looking at the design of the external features of business premises as in the case of the Hoover building on the A406 or Dudley's on the A12, the former a design classic and the latter a modernist wonder, (both now closed), to tell at a glance what might be happening within its walls. Some factory owners used exotic styles of architecture to depict the country of origin and the main staples used in factory production. The Doulton factory on the south side of the Thames or the Bryant & May factory in Bow, East London, illustrate this. Sadly, many of the warehouses once used to import jute, tea, coffee, or ivory were destroyed in the 1970s. Such buildings reflect the nature of the labour taking place within it but not its inner character.

The division of labour lay at the heart of Victorian labour processes. Morris believed that the effect of Useful Work on society would be deep and revolutionary and hoped it would give an opportunity to do away with this division. This would spell an end to 'useless toil' as well as the repulsiveness of the conditions in so many factories. Adam Smith, amongst others, had described the division of labour and Marx had dissected, depicted and laid great emphasis on it in *Capital*. To Marx it was the dehumanising and alienating core of capitalist production. Morris said, "it is not only the labour that is divided, sub-divided and portioned out betwixt diverse men: it is the man himself who is cut up … "

Useful Work would change the relationship between the mind and manual labour producing what he termed 'thinking hands' work. It would also change the relationship between town and countryside as well. Cities are built around concentrations of population as production requires easy access to the extraction or obtaining of raw materials and historically or environmentally determined means of transportation. Changes in production would result in alterations in the urban concentration of production and how the cities regarded the rural communities who supplied them with labour and food. Concentrated intensive labour is, generally, factory work. When concentration of labour grows less so does the need for factories, and Morris believed that this would be a natural consequence of a shift from useless toil to Useful Work. Although much of what he strived for has come to pass, other factors have contributed to the process of breaking down the intensive use of labour.

The nature of ownership has contributed. Globalisation and foreign ownership has resulted in a dispersal of production across a number of units internationally, all producing parts of a single product. Today, few cars are totally the product of any one country. Technology has resulted in fewer workers being needed to increase levels of production. Where capitalism relied on a large number of people in the nineteenth century today it seeks to exclude people from the physical process of production or reduce their involvement to a minimum. Usually, the smaller the workforce the smaller the workplace. Where it has been possible to outsource, workforce numbers have been reduced. Where production processes have become more diversified or more complex, instead of bringing all the necessary parts for the process under one roof, smaller 'supply' companies are established to contribute to the finished product. It is like a giant ecological food chain, except it only contributes and then only to the extent, that profits are increased.

Morris thought that a move away from division of labour and factory production to handicraft would lead to a massive relocation of production to rural centres. Those workers given the opportunity would opt automatically for country life. He thought that it would, for the same reason return to the home, so that work could take up a natural role in relation to family and community life, rather than push against it.

At the same time he saw a basis for socialism in the collectivism and socialisation of labour. For a long time one would have seen a glaring contradiction here. Surely workers were best organised and evidenced greater class-consciousness where they gathered in bigger numbers and worked in complex production arrangements based on a division of labour? Yet nowadays, groups displaying advanced collective consciousness and a strong sense of identity such as doctors, engineers and even prison officers, work in small units or extended networks of labour. This issue merits deeper analysis but it is unlikely that Morris could have foreseen such changes. What is certain is that the essence of cooperation in industry, without which there is no production, has little dependence on the numbers involved. A workforce of five can have at least as sophisticated a level of cooperation as fifty or more.

For one who supposedly sought dispersal of industrial concentrations and a near impossible return of labour to a pre-industrial state in the home and community, Morris attached great importance to the role of the factory. He saw in factories a critical area of shared skill and experience, a place for learning and a potential hot-house of ideas, especially through the prevailing apprenticeship system. The anonymity of large groups also allowed the worker space to organise. So, despite the factory's obvious faults, it was at least a social centre and a place where some found love and partnership. Could science be applied at workplace level to improve the quality of working life, getting rid of noise, danger, pollution and dangerous noxious substances or emissions? Morris was ahead of his time.

This thinking was possible because he was able to separate the reality of production from the cause before which all gave way – profit. Once freed from the notion of profit as the sole motivator for production, many of his advanced ideas did indeed flow naturally. As workers began to organise themselves and protective legislation was introduced, more space appeared, which Morris saw as an opportunity to fashion production and factory life with an entirely different emphasis – from making profit to making things for people.

Some of his ideas for redesigning work may now appear schematic. Surely shortening the length of the working day, breaking up centres of production or the expense incurred in applying science to labour at workplace level would all amount to significant increases in the cost of production? Yet stripped of its profit motive, each of these factors could increase the true value of the end product and allow work to become art, which could consequently raise demand. For one who claimed no interest or expertise in political economy Morris's conclusions are extremely sophisticated. But can they stand up to close scrutiny?

Morris contends that the cost to production of any of these above-mentioned factors would tend to reduce over time. Furthermore, each cost could be contained within the total surplus money freed up, because workers were no longer engaged in useless toil expending wasted effort on unnecessary wares. He was not the first to realise or the last to prove that a system involving long working hours is injurious both to the body and production, even in the short term. This kind of culture is a form of deferred cost. Nurtured within the factory environment, the cost of dealing with the resulting effects of stress, ill-health, family break-up and children with absent parents, do not affect the employers of labour. Instead, they are passed onto society in the form of social insurance, the health service, social services and the police force.

Morris goes much further by pointing out another factor that has a significant bearing on costs. Suppose the element of compulsion to labour is reduced to a necessity to work, free of compulsion. The collective could perform a great deal of work, shared round on a voluntary basis – that would have been performed by one discontented individual. Pleasure in and of work would result in an increase in production. Work that was useful would be work performed with gusto. This might sound outlandish until we begin to quantify the amount of voluntary work performed today that was once paid labour, like caring for relatives, once supported by social services or through industrial injuries schemes. There are volunteers for so many vital functions nowadays from manning lifeboats to maintaining National Trust properties, and there are many who work for charities that step in where foreign aid once did and now no longer does.

Morris asserts that individuals or associations could carry out such forms of unpaid labour on a different basis. They are secure in doing this because other aspects of their new economy would be underwritten by paid labour produced by Useful Work. In truth, we have come to define the value of productive labour only in terms of the cash nexus and find it difficult to imagine employment – other than the temporary, voluntary and incidental – on any other basis. One writer has posed the view that the reason science fiction is so popular is because it is one of the few branches of literature that regards society and development in terms other than those completely suffocated by money. It is certainly true that the trade unions, where 'visions beyond capitalism' once held general currency, and at times before the First World War and immediately after the Second, actually held sway, are only now beginning to question the philosophy and value systems underpinning today's political economy.

Morris never refers to an age for retirement or a specified cut-off point when working life suddenly ends. One reason may be that an age for retirement did exist in medieval times, outside legislation and regulation, but accepted and handled as a cultural norm by the working population. It was not extant in Morris's time where the norm was, like Steptoe's horse, to die in harness – and to die relatively young at that. A notion of retirement returned with the introduction of pensions by the Liberals in 1911. For Morris, shorter days and fewer days were the answer. Workers could work to an age that either suited them or was the culturally accepted norm within their craft or industry. Probably he felt that if Useful Work succeeded, the worker would be able to engage in their craft for more years than when in the service of profit where the rate of exploitation was greater. It would be possible to systematically reduce working hours and thus increase the time allowed to leisure and rest. The craft, industry or company would benefit by being able to return the accumulated wisdom and knowledge of the older worker for as long as possible.

Morris acknowledges that there is room for both points of concentration in production as well as decentralisation. In fact he does so with no difficulty because his aim was to save the worker from the burden of repetitive labour,

which is best done by a machine. However, no machine is more intelligent than
its operator. It may be quicker in some respects or more accurate, but a person
has set it to work and make sure it keeps at it. He believed that machinery had
a role in lightening fatigue and the depressing alienation of repetitive and back-
breaking work, but it could never be a substitute for brainpower. Even if that
were desirable, it is doubtful it will ever happen. Morris thought a worker
might work one day at home on craftwork, the next on a machine in a factory
for a period of concentrated repetitive work and that this variation of the kind
and location of the work would prove stimulating and enjoyable for the
employed.

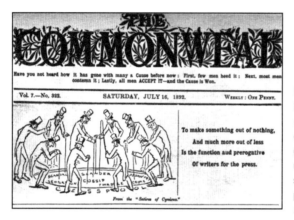

Bankrolled and edited by Morris.
For much of its existence, *The
Commonweal* played a key
educational role for the new
generation of socialists and trades
unionists. Carried on its pages, in
serial form, can be found such
pathbreaking work as *A Factory As
It Might Be*.

Break-up of the factory system

In a series of articles in Justice and later, in Commonweal, entitled The Factory – How
it is and How it Might Be, Morris elaborates on the role of individual and collective
labour. In it he illustrates what impact the new factory-based concentration of
labour may have on the organisation of work and the physical construction of
the environment.

Morris was unwilling to outline a blueprint of socialism or elaborate a 'big
bang theory' to which many at the time subscribed. He felt this was a job best
left to those "lucky enough" to be born into a new society, who could come to
it without the scars and distortions of the old one. Instead he chose to elaborate
on "the conditions of pleasant work in the days when we shall work for
livelihood and pleasure and not for profit." To do this he focuses on the factory,
an interesting, but unavoidable choice for one who supposedly felt uneasy in
the company of machinery. Having said that, it was really unavoidable, because
the factory was the crucible of capitalist production and if one was to

comprehend it, criticise it and then suggest something different and better, it served as a touchstone and point of departure. In criticising factory life as it was, Morris was able to describe a new social way of living. His analysis of work *as it was* enabled him to project an image of work *as it might be*.

In contrast to the factories, many of which were then little more than "temples of over-crowding and adulteration and over-work", it would be possible to create conditions where factories were run in harmony with the communities whose livelihoods they provide.

Morris thought that factory buildings should reflect externally, the new way that processes were conducted and people worked inside. They should be full of light and air, situated in parkland, and should not foul local waters or billow smoke from chimneys. Instead they should blend harmoniously with the local natural and built environment. Architects should be used who are committed to an integrated landscape using new materials, techniques and standards that meet the needs of *all*. By '*all*' is meant those who work in them and in whose space they are erected.

Factories would colour the nature of a locale especially if it was at the centre of low wage economies, extensive networks of support trades and suppliers. Outworkers in one street would supply buttons, in another, hooks and eyes – and there would be dozens of streets and alleyways, all focused on the centre of production. Morris asked, "as to the factories themselves; why should there be scarcely room to turn round in them? Why should they be, as in the case of the weaving sheds of oversized cotton, hothouses for rheumatism?"

Despite such misgivings, Morris could see that the factory had emerged as an important landmark in the environment of capitalism and indeed in the social construction of the working class. Neither was it likely to go away. In this series of articles he sets aside his original hope for reviving manufacture in the home. Now, rather than seeking to get rid of factories and return to some idealised pre-capitalist community organisation of production, he wanted to change the way factories worked from within, and therefore influence what happened outside them. Many today see Morris as one of the first champions of the environment, but he was a campaigner for an environment existing hand in hand with industrial production. In the same way as the external features of a factory reflect the work regime inside, so, change in the factory is an indication of evolving power relations in the internal work ethos. Morris believed that to change fundamentally from within, it would be necessary to shift away from the division of labour.

He reasoned that as this process unravelled, the factory could begin to serve as a social hub for the locality, incorporating dining facilities, nurseries, schools, medical services, opportunities for training and job variation, libraries for the enhancement of knowledge, clubs to advance interest in sciences and languages and a technical school for the improvement and development of trades. It could even be used as a transport centre, making travel to and from work easier and faster, thereby freeing up more time for rest and leisure.

He thought that the search for higher standards would inspire workers to introduce art into the building structure as well as its internal design and products. Many workplaces and centres of community do now reflect this process, which Morris and those who founded the Arts and Crafts Movement considered organic. Consider a school of today. Most display pride and confidence in their pupils – no matter what state the school building is in – by prominently displaying their achievements and work on every available wall space. Posters abound encouraging students to respect each other, work together, and take an interest in the lives of others in the community and around the world. They display, through artwork, how they have progressed as individuals, as a class, and in a developmental manner as they grow more mature. Through this art they also show pride and joy as well as concern. Students talk to each other through art and reveal something of their inner selves: there is a similar communication of anxiety and hope between student and teacher and the impact of school-based art on a parent or other outside visitor can be a shock and a revelation. Art is a sign of collective confidence when the Inspector calls for it is a natural process that reflects the kind of relationships and struggle to advance going on in the school at any one time. More and more schools have become centres of united and individual effort as pillars of community. They represent the kind of process that Morris believed would ensue if factory work exchanged useless toil for Useful Work. However, to earn the respect of the community, there would need to be a move away from "adulterated wares" to the production of quality artefacts.

Morris foresaw the possibility, of situating the factory in the centre of leisure parks, estates, gardens, orchards and fields, producing all kinds of food that would be made available to employees and the local community. He contended that this was already being done except that the estates were being kept for the 'masters'. In the past, beautiful workplaces have been built, so fine in fact that, when they have ceased functioning as workplaces, they have been transformed into dwellings or national monuments.

Morris recognised industry as a great achievement for human beings, that separated them out from all other life on earth. It was much more than a gathering of people set to work to produce a mass of commodities, for it was collective, increasingly complex, and spanned the globe. It was a repository of 'hope' and provided a sense of purpose. It improved life and, its rationale was constantly questioned. For each technical challenge posed a philosophical one. Today genetic engineering is a good illustration of this moral dilemma.

If production were the only *raison d'être* for industry, factories, where processes are concentrated and reach their zenith would surely be "palaces of industry"? Most factories had 'growed' like Topsy, with little thought for their position in relation to the surrounding community or the influx of raw materials and outflow of finished goods. This left scant room for expansion and development and almost nothing for the welfare of the surrounding community. Consequently, growth consisted of bolt-on floors and annexes, and the conversion of production space made only at the expense of staff facilities. At worst it meant invading the space of local communities.

Factories had a direct bearing on the state of their local environment and could take the lead in setting it in some sort of balance. Morris thought that science would play its role in, "teaching Manchester how to consume its own smoke, or Leeds how to get rid of its superfluous black dye without turning it into the river, which would be as much worth her attention as the production of the heaviest of heavy black silks, or the biggest of useless guns."

Even where factories were newly built and towards the end of Morris's life they were growing in number and size they were handicapped by blindly putting production for profit before all else. Communities were not consulted and it was common to subvert local regulation and planning permission, rather than work with it. The workforce was simply ignored.

Morris argued decisions like the siting of factories should be taken by the community as a whole, not by individuals. He reasoned that even the most philanthropic of factory owners could die, move on or be bought out by others less concerned with the impact a factory made on a community. Therefore, some form of regulator, external to the company, needed to be included in the decision-making process, and preferably one that enjoyed a popular mandate.

As we have learned previously, in the factory, production was for profit. Morris considered what would happen if excess profit was ditched in favour of the production of quality goods for use? What would happen to the ill-maintained and dangerous machinery that had been run into the ground in search of maximum profit? What if machinery only be used to save human labour and not simply to replace male with female workers or women workers with children? Surely much less labour would be required and there would be more time to concentrate on the quality of the product, the suitability of the factory environment and the welfare of the workforce? Not all work time would need to be spent on "mere machine-tending". Where this was necessary, a worker of average intelligence could quickly master first principles and work on a range of different machines. Work would become raised as an art. Morris goes the whole way. If such opportunities were seized, and the change in priorities result in a new way to labour, people would seek out repetitive machine work as a means of relaxing from the much more intellectually challenging work of striving for quality and manufacture as art. Now that is a world turned upside down.

So the factory would continue, but the factory system would be broken up. Socialisation of labour would continue and be enhanced but appropriation of surplus value would be for the common good rather than for the benefit of a private individual. Morris thought that this would occur when it became possible to do away with what he called 'repulsiveness in work' and replace it with 'hope'. Repulsiveness in work was labour without aim or strategy to achieve it. It was the treadmill towards the workhouse, for in his time it was often a close call, which was the factory and which the workhouse. If this could be removed and 'hope' restored it would be possible to begin to envisage the factory of the future "where people would work for a livelihood" and "harmonious co-operation towards a useful end, would itself afford opportunities for increasing the pleasure of life."

To Morris, workers would never embrace socialism as a result of their suffering, they would be more likely to reach for the liquor bottle. They would only embrace it as a result of their collective experience, comprehension and intelligence. So, in Morris's eyes, the factory should become a great school: both a centre for education for the families of workers; and for the workers themselves, in their trade.

A factory would be especially interesting for children because of their natural inquisitiveness about how things are made. There would be technical instruction and a thorough apprenticeship to a craft. The education, "so begun for the child will continue for the grown man". The worker should be especially encouraged to study the science on which his craft is founded. In Morris's factory every worker would be a craftworker, multi-skilled to suit his talents, and working cooperatively on the more onerous tasks which machinery cannot do. There would be time and space for collective work and experimentation in the craft, relating theory to practice – what we today call research and development. Literature and the arts would be studied as well as science and art.

Morris thought that factories could even be made of transparent materials so that the public could watch the work and observe the processes. The doors would be thrown open so that they could be brought in both to learn and teach. If competition were killed off "no detail of improvement in machinery would be hidden from the first inquirer". This is a way of being that Morris returns to time and again.

Discarding the ethos of the monopolist and profit-seeker was an opportunity to truly liberate labour. Another aim was to raise the standing of work, as a collective and social requirement for human beings, free of compulsion. Morris reasoned that in this way work could be put in its proper perspective – at the centre of our lives, a joy and pleasure, not a domineering and stark fact. The work of the factory would become the focus of interest for the whole community. Putting work in its rightful place elevates it and magnifies the desire for standards of excellence and quality.

Morris contended that labour was not elevated but dragged down to a morass of shoddy and cheap goods on the one hand, producing on the other hand, useless goods at inflated prices for the few who do no work and pay too few taxes. What is more, the labour was performed by workers compelled to do it so they could eat. Open factories would produce an educated community who could spot poor work and reject shoddy goods.

Morris's vision of socialism was essentially based on a combination of *Useful Work* and the establishment of a network of *Factories As They Might Be*. He felt that these conditions were essential for any re-emergence of art. Art was the litmus test of the health of true society. If one networked the concepts of the *Factory As It Might Be*, first across and between related industries and then between the rural and urban workforces, a new basis for society would take shape. It was for reasons such as these that Morris opted not to join the many middle class art movements of the time. He declared that he would not do so as long as art remained cut off from its natural source, the working people.

"Surely, " he wrote, "anyone who professes to think that the question of art and cultivation must go before that of the knife and fork … does not understand what art means, or how that its roots must have a soil of a thriving and un-anxious life." Morris believed that art makes a restless man, less so. The labour that produces art cannot be based on compulsion, but is voluntary "partly undertaken for the sake of labour itself". It is also based on hope that the practical outcome is of use, enriches the life of, or brings pleasure to the senses of the end user. 'Art' in Morris's mind is not about one piece of work no matter how stunning or glorified. It is a social product and it takes centuries to develop, the subject, style and genre. For Morris it was all or nothing. Under capitalism, the arts and craft could only wither and die – crushed forever under the clatter and clang of machinery. Yet much of it has survived.

He thought, perhaps mistakenly, that literature would go the same way as art. Instead, critical writing rescued literature and laid the basis for its uneasy relationship with capitalism. Morris underestimated the capacity of people to rise above their predicament. At that time he probably was not able to evaluate the effect of mass education, science and rationalism, nor the sheer practical nature and dogged empirical prowess of working class people in their quest to survive and advance. Factories may be the centres of so much wealth creation but even today they are still regarded with anxiety and distress. The young consider them a second-rate option, an alien repository of mind-numbing and repetitive labour. Morris's challenge remains very much unfinished business.

"Remember always form before colour, and outline, silhouette, before modelling; not because these latter are of less importance, but because they can't be right if the first are wrong..."

Art and the Beauty of the Earth, a lecture given by Morris in 1881

Architect of the Human Landscape

Morris came to socialism through art and to art through architecture. To him, architecture was the big picture into which all else had to fit. He was a true architect in the sense that form was important but context was key. In architecture, and through it, he saw all that he considered wrong with 'civilised' society. Also it could be used to reflect things being put right. Although he studied as an architect for less than a year before abandoning his articles at GE Street for art, he has, arguably, had as much enduring influence on our architecture today, as any other figure of the nineteenth century.

For Morris, architecture was the starting point, the 'crown' of so many things. It was also the point of departure for taking a stand on what kind of society he wanted. It was the laboratory in which he could test his theories about the relationship between what was made and built and how it was achieved. As we have seen, for him everything turned on the way the craft worker was set to work and the nature of the labour performed. He reasoned, that architecture was the *master* art, "the moulding and altering to human needs of the very face of the earth itself."

Architecture – the crown of things

Morris wrote, "The untouched surface of ancient architecture bears witness to the development of man's ideas, to the continuity of history and, so doing, affords never – ceasing instruction, nay education ... to the passing generations, not only telling us what were the aspirations of men passed away, but also what we may hope for in the time to come."

There was the simple beauty of it all especially those church steeples reaching for the sky. There was in each building, in every brick, an expression of sentiment of the builder many of whom would not live to see their castle, or harbour, or church completed, but knew that successive generations would scrutinise and marvel at their work. "Untouched" was to become a most important factor in his outlook.

Of course, as Morris pointed out, history is often conveyed through books by those who could or were paid to write by those who wanted to be remembered. But 'architecture' was different. First, it was a living history as most buildings that he wrote about continued to be used. Secondly, although built for a King or Pope, who could only live or pray in them when they were alive, the building would endure for centuries more. Most importantly the building was an expression of and a monument to those who built it, regardless of who inhabited it. Architecture forms a record, a history of the people, how they saw themselves, how they fashioned available materials and the innovation they brought to the challenge of making each building better and more technically advanced than the last. That is why we remember Whitby Abbey by the name of its location and what it is rather than the ecclesiastical authority or Bishop who commissioned it. The same goes for Caernarfon Castle, Westminster Abbey, Tilbury Fort and the Tower of London.

The surface of an ancient building was "the *handling* of the old handicraftsman". Such buildings would have to remain untouched as it would be therefore impossible to reproduce them.

As soon as Morris repulsed attempts to reproduce or renovate ancient buildings – the number of campaigns to maintain ancient buildings that he was involved in runs into the hundreds – he would immediately talk about the conditions of the craftsmen that produced them, from classical times onwards, and contrast them to social problems of the day. It is a link we rarely make today and our understanding of contemporary society suffers as a result.

Each architectural work "is a work of cooperation". The designer works under the influence of tradition. Each worker who has his designs set to work subordinates his exertions to the general body of effort. At his best the handicraftsman's work will reflect his living and working conditions, the material available to him, and the cooperative spirit expressed in a shared quest for the highest standard. Integral to this was the apprentice who, once engaged, was sure to go on to become a master.

Nowadays, we have a 'great discovery' that the greatest works of Leonardo and Michaelangelo may have been part produced by apprentices. But this could be no other way as apprenticeship was integral to the process of craft practice. Each of these factors differs from age to age. Hence we get a sense of forward movement (at best), or just of change – a kind of differentness. The buildings built by slaves will differ from those arising from independent handicraftsmen working in cooperation. Cooperation in one sense means 'together', but in another reflects the effort of a multiplicity of handicraftsmen working the same tools, such as sawyers or masons. As society developed, projects grew in size, scope and time range. Handicrafts were drawn together in greater and greater numbers.

These craftsmen organised themselves into work combinations called guilds. The guilds were pre-Norman and came to the height of their power in the fourteenth century. They regulated and protected standards of work, apprenticeship, supply and cost of labour, price of product, and the craftman's right of direct access to the consumer. As such, the guilds held commerce to the role of trade and exchange of wares keeping pure profit-making at bay. The craftsman in such days may live, in the words of Morris, indeed, in our eyes, "roughly", but he had a real degree of independence and freedom. His "closed shop" guild kept the excesses of feudalism at bay and even kept Kings at bay occasionally and what's more he had access to food through common ownership of communal pasture. As such he was, truly, independent.

The guilds had one other special contribution – too big and important to be dealt with here, except in passing. The craft guilds were strongest where the Latin Church was weakest. Guilds were most powerful in Denmark, Germany and in Britain and played a role in moving religion onto a non-papal basis. The guilds mobilised their biggest effort to support Cromwell and the Republic during the English Civil War.

In these days with craftsmen enjoying greater leisure time, art was a general talent rather than an exceptional talent for a few. Buildings were considered great works of art in their day and news and views of their construction passed worldwide by word of mouth and book illustration. Ironically, as most people had artistic ability, wage rates tended to be narrower and more stable across the country.

Soon, as trade and towns grew and labour became less regulated, merchant guilds and some in the craft guilds, set up new ones no longer based on democracy or fraternity, but on accumulation of capital.

It was during the sixteenth century under the Tudors, that Britain passed from a craft guild and village-dotted landscape to a giant sheep farm sold on 'profit' – illegal in earlier times. Morris castigated Henry VIII for allowing so many important, ancient public buildings, to become dilapidated as a result of his raid on the church and its funds.

Where under the old craft order, a building process involved craftsmen working from the beginning to the end of a project, handicraft began to give way to manufacture and then to factory production based on work on parts.

Under manufacture a division of labour began to appear which was more incisive and led to a greater dispossession of the crafts.

With this downturn went the decline of a golden age in architecture. In later years, many projects were selected, by men anxious to exaggerate their own importance and who despised the really great men who together built the best. In Morris's view this affected, not just the great cathedrals, but all buildings, down to the form and style of the smallest home or countryside church.

Morris believed that society could only protect its ancient buildings when it was mature enough to acknowledge them, not as good or bad, but of our lives, our historical continuity.

His point of concentration lay in the decorative arts, in which he included printing, "that great body of art, by means of which men have at all times more or less striven to beautify the familiar matters of every day life". His influence in the visual arts is still immense. The decorative arts all stood or fell on the nature of the architecture. Architecture was the "roof over our heads without which life was limited in quality and extent." The decorative was what was put under that roof. It brought the noble and ancient crafts together into one industry, painting, joinery, carpentry, metalwork, pottery and glass-making as well as weaving and other textile crafts. Of course there was often a tense and dynamic interrelationship between the two. The skill of those who made and laid beading or who cut a cornice, was directly related to those who constructed houses and buildings, whatever their purpose. But for Morris architecture was important for another reason.

In *Making the Best of It*, a lecture given before the Trades' Guild of Learning and the Birmingham Society of Arts in 1879, Morris elaborated on the role of art in architecture. Arts he wrote, "are the sweeteners of human labour, both to the handicraftsman, whose life is spent working in them, and to people in general who are influenced by the sight of them at every turn of the day's work: they make our toil happy, our rest fruitful..." In a period of 'weak' media, art and architecture were a means of influencing and shaping the world through the portrayal of styles and movements and the sharing of rules that gave the craftsman guidance. The division of labour was destroying crafts whose rules were laid down so long ago that few knew why crafts were as they were, only how to acquire them and put them into practice. Rebellion against the age of commerce was in Morris's eyes a struggle to re-establish the laws of nature, whose ancient and long-forgotten rules had been usurped. This was a daring concept to put before an audience because commerce claimed to act on behalf of God and the laws of nature. Morris posed the same question to his audience as he had often asked himself – what could be done to improve the form and function of the dwellings of the millions? There was a pressing need to act because the millions lived in dwellings that were, "the ugliest, and most inconvenient that men had ever built for themselves, and which our own haste, necessity and stupidity, compel almost all of us to live in." He looked forward to a time when the craftsman would be guided "to work in the way that she (nature) does, till the web, the cup, or the knife, look as natural, nay as lovely, as the green field, the river bank or the mountain flint." The building and its contents should originate from, contribute to and expand nature.

Morris argued that the building of existing dwellings had been based on "no dignity or unity of plan." Yet the potential for such a plan existed at a local, municipal and community-level. Morris thought it important that a certain standard be agreed, through discussion and consultation, between builders and potential dwellers. He reasoned that all new dwellings should be built solidly, and conscientiously, with beauty, common sense and convenience in mind. They should represent the "manners and feelings" of their times. He disparaged the tendency to reproduce styles from the past. In the people he saw honesty, independence, elevation of thought and consideration for others. What kind of dwellings did these people deserve? "They should be fit for people free in mind and body."

Anticipating action that would not come for another half century, he argued that lesser arts could be used to improve dwellings that already existed. He binds this closely to the idea of "content and self respect for all craftsmen." In other words, treat the builder like a human being and you will get dwellings fit for human beings to live in. The lesser arts, would reflect the craftsman's condition of labour and character of employment, in a way that housebuilding always should, but often does not. Further, in the same way as the malaise of the craftsman reflects his separation from access to capital and ownership of the labour process, so too is he excluded from the design process, divided from others in the chain of production and barred from working with those who are to live in the house he is building or decorating. It is likely that those who build houses and those who live in them will never meet.

But for Morris there was yet another sense in which architecture was important. The 'build' – its structure, form and style, was a reflection of the artisan who made it and, as he was increasingly to understand, it was as much a reflection of the mode of employment of the artisan and his social relationship with production. In the days when the artisan had some control over the nature of production, owned his own tools, was responsible for the development of his own skills and worked in teams for a fee with profit not the driving force, it was possible for architecture to combine the functional and the beautiful. Art and Labour were as one. The craftsmen's mastery of time – those who built determined how much time the build should take – gave him space to fuse diligence with art.

Each weekend millions of people visit a building that meets this description, from the humblest village church to the most magnificent cathedral. Together, the National Trust, English Heritage and the Society for the Protection of Ancient Buildings, are responsible for much of this interest, which is enormous, enduring and across the social board. The National Trust is the largest single voluntary membership organisation in Europe. Most of the buildings they own remain exactly as Morris saw them. They are of such interest they attract this following in some cases a thousand or more years after they are built. Still we marvel at them. Still we ask – how could such extensive buildings be erected and still revered centuries later, when others built in the 1960s, have to be pulled down?

Morris had an answer. Buildings were then the work of noble men of lowly birth whilst men of noble birth, lived a listless and drab existence in them. The buildings were a reflection of the artisans that made them and a memorial to their skill and foresight. To them art was not labour but a natural extension of their social existence. They worked for the work, for the quality of the result of their labour, rather than because their noses were set against the kinds of mechanical repetitive drudgery of the factory system which Dickens described as Gradgrind. Capitalism, because it stripped the artisan of his independence and ownership of the means of production reduced him to a form of slavery in a country where the tradition of chattel slavery was scant. It reduced him to a wage slave who worked only so long as he could find an employer to buy his labour. He barely earned his keep, and only then because he sacrificed quality work in his need to work fast and cut corners.

The other avenues of life he had inherited as an ancient right became increasingly closed to him and brought under the catch-all of property rights. The bond between art and labour came apart. Henceforth art was an additional extra that had to be paid for. Morris concluded that only socialism could stand architecture back on a sound footing and bring art and work together again. He long pondered this dynamic relationship of art to labour and to workers. He later wrote, "It is the province of art to set the true ideal of a full and reasonable life before him, a life to which the perception and creation of beauty, the enjoyment of real pleasure that is, shall felt to be as necessary to man as his daily bread, and that no man, and no set of men, can be deprived of this except by mere opposition, which should be resisted to the utmost."

By 'opposition', he meant self-limitation or as so many of today's socialists would recognise, cultivation of an outlook restricted to opposing the fact of capitalism, its appearance, rather than actively working up measures that would restrict and replace it.

He was, as we have shown, arguing this long before he became or began to call himself a socialist and certainly years before he called himself Marxist. In this sense Morris is always a pioneer and visionary thinker, in the same league as any of the nineteenth century trailblazers. Morris's view of architecture gained immeasurably from his class background that opened avenues to him that could never have been available to someone born into a poorer family. Whilst he was a quintessential Englishman and a true patriot in the Blake mould, he also had a world-view. That philosophy was gained first-hand through travel and discovery and as a result of his schooling and the opportunities he had to study in libraries and museums. The cocktail of patriotism and the *Weltanschaung* were a dynamic mix and when abroad he brought back the passion he gathered for architecture to England, as a defender of the old and an originator of new.

Morris did not dwell especially on the shape of buildings – for him they were simply a reflection of the community and art of labour that designed and built them. They would change as that community grew. There is much of Ruskin in him in this sense. He wrote in *Aims of Art* (1886), "I say it is the *aims of art* that you must seek rather than the *art itself*..." As an unreligious man, after he turned thirty, he was still capable of defending every stone of an ancient church without having the slightest interest in what went on inside. In this sense he was quite unlike Ruskin. Neither did he dwell on any one building in isolation. Where one man might see a particular building, Morris saw a skyline. For if a building was a summary of the effort, skill, knowledge and intellectual capacity of the working community that produced it, it also reflected the social code they lived by in their relationship with production. A neighbourhood or a city was a reflection of an aggregate of those social relations. When referring to a city as 'ugly', Morris was apt to be describing not just an absence of beauty and art in the form of its buildings, but the conditions under which its citizens were employed and the nature of that employment.

Poor conditions and a workforce separated from the ownership of the tools of production resulted in bad architecture and ugly cities – where the rich could surround themselves with beauty, whilst sewers went unbuilt. For

Morris, socialism did not mean sweeping away such ugliness. Indeed his starting point was to campaign to retain buildings – both at home and abroad – and to keep them free from renovation and he did this very successfully. His job as he saw it was to keep unchanged, the many landmark buildings erected in times when art and labour were as one. Socialism would change the shape of architecture – which to Morris was the same as changing the shape of life – by changing the producers relationships to production. Once free from jobbing, profiteering, the cost-cutting that Robert Tressell so brilliantly exposed in the *Ragged Trousered Philanthropist*, and private individual appropriation of profits by employers, shoddiness would evaporate and art and labour could be once again restored. Morris saw capitalism driving a wedge between the intellectual arts and the decorative arts. He wrote, "In all times when the arts were in a healthy condition there was an intimate connection between the two kinds of art." Further, "the best artist was a workman still, the humblest workman was an artist. This is not the case now..."

His sharpest condemnation of capitalism was that it made two divisions – those who conceived and those who made. The professional artist was divided from the wage-earning worker, the architect from the stonemason, the pattern-maker from the weaver and the designer from the printer where they had once been one and the same. To Morris, the idea of a professional artist was anachronistic in the sense that *all* were artists, only the class nature of employment meant that only a tiny few were free, with time and space to create 'art'. To him, all good art was popular in origin and the idea of a professional artist led to the wrong kind of art because art became separated from the people and their daily experience. Once separated, it is not just art that suffers, but work too, as it is stripped of its creative core.

The concern was that the worker would become alienated, not just from the tools of his labour but also from the essence of the labour itself, the power to use initiative and direct his own work. Morris thought that if this freedom could be restored to the worker, he would naturally bring to his work the creative inner urge that had been sustained in his class by guild and then by union for generation after generation. Those wishing to educate themselves in the politics of William Morris and seeking to discover his contribution to socialism, who turn first to his later political writings may be looking in the wrong place. Yet they may be surprised to find his reports to the Society for the Protection of Ancient Buildings most fertile ground. Indeed we cannot really talk about Morris's political writings at all as he managed to politicise virtually everything he wrote.

Town versus countryside?

Capitalism did not just divide people as individuals or even classes but physically separated living spaces too. In addition, to physically mould the very face of the earth itself did not necessarily mean it would be for the better. Morris asked, "Is money to be gathered, cut down the pleasant trees among the houses, pull down ancient and venerable buildings for the money that a few square yards of London dirt will fetch; blacken rivers, hide the sun and poison the air with smoke and worse, and it's nobody's business to see to it or mend it; that is all that modern commerce, the counting-house forgetful of the workshop, will do for us, here in."

Morris analysed how capitalism had driven a wedge contrasting town and countryside. Again, and unbeknown to either, Marx had cited precisely the same problem as one of the biggest challenges posed by capitalism. Where for both Marx and Morris, the division between mental and manual labour – expressed by the division of labour – was the challenge posed in production, the division of town and countryside – the setting of each against the other – was the challenge posed in the community.

Opposing this he asked, "Is it possible to make the town part of the country and the country part of the towns?" He summed up the separation with beautiful simplicity. Town life meant that one needs to drink milk but cannot keep a cow. Now the problem is compounded into one whereby most who drink milk would not know how to get it out of a cow if they were sitting next to one. What's more how much of milk is produced by cows and how much is a product of the industrialisation of milk production with treatments, additives or synthetic alternatives?

Somehow – and he laid the challenge for socialism to resolve – it was necessary to bring "the beauty and incident of nature" back into people's lives.

In Roman times when manufacturing was in handicraft and both country life and work were blighted by the use of slaves, life was both bleak and unrewarding. Yet the Roman city "with its handsome buildings and gardens, its public baths," resembled an embryo form of municipal socialism. In such times a town with its market centre, acted as a kind of high point in the concentration of agriculture that dominated the district. It also served as a focus for trade across districts.

With the demise of Roman rule, the town as a distinct way of living declined and was not to be resurrected for centuries. When towns did re-emerge it was not so much the houses that made the town as the constitution, the freemen and the guilds, which gradually grew into the corporation. Much of the town property was held in common by the freemen. The town in the Middle Ages was interlinked in many ways with the countryside.

The strife between the two, Morris believed arose from the sheer scale of the major towns like London, Birmingham and Manchester that burgeoned with the onset of industrial capitalism. As these towns grew, the countryside became "a troublesome appendage." It was almost as if town life was baulking at nature. The ability to service these towns and to create environments that were healthy posed enormous challenges. However, as towns grew and used economies of scale to develop lighting and heating systems, the countryside felt the division even more.

There was a mismatch of resources between the town and the countryside. The spread of population becoming a problem rather than a source of strength. To survive, agriculture, which dominates life outside cities, has sought to emulate town life: it has concentrated ownership, standardised, mechanised, automated and applied science. It has applied to the government for support when it needed it and opposed the government at other times. In many ways the bitter cry of the outcast smallholder, echoes that of the nineteenth century craftworker. With the surge into cities and the full enclosure of so much land, the countryside became denuded of able-bodied adults to work the harvest. Now, one and a half centuries on, the plight of the country village resembles that of the inner city, with core resources and infrastructure, from post boxes and banks, to bus services pulled out.

Morris wanted the town to be impregnated with the beauty of the countryside and the countryside with the intelligence and vivid cultural life of the town. The town would become, in his vision, "a garden with beautiful houses in it."

One of Morris's most interesting contributions to an understanding of capitalism lies in his search for a new form of production, free of the division of labour. He reasoned his approach in this way. The craftsman carried a burden that was the accumulated legacy or historical tradition of the craft or 'incorporated trade' within which he worked. It was an incremental body of knowledge and access to it was often restricted to members of the guild or craft. It was passed on in rites and memories through the apprenticeship system and the guild and was reinforced through the journeying system.

The collective memory of the guilds stretched across many generations. The guildsmen of Edinburgh for example marched under an ancient blue banner first flown over the walls of Jerusalem in the twelfth century. It needs to be remembered, and with an abundance of television programmes to fill in the gaps in our knowledge there is now no excuse not to, that when we talk of a craftsman in the Middle Ages, we are often talking about a highly cultured, literated individual, schooled in the arts, numerate, with an interest in the sciences, and also well travelled. Morris saw capitalism seeking to do away with tradition because where once the object of production was in its value for use and aesthetic character, capitalism sought exclusively the maximising of profit. This did not mean that beautiful buildings were not made. Only they were made to the extent that they facilitated the maximisation of profit. As only the rich would be able to purchase beautiful things, beauty would be torn away from the life of the working class. Indeed, beauty would be stripped of its universality, as it would only be available to those who could afford it. As only one class could afford to enjoy its benefits, art for them could only reflect a two-dimensional reality. It would be distorted and bar them from the true source of life both spiritual and physical, for it would alienate them from most of their fellow men. There would be no joy in it.

Tradition played another role too, one that we can more fully comprehend as notions of time and space have accelerated. From the beginning of civilised man until the mid-nineteenth century, large-scale building projects like monuments, abbeys, cathedrals, castles, fortified ports and roads, were built by large groups of highly skilled men working as a team. Only those who did the building or could share this skill as a result of their membership of the guild, knew how to build. The knowledge was written down but was mostly passed down the generations orally. This is because such huge projects could rarely be built within the lifespan of one generation alone, and it could well be a worker's grandchild who puts the finishing touches to a building. So tradition was a handing down from one group to another and this information was added to continuously – a sort of knowledge database.

When the first Industrial Revolution took hold, some of the guildsmen managed to transform themselves into trade unions. Others falteringly, held together, to keep local combinations that were not really guilds but a kind of proto-union with a limited geography. Yet others became Royal Colleges. Where once the guild had included both employer and worker as a combination of mutual self-interest for the furtherance and protection of the ways of the craft, the Industrial Revolution resulted in division. Employers of differing crafts and guilds began to look to each other in recognition of a mutual self interest that was greater than that enjoyed by fellow guildsmen of the same craft. Most guilds became dominated by richer tradesmen and then were usurped by those who bought in to guild membership but had never practiced the trade of the guild to which they belonged. The guild was used as an instrument to gain influence in town affairs and lost all of its inner rationale and integrity.

Workers continued to combine during the Industrial Revolution but were now subjected to capitalist competition both individually and in groups and companies. Morris believed the quality of the finished work was the first casualty of this, because it was a reflection of the quality of life of the craftsmen and the character of the organisation of the relations of production. Tradition was a casualty too as the work became increasingly alienated and segmented into tasks that could be reproduced or repeated as simple repetitive steps in which the worker became a mere cog. In textiles this happened quickly, taking no more than two generations. Crafts were divided more slowly, for example, the tools of building construction changed very little until the end of the nineteenth century. It was not until well into the twentieth century that the building worker was displaced by machinery. Meanwhile, the collective memory of how and why things were done, decomposed. Machines embodied, but did not pass on collective memories and knowledge.

What effect did this alienation have? The worker began to lose his individuality and so his skill suffered. His level of expertise was a measure of his understanding and mastery of traditional knowledge. When this suffered his contribution to his trade was diminished. Morris concluded that only socialism could restore his special role in production as an active, thinking agent. Where machinery was designed to iron out all inconsistency and unpredictability in making things, human beings could take pride in these very features. The architect, the builder, the craftsman did not just 'do a job'. They mastered whole processes of construction and could handle a wide range of functions and disciplines. They would carry out research in their own field, then design and make the product, be it a bonnet or a bell tower. They knew how bricks were made even though they only had to lay them, or how the stress of a roof could be upheld even though they did not themselves erect it and could work out how to run piping or guttering to relieve the stress and support the building within its environment. They would draw on the skills of the architect, the designer and the artist to make what they made beautiful, and had pride in their achievements. If the reader doubts this, take a trip one Sunday to the fine Cathedrals of Ely or Salisbury, or spend some time exploring any one of the hundreds of churches, ports, castles or encampments whose remnants still remain as a testament to the scale of vision and achievement of the time.

The Industrial Revolution gradually eroded tradition, localism, and the medieval kinds of relations with production, by destroying both individual and collective handicrafts. Instead it caused workers to be driven from land enclosed and herded into profit-centred workshops, building gangs or the factory system.

Morris is often criticised for harking back to the Middle Ages yet his view of it is not out of step with many thinkers of his day and some heavyweight ones at that. Some of his assertions about feudal England, "the unspoiled country came up to their very doors", are questionable. Others are both accurate and have stood the test of critical analysis. Thorold Rogers, a critical figure in the development of research standards in industrial history, and whose study *Work and Labour over Six Centuries* is still an authoritative work today, a century after it was written. He wrote "the best times were in the fourteenth century." Was there an absence of exploitation in feudal times? Obviously not. But between the thirteenth and sixteenth centuries, a craftsman was a craftsman. Each building epitomised the accumulated grief, joy or hope in generations where "there was no Plato, or Shakespeare or Michelangelo among them. Yet scattered as it was among many men, how strong their thought was, how long it abided, how far it travelled." What's more the community of town and countryside was the backbone of unity across the Isles.

Morris on nation building

Many refer to Morris as a quintessential Englishman. It is an entirely accurate observation in the sense that he typified what we have come to think of as 'Englishness'. We have looked at England's view of him, as a master craftsman, public conscience, and a dangerous revolutionary, but what did he think of England? How did he define it as a nation whilst remaining true to his lifelong internationalism? And, did he really think it would ever become a civilised country?

Morris was steeped in the cultural framework of the nineteenth century, a peculiarly British one, shaped by the effects of the onset of the Industrial Revolution, the break-up of village life as handicrafts dwindled and the burgeoning of the roots of industry and then the Empire. Early on, he enjoyed the advantages of a Victorian bourgeois family upbringing, becoming well versed in the classics and the history of England through architecture and popular mythologies. His mastery of languages and his travel abroad allowed him to see England in perspective, enabling him to compare and contrast. He understood both imperialism and internationalism in a personal, immediate sense, for each affected things he loved, from art to family. His brother was Colonel Arthur Morris who, along with his regiment, was stationed in India.

The concept of nationalism was an open one during his lifetime. It was a constant challenge as the nineteenth century was one that epitomised it. Few countries managed to carry their national character and boundaries from feudalism into capitalism largely unscathed. China, Korea, Japan and the Iberian and Scandinavian countries did manage it, but in most instances, nation building, as in the USA, Germany, Italy and the Balkan and Latin American countries, was tied to the development of capitalism. England was in the first category and Morris was able to look back on an unbroken history spanning many centuries, nearly a millennium.

In looking at England, Morris emphasised nature, the physical and human landscape, and history. In history he looked for a consistent thread, which, along with Carlyle and Ruskin, he found in the craftsmen, Britain's men of oak.

To Morris, the craftsman *was* England. This outlook, inseparable from the unceasing class struggle that emerged in the 1800s, formed the core of his thinking. The craftsman was the leading figure of a new proletariat embodying ancient attributes such as 'hope' 'stoutness' 'fidelity to community' and 'natural justice'. He was the bearer of ancient rights. In the Middle Ages, the monarchy and the aristocracy, later brought to heel by the English revolution, had opposed the emergence of the craftsman as a political force. In the Industrial Revolution the craftsman initially found himself in opposition to a rising class of capitalist who enclosed land and shepherded millions into cities and thousands into 'satanic mills'. Later, this capitalist class drifted into imperialism and, from the time of the civil wars in the USA, when workers opposed the slave owning states whilst many capitalists supported them, the craftsman became estranged from the Empire and looked on it with deep suspicion. Britain's slavery policy abroad was mirrored by child labour at home. Later in Morris's life imperialism and international rivalry resulted in war after war, coupled to imperial adventure. He considered the role of monarch to be an unnatural social state, ruling by birthright rather than the choice of the people and wondered how the person could be both Queen of England and Empress of India. Riding two horses was nearly impossible and the spectacle quite ridiculous.

To Morris, the divergence of class opinion as to what constituted England and what her aims should be did not result in personal rejection of his country. He believed that those who wrapped themselves in the national flag to advance their own business ends usurped the natural character of England, which he knew manifested itself best in ordinary working people. This mirrored his outlook on industry and the community and the inherent qualities of collective labour and skill, which he believed, had been usurped and disfigured by the merciless tide of capitalism. Morris was aware that class interests spanned the nations and each national band of workers whilst speaking in different tongues had more in common than they did with the employing class of their own nation. He felt that internationalism was not the opposite of nationalism but was essentially the same thing, one an extrapolation of the other. In 1887, he wrote, "the Indian or Javanese craftsman may no longer ply his craft leisurely, working a few hours a day, in producing a maze of strange beauty on a piece of cloth; a steam engine is set a-going in Manchester, and that victory over nature and a thousand stubborn difficulties is used for the base work of producing a sort of china clay and shoddy, and the Asiatic worker, if he is not starved to death outright, as plentifully happen, is driven himself into a factory to lower the wages of his Manchester brother worker..."

Morris's social project, socialism, was about nation building. It was based on education, enlightenment and a working-class renaissance and was about the restoration of art as a result of enhancing the skills of the people, removing any compulsion to labour and the re-emergence of collectivism and community over private appropriation of profit. This was a huge project. However, the Teutonic peoples embraced it first. Morris saw it as a shared project spanning national boundaries, whatever he was involved in, be it the manifesto of the SPAB or one of his books, they were always translated into several languages.

Morris loved England. His England. He abhorred imperialism, seeing it only as a dead end. His loyalty was to his nation: a sort of working class nation. His fidelity certainly did not extend to the state. Englishness was one of the unsettled and unsettling issues of the nineteenth century. So much of what Morris considered English, even the physical landscape itself, was being changed and rapidly so, by commerce: a seemingly unnatural and certainly unwelcome imposition of mankind on a suspicious and wary nature.

Overwhelmingly, Morris drew inspiration for his life's work from a feeling for the innate characteristics of the English as a people and from its landscape. These were lifelong considerations stretching from his childhood days, when he explored Epping Forest to his work with the SPAB when he reclaimed many architectural antiquities for everyone to enjoy. Some of his most lucid thoughts came to him as he grappled with industrial processes that were unique to England, although he did not hesitate to draw on the latest ideas and advances made abroad. The majority of the designs which made him famous, were inspired by his immediate surroundings, especially his gardens. To Morris, Englishness and the qualities that defined it, had been debased by 'civilisation'.

What is worse, they had been robbed of their identity and run up the flagpole as a banner of free enterprise and empire, when it would have been more appropriate to fly the Jolly Roger.

The uniqueness of England lay in the conditions it provided for the Industrial Revolution.

There was nothing accidental about it. Nor was it imported. It was an unravelling of processes that had been set in train for centuries. It did not depend on the discovery of the New World in the sixteenth century, the revolution in science in the seventeenth century or the advance of industrial technique in the eighteenth. All played bit parts. For in Britain, uniquely at the time, capitalism developed from within, firstly from agriculture, which dominated the industrial landscape, and later from industry. Enclosure was pivotal: important too the evolution of the guildsmen who could live only so long as they multiplied their capital, and also the workers who had nothing to sell but their labour. Britain was already more or less one nation for all the core factors of nationhood were in place. The English, Scottish and Welsh were united as a single island people, largely spoke one common language and had a class system that crossed every community. This served to speed the advance of commercialism.

No place in Britain is further than 75 miles from the sea, so transport and travel was relatively cheap. Literacy was high and widespread. At first only a relatively small amount of capital was required and expansion was financed out of profits. Britain had a highly skilled workforce, so no major trigger was necessary to set the Industrial Revolution in motion. Britain soon found that military power was less effective in impacting abroad than free trade, and few internal barriers to capitalism existed. So Britain had a national market with a single language, few cultural divisions such as religion or regionalism – certainly amongst the common people. And this situation existed as early as the seventeenth century.

Britain did not even need moneychangers because, unlike any other European country, she possessed only one currency. So our unique development was intensive rather than extensive. In Britain the state took the role of enabler rather than opt for direct intervention as Germany did. It did not need a state to wash away internal boundaries and separate tax systems, so even this emerged in a unique way in Britain, for she was no prison house of nations. Yet Morris held on to his personal notion of England because, although he had travelled extensively in Scotland and Wales, he did not feel a need to speak for areas that were not intimately his own.

As the ascendancy of capitalism was so complete, the working class were unable to mobilise on the basis of "Liberty, Fraternity and Equality" which had been the watchwords of the capitalists when they opposed the aristocracy. These were the weapons of a struggle against absolutism. For Morris the dominant character of the internal contradictions in Britain was one of capital against labour.

Englishness had its roots in history and these were firmly set. It was stout, rugged and communal, involved justice, freedom and the good sense of peers rather than masters. It meant understanding the tradition of ancient rights and bringing them into the present in a struggle for 'hope'. It was through these efforts that 'truth' would and honesty eventually emerged. Many of the rulers who spoke for England were the descendants of the Norman Yoke who had originally stolen the land. England was at her best when seeking to build democracy or sustaining others wanting to do the same. It was our special contribution. Trade Unions were a modern expression of that democracy; something Britain contributed to the working world. Morris therefore thought that socialism alone could rescue Englishness because it was in itself an advanced form of democracy.

How ironic that Morris was provoked into a political life by the mass murder of one group of foreigners by another in a strange land.

His support for democracy and national independence was unyielding. When, in 1885, having returned from abroad, his daughter asked him what news she had missed, Morris commented on the death of General Gordon in the Sudan, "What has happened? Khartoum has fallen into the hands of the people it belongs to." So, if democracy and independence were good enough for England they also had to satisfy anyone else.

The special characteristic Morris observed in the history of the English people was fellowship. Where John Ball was looking back, William Guest in *News from Nowhere* looks upwards and to the future. He thought King Alfred "was the one sole man of genius who ever held an official position amongst the English." Morris's communism did not extinguish his understanding of the good, the positive and the stimulating arising from national differences. In *Socialism Its Growth and Outcome* he talks of a world without boundaries, a worldwide federation of different countries. It would be led by a "great council of the socialised world" which would oversee "federations for localities arranged for convenience of organisation."

Morris drew heavily on a concept of a federation of northern peoples. This was reinforced by his love of Iceland and the Icelandic way. Were not the

English, Teutons by origin, he reasoned? However, he employed these ideas quite differently from those who used them to make spurious declarations of racial purity, superiority and domination over others, although he was aware that such countries appeared to have embraced the conditions which would give rise to socialism. Morris was eager to demonstrate that love of one's country did not mean universal approval for all it entailed and for everything done in its name. Far from it. Neither did it mean that what was accomplished in England was necessarily better than what was achieved elsewhere. It was different, that was all. However, all would be judged by the extent to which change and action moved peoples in the direction of socialism. What was important was that England wanted to do the best she could. However, under capitalism Morris believed that this could never be more than the best of the worst.

It should be noted that Morris was consistent on the Irish Question. Indeed when the Liberal Government passed an Irish Coercion Bill in March 1881 which suspended Habeas Corpus and authorised arbitrary prevention and arrest, Morris was driven to look outside the Liberal Party for a vehicle to express his ideas

To create a country is one thing. Yet, while all countries consider themselves, or at least like others to consider them, as civilised, few are later remembered as civilisations. Civilisations played an important part in Morris's schooling and the literature he read all his life. The Hammonds could have been writing about him when they wrote, "Education had given to the English governing class an insight into a civilisation in which the conduct, the relations, the difficulties and the purposes of social life had been the subject of endless experiment, of penetrating discussion, and of the most exquisite compositions in history, philosophy, poetry and drama. The best representatives of that class were steeped in the humanism of the classics". Elsewhere they wrote, "It was from the classics that men of liberal temper derived their public spirit, their sense of tolerance, their dread of arbitrary authority, the power to think of their nation in great emergencies as answering nobly or basely to some tremendous summons." Whether they were writing about him or not, it was precisely this tradition into which Morris plunged himself. It was the tradition of Cicero, Tacitus, John Milton and Thomas More, who opposed the enclosure acts of early capitalism. And it was a summons such as the Balkan massacres that brought Morris into active politics.

Names like Venice, Byzantium, Babylonia, Greece and Rome had a resonance to them. They had achieved such status according to Morris, because they could act as exemplars for others. Each had a distinct contribution to make that enriched the general level of civilisation across the world. England had the ability to aspire to such levels but her contribution was of limited value because it was distorted by commercialism. Morris felt that the test of a civilisation was dependant on the passage of time for he believed that the ability to influence must transcend the rule of a single leader or generation. A civilisation must break new ground and go beyond what has been accepted as normal – it must change the way things are done, way beyond the influence of an immediate circle: the influence of Greece on democracy comes to mind. It should raise expectations and standards in a similar way.

Where Greece gave us democracy, Rome brought Public law and Constantinople the unified efforts of peoples in pursuit of knowledge. William Morris saw an Elizabethan England in which great voyages and events, majestic architecture, the wellbeing of the people and a world vision governing trading patterns that have remained to this day, as one such civilisation.

No less a writer than Richard Tawney called Elizabethan England a watershed in our economic history. Morris thought that what was special was in its industry and art. Capitalism began early in textiles, coal mining and metalworking. The capitalist thought of industry and profit. There could be no middle way. How this clash of ideas, interests and power would be resolved would either qualify Britain for the status of a civilisation or condemn it for ever. A further definition of civilisation is that it brings change that is irreversible, and forever alters the life, custom and intellectual purpose of a whole people. In his early years Morris saw the negative side perhaps more strongly than the positive. He was born in a time of violent population change and migration, into a world virtually turned upside down, but within this seeming malaise, Morris saw a force for civilisation – the working class, who, at that time were working in the least civilised conditions.

That working class, seen by Morris as the dispossessed inheritors of the mantles of the craftsmen of Elizabethan times, could decide to destroy civilisation or transform it and give it new powers. Until about the 1850s it was probably in favour of destroying it, but after this workers began to accumulate forces to regain what had been lost since Elizabeth's time. Where once the Statute of Labourers ensured a safety net for all, now it was to be the New Jerusalem. It set about reconstructing notions of law, custom, justice, and the combination and articulation of separate class interests.

In his later years, Morris became increasingly concerned at the threat of war arising out of rivalry between competing empires. In the event of a war between France and Germany, he urged workers to "refuse to allow themselves to be dressed up in red and be taught to form part of the modern killing machine for the honour and glory of a country in which they have only a dog's share of many kicks and few half pence..."

"So, there I was in for a fine pessimistic end of life, if it had not somehow dawned on me that amidst all this filth of civilisation the seeds of a great change, what we others call Social Revolution, were beginning to germinate."

How I Became a Socialist, an article in Justice in 1894

Developing a Sense of Purpose

Morris brought new forms of thinking and a new sense of purpose to so many aspects of life. How did he set about giving these ideas an organisational form? He had long left the Brotherhood behind. The Company was acknowledged as leader in its field, yet he yearned for something different, something more. Elsewhere we have seen how he took prevailing notions of wealth, labour and service to the community, and turned them the right way up. He had a similar impact on ideas of skill, machinery and the ownership of property. He was to do the same on the all-important issues of what was natural, 'hope' and 'fellowship', each a vital ingredient in the notion he had developed as a modern interpretation of the Commonweal. He played a critical role in defining what socialism meant and developing ways it could be applied in Britain.

We have seen how Morris developed a critique of capitalism, his views on machinery and the evolution of the concept of Useful Work. Morris had, by the age of fifty, begun to systematise his views. It was not in his character to accept a role as observer or bystander and he was drawn into a decade of intense activity. We can now turn towards considering the factors that contributed to his new way of thinking and his attempts to propagate it. Here we look at how socialism came to dominate Morris's thinking. That's the historical part. As important, but a more difficult challenge, comes when we look at what Morris put back into socialism.

When describing himself, Morris used the phrase Communist, in the sense that he believed the problems of capitalism would only be fully resolved when human development had removed the obstacle of class and the need for class conflict. Communist was but a modern version of the ancient concept of Commonweal which had become part of popular culture since it was adopted by Cromwell against the monarchy. For the purposes of agitation he saw himself as a socialist and, at a time when many questioned whether such an idea, despite any merits, was possible, he saw himself as a practical socialist. His embrace of socialism developed not from a general abstraction, nor even from sympathy for the downtrodden. It grew from a realisation of how, under capitalism, things worked practically, and how, if in practice things could be arranged differently, life for all would be richer and more rewarding.

It is not difficult to ascertain the main sources of his new thinking because Morris outlined them for us in many a lecture and article. He not only held to these views when he had passed middle age. He asserted that they had been with him all along. "This view of socialism which I hold today", he wrote in June 1894, "is what I began with; I had no transitional period, unless you may call such a brief period of radicalism during which I saw my ideal clear enough, but had no hope of any realisation of it."

So, what were these sources? There was his character, one that would not rest with half-baked ideas going off at half cock. He was an intensely practical man with a unique insight into British history and, in particular, that of the common people. He developed his new thinking at a time when the common people were accruing a power, organisation and influence that had bypassed the generation who suffered the first shocks of the shift to industrialism. He drew on Ruskin and Owen. He read *William Cobbett's Rural Rides* and studied it closely. He saw a need to redefine man's relationship with nature. Much of this came together as a result of his establishment of the Society for the Protection of Ancient Buildings (SPAB) in 1877. Here he developed an ability to muster and direct a 'big vision' and displayed the leadership qualities of someone who wanted his organisation to actually make an impact, rather than generate hot air. His activism began with his role as national treasurer of the Eastern Question Association. He read *Capital* and came into working contact with workers organised into a trade union for the first time, and adamantly supported popular sovereignty and inalienable rights.

During the English revolution, which as we have seen exercised a deep influence on Morris, Richard Overton, a traveller and a radical who took part in the Putney debates, expounded his historical theory of 'popular sovereignty'. If property was the most important issue of the time, Overton asserted that the supreme form of property was 'self propriety', by which he meant equality and self preservation. Property was mankind itself. On this basis all land belonged to the people and the citizen's rights were inalienable. What's more, the supremacy of the nation was derived and drew nourishment from the sovereignty of the people, its class organisations and institutions.

This broadly accepted view, apparently at its height during the Middle Ages, endured well into the nineteenth century finding its apogee in Chartism. Chartism did not simply evaporate. As its last embers dimmed, individuals emerged with ideas so advanced that they would not be realised for a century. There was Ernest James call to nationalise cooperation. "What then is the only solitary basis of cooperative industry?" he asked. "A national one. All cooperation should be founded not on isolated efforts ... but on a national union which would distribute the national wealth." Exactly what government did in the two great wars of the twentieth century.

Ellen Meiksins Wood recently wrote, "Tom Paine's *The Rights of Man*, remained the most widely circulating radical text throughout the first half of the nineteenth century, but its injunction to abandon appeals to historical precedent in favour of rationalist theories of natural rights never succeeded in displacing popular constitutionalism as the dominant radical discourse." Morris now took Overton's 'popular constitutionalism' and the 'natural rights of freeborn Englishmen' into socialism. As if that were not sufficient, there were the trips to Iceland!

Morris travelled twice to Iceland in 1871 and 1873. The first visit was to last a year, as Morris wanted to translate the Icelandic sagas. Being the man he was, this could not, of course, be undertaken from the British Library; it had to be done on site. Travelling with his long-time friend Erik Magnusson, he was keen to improve his understanding of an island he called a "romantic desert". In the people of Iceland he was looking for qualities of independence and courage – Morris called this latter the great virtue of the human race – and an utter unconventionality that "took my heart by storm." He found an extra-special lesson there for here was a country where people had learned to survive in the face of adversity. Where he had already developed a critique of capitalism from the standpoint of medievalism, which of course was pre-capitalist, Iceland, although not capitalist, was contemporary. With Magnusson's help he went on to translate and publish, *The Story of Grettir The Strong*, a set of six sagas entitled, *The Northern Love Stories* and an Icelandic version of the *Niblung Tale*, called *Volsunga Saga*.

Morris was happy to acknowledge the influence in his life of both Ruskin and Carlyle. Ruskin criticised capitalism from a different standpoint to Morris but was an especially important thinker and source of ideas after the eclipse of Chartism. Writing in the 1880s Morris thought, "how deadly dull the world would have been twenty years ago but for Ruskin." Morris took the ideas of Ruskin in his stride and in the 1860s fused them with his own saying, "It was through him that I learned to give form to my discontent." The similarity of message is evident in the style of much poetry, prose and visionary writing of the time. For example, in *Unto This Last* Ruskin wrote, " The prosperity of any nation is in exact proportion to the quantity of labour which it spends in obtaining and employing means of life … that is to say, not merely wisely producing, but wisely distributing and consuming … wise consumption is a far more difficult problem than wise production … The vital question for individual and nation, is never 'how much do they make?' but, 'to what purpose do they spend?'"

This was a different treatise to any previously written by Ruskin. In *Fors Clavigera*: serial letters to the workmen and labourers of Great Britain Ruskin had sought to enlighten a bourgeois readership, seeking to impress on them their need to take their own reform in hand. *Unto This Last* is addressed to the working men and is a seminal work. Ruskin wrote a scathing critique of capitalism in serialised form, rendering the Manchester School senseless. However, he was terrified of the Paris Commune which seemed to imply to him that the new continental – and British – proletariat was capable of tearing capitalism down but not putting anything up in its place. In these early formative years, Morris too was concerned with the actions of the proletariat. After all, the Commune of 1871 – the first workers' government, had stood by whilst a mob burned down the Louvre. Morris found this act abhorrent, and it prevented Ruskin from seeing the workers as harbingers of a new era. Morris realised then that if he was to be a revolutionary, he would at times have to stomach the unpalatable and even endure the unacceptable, in order to focus on the big picture. He was not far wrong and it is likely that his understanding of the English revolution found him better prepared than Ruskin. Was not the English Revolution fought between brothers, and a destructive and bloody affair? It often happened that the beautiful things in life were the first victim in conflicts such as these. Therefore he was inspired to be even more active, certain that he had a part to play which could positively influence and direct the actions of the mass of people.

Eastern Question

The Eastern Question forced itself on Morris from around 1876 and drew him in to activity of an openly political kind. In October of that year he wrote to the Daily News, "I who am writing this, am one of a large class of men – quiet men – who usually go about their own business, heeding public matters less than they ought, and afraid to speak in such a huge concourse as the English nation, however much they may feel."

His fear was that, as a result of the atrocities in Bulgaria, Britain might take up arms against Russia in support of Turkey. In the formation of his new thinking, 'taking a stand in the concourse of the English nation', was important because, for the first time it brought him into contact with the working class and trade union organised workers. This life was far more harsh than the one that he had been born into. Organised thugs and gangs broke up Eastern Question meetings: "in Stepney we had a bare majority in the meeting" and in Trafalgar Square he had to take refuge and hide in a cellar. Only the Unions and, to his credit, William Gladstone, – whom Morris had worked with – stood firm when the Russians made war on Turkey. His influence grew to the point where his presence as a figurehead, made a difference. The opening of the Workmen's Neutrality demonstration in 1878, at the height of the crisis, was marked symbolically with the choir of the Stonemason's Union singing a Morris song, 'Wake London Lads'.

In addition to testing him on a national stage on a point of principle, the Eastern Question agitation taught Morris the limits and challenges of public action and liberal radicalism. He only leaned towards liberal radicalism at this time because he had not yet found any other peg on which to hang his coat.

In his twilight years Morris came to look upon his involvement in the Eastern Question agitation as a turning point. True he was a socialist in all but name for the first half of his life, and openly so thereafter, but the agitation over the Eastern Question held a special significance. Firstly it offered a chance for practical campaigning at a time when he was in a period of intense reflection and writing his lectures on 'Art and Labour'. Secondly, he "thoroughly dreaded the outburst of chauvinism which swept over the country, and feared that once we were amusing ourselves with an European war no one in this country would listen to anyone on social questions." Nowhere at this time, was there a party more radical than the Liberals, especially one with sufficient clout to stop the war and defeat the government, but unbeknown to Morris, a large group of the most advanced and class-conscious workers had drawn the same conclusion. Thirdly, the agitation actually brought down the Disraeli government, proof that government is man-made and can be undone when popular legitimacy and mandate is forfeit. He had few illusions about the Liberals, but many of the trade unionists he was to meet, did. When the Liberal government published the Coercion Bill and in turn, made war on Egypt, he set about deserting the Gladstone ship. Although he hovered for a while, not wishing to cut himself off, and joined with those same leading trade unionists to form a kind of 'save the party' committee, the endeavour was short lived.

Morris saw the Eastern Question in class terms. In May 1877 he addressed a Manifesto to the Workingmen of England. He asked, "Who are they that are leading us into war?" concluding that they were the "greedy gamblers of the stock exchange, idle officers of the army and navy (poor fellows!), worn out mockers of the Clubs, desperate purveyors of exciting war news for the comfortable breakfast-tables of those who have nothing to lose by war; and lastly, in the place of honour, the Tory Rump."

Society for Protection of Ancient Buildings

His class sense became sharpened when he established the Society for the Protection of Ancient Buildings in 1877. This counterposed him to the work of 'official' or 'culturally endorsed' architects such as Sir Gilbert Scott, and against the church. Much of the mid and late-Victorian movement for restoration of ancient churches was funded or sponsored by the ecclesiastical authorities. He called for "an association ... to keep a watch on old monuments, to protest against all 'restoration' that means more than keeping out wind and weather, and ... to awaken a feeling that our ancient buildings are not mere ecclesiastical toys, but sacred monuments of the nation's growth and hope." Restoration, according to Morris, was more often than not a euphemism for destruction. The Society for the Protection of Ancient Buildings became a byword for gathering together the cultural faces of the nineteenth century who did not quite fit – Thomas Carlyle, John Ruskin, Sir John Lubbock, William Holman Hunt, Lord Houghton and the radical liberal trade unionist AJ Mundella. In the Society for the Protection of Ancient Buildings, Morris was on firmer ground than when active on the Eastern Question.

William Morris's favourite church near Kelmscott, St John the Baptist. Morris would often visit this thirteenth century church – with roots dating back to Saxon times. Saving such buildings as living testimony to the work of previous generations from the predatory church authorities of the Victorian age constantly seeking to 'renovate' was a driving force behind Morris's formation of the SPAB.

The Eastern Question had aroused his passion and sensitivity as an Englishman committed to liberty and justice. In addition to his heart, The Society for the Protection of Ancient Buildings could employ his hand and brain. Here, his achievements could come close to his vision. It was a particularly interesting period in his life. He met many great characters of the age including Joseph Arch, the father of rural trade unionism, and past leaders of the First International Workingmen's Association. However, he did not meet Marx and, in fact, took a distinctly dissimilar position from him on the Eastern Question. In 1879 he enlisted the support of Gladstone and Disraeli in a campaign to save St. Marks in Venice.

The Society for the Protection of Ancient Buildings brought him into contact with the 'big works' of times past and this increased the scope of his thinking and expanded his vision. Morris has sometimes been associated with the idea that small is beautiful, but in fact he never embraced this. He attracted a group of highly skilled architects to the Society for the Protection of Ancient Buildings. Many gave free advice to those seeking change before plans were actually implemented and the work of restoration begun. Morris knew that getting in first and capturing the high ground would put him in a strong position.

His campaigns had practical and immediate results. Some, such as the rescuing of Christopher Wren's City Churches played a critical role in shaping the cityscape that we today take for granted. Without Morris these were nearly lost. As Morris believed that such buildings were "monuments of the nation's growth and hope", he cut across the property rights of capitalism citing them as "national property" and therefore adroitly placing them beyond the control even of the church authorities. Drawing on the thoughts of Ruskin and Carlyle he argued that such monuments could not be touched as "They are not ours." He believed that they belonged to those who had made them and the successive generations who had used them. It was necessary to preserve the past, maintaining it as a living reality in order to gain a true perspective on the present through the history they portray. He wrote in the *History of Pattern – Designing* that architecture "bears witness to the development of man's ideas, to the continuity of history, and, so doing, affords never-ceasing instruction ... to the passing generations, not only telling us what were the aspirations of men passed away, but also what he may hope for in the time to come." Archaeology was the "record of man's creative deeds" and each work of architecture embodied a spirit of cooperation.

The architect and designer, no matter how original or brilliant, worked under the influence of tradition and was in conflict with a historically determined set of conventions. He could not wish away what the past had trusted him with. Once lost it would be too late. What would happen, he asked of those seeking renovation, if, "their sons and their son's sons, would one day fervently long for buildings that no longer existed and which no wealth or energy could ever buy again for them?" He did not need to look far. Next to his works at Merton Abbey was the remains of the family home of Nelson who lived there following the Treaty of Amiens in 1802. It was 'renovated' out of existence.

The same guiding principles of construction, and probably some of the tools themselves that had been used to build the most recent of architectural achievements, had been in use for centuries. In *The Nature of The Gothic*, which describes in detail, the organisation and skills of the ancient craft workers, Morris deduced that it was not the tools that had changed but the relationships between those who now built and those who used to build, but now instead, lived by employing the labour of others. Britain had a special duty in this respect, the extent and impact of her history ensuring that there was much to preserve that needed saving.

Morris took a firm and unyielding position. The extent of his influence was bewildering. Many a church parishioner came to see him as a saviour of their local church, saved at the last minute from builders clutching renovation plans drawn up by church authorities. Writing to the *Athenaeum* in March 1877, Morris asked, "Would it not be of some use once for all … to set on foot an association for the purpose of watching over and protecting these relics, which, scanty as they are now become, are still wonderful treasures." Ancient buildings should be left to be just that. New ones could and should be built, but there was little worse than new buildings mimicking old designs or old ones being made over in the style of the present. What would Morris have made of the dock and warehouse clearances in London in the 1970s and those on the Clyde and in Cardiff Bay in the 1980s? Many of these beautiful buildings and warehouses, had been constructed to stretch the imagination, but came to be associated as with long hours of toil and sweat, and were despised as such. So few people were around to speak up for them when plans were made to pull them down.

In the Society for the Protection of Ancient Buildings Morris argued for a century-long truce on renovations so that a public debate could take place. Hardly known for their long term thinking, apologists for capitalism and renovation gave him short shrift. The Society gave Morris confidence and some idea of the extent of his influence, but above all, it meant he was involved in building works and shaping the future in a practical way. It is certainly true that when Morris wrote a letter to *The Times* it was usually printed. For the first time he was the directing influence of a national and public organisation. It proved effective. This work laid the basis for the growth and stability of the National

Trust and English Heritage, while The Society for the Protection of Ancient Buildings continues its so valuable work today.

Where the SPAB, the EQA and his visits to Iceland had given him a sense of purpose, he now sought out some unity and between the demise of the EQA in 1878 and his adoption of socialism in 1883 discovered a steep learning curve.

Onto firmer ground

Morris left the Liberal party and set about deepening his analysis of capitalism, which he saw as a competition of cheapness, not of excellence. Quality, important in itself was very much in the interests of the worker and not only did they have such interests at heart but the "seeds of order and organisation which makes that duty easier."

He turned from the personal to the political. Before 1883 Morris had sought to educate artisans in the fine arts, rather than organise them to assert the skills that were already theirs. He began to realise that the Firm, established more as a centre of art than of commerce, would in itself have insufficient impact on society. His lecturing took him to new places and exposed him to a broad slice of city life, and at this time he also moved to Hammersmith. It was the city life that needed to be changed. Ironically, the Firm's greatest success was to be its absorption into the cultural world that Morris so despised – that of the bourgeois, so Morris sought his own personal salvation through engagement with the movement that the bourgeois despised in its turn. Partly because he came late to socialism, his lectures such as *Making The Best Of It* are a retroactive attempt to make the Morris creations into something of direct and immediate use to those on lower or restricted incomes. Socialism led Morris to discard much of what he saw as clutter, and his later designs are simpler in form and less ornate.

He carefully selected his lecture audience and he gave many interesting talks during this period: *Art Under Plutocracy* (1883); *Art And Labour, Misery And The Way Out* (1884) *The Political Outlook, The Origins Of Ornamental Art, True And False Society* (1886), *Early England and Society of the Future* (1887). Areas of his life were now coming together. Nowadays he would have the luxury of finding a niche for himself in a wide range of campaigns and organisations that already exist, but in England in the 1870s and 1880s there was little in train and many of Morris's activities had to be self-generated. The contending schools that did exist were weak and the walls between them were permeable and ill defined. A socialist might be a member of a trade union, a radical club, an association for the promotion and advancement of the arts and sciences, or a single-issue cause. He or she might agitate for Home Rule, universal (including women's) suffrage, or temperance, or be involved with any number of mainstream or dissenting religious group, or even the republican movement, which was then gathering pace. The 1867 Reform Act had been secured, and a million more workers had gained the vote. Although not yet strong enough to field its own candidates the working class could now emerge as an electoral force. It was a period of radical development of ideas, indeed a time when there was no discernible front line. Chartism and the First International had passed on, frustrated in short-term achievement, though each had real long-term influence on important issues such as obtaining the vote and the introduction of the eight hour day. Radical clubs flourished and the more advanced workers were beginning to look for something beyond the Liberal party.

Club world

Who was Morris's audience? In the mid-century active workers, especially miners, engineers, bootmakers, cabinetmakers and tailors gathered in working men's clubs. These were radical even by today's standards, for they remained steadfast during rocky times when support for the Paris Commune was tantamount to subversion. Yet they were also active as craftsmen and mechanics in their trade societies. Some had a pedigree going back to the 1830's: active as Chartists. Others were attracted by and to Marx and the First International Workingmen's Association. Unlike many at the time, they championed universal suffrage in its true sense – to include women. The working man's club was a social and political centre, where it was also possible to find work, but its chief role was as a home for adult education. Its lecture circuit was formidable, reaching every corner of the country. A speaker would deliver the lecture and then a debate would follow. Many new and radical ideas such as atheism, which today we take for granted, were encouraged. The men and women of the working men's clubs were the first to embrace the Social Democratic Federation and the Labour Emancipation League that attracted the more radical trade unionists only recently in the Liberal Party.

The club network in the late 1870's reached a high of 130 establishments in London alone. These were radical associations, Jewish and Christian Clubs, Mutual Friends, the Dialectical and Radicals in Stratford, Debating Societies, Robert Owen Societies; Science Clubs, Artisans, the London Tailors; Cobden Societies; Democratic Clubs; Progressives and followers of James Bronterre O'Brien – the social chartist who saw the Labour question at the centre of democracy. Club members were expected and encouraged to use their own skill and knowledge to enlighten citizen club members. One writer, Stan Shipley, in his brilliant reconstruction of Club Life has referred to them as 'Artisan Universities'. O'Brien wrote, "A people ignorant of their true political and social rights will never elect a Parliament of real political and social reformers." O'Brien was, along with others such as William Benbow, amongst the first (certainly before the 1840s) to advocate nationalisation of the land, mines, fisheries and turbaries (peat bogs). Later he added docks, railways, canals and utilities to this list.

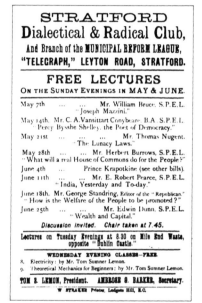

The Stratford Club (formed 1880) was a leading radical force in the 'club' galaxy. Formed out of a split in the National Secular Society. It attracted characters such as Ambrose Barker, Frank Kitz and Tom Lemon. Lemon helped form the Labour Emancipation League. The Club based itself on six points of the Charter to which it added "equalisation of wealth" and "socialisation of production".

They gathered at the Freethought Institute in Walworth and the 'Common Wealth' in Bethnal Green. Tom Mann formed a Shakespeare Mutual Improvement Society. It was a time of great openness to new ideas. One meeting place was called the Eclectic Hall. These were almost exclusively centres of working class cultural formation, in which Liberals and philanthropists – contrary to the popular picture – played no role. Just a glimpse of the addresses of the clubs shows that they were situated at the very heart of working class areas. In this period their role was even greater as many craftsmen and mechanics worked in the locality of their Club amidst thriving and rumbustuous communities. There was the Patriotic club in Clerkenwell, the building now part of the Marx Memorial Library, as well as 'coal clubs' to save for winter fuel. There were clubs for poetry, music, cribbage and dominoes and one, which met in Foley Street, was also a 'House of Call' (employment exchange outside the state apparatus) for the West End No. 2 branch of the Association of Cabinetmakers. A Wednesday Club for Theoretical Mechanics for beginners was also held.

A key role fell to the organisation of the National Secular Society with its 'Hall of Science' in Old Street. Many people have struggled to understand the working class ambivalence towards organised religion, yet this has its roots in the determination of the NSS to take the secularist message into the poorest working class areas where few others would venture. They combined secularism with a struggle against poverty and backward ideas, for the poorest parts of London, even in 'The Jago'. The Church were landlords, so the fight against poverty was often against the Church. By the late 1870s and certainly by the 1880s, Marxism began to gain ground in the NSS and some of its affiliates wanted to form a new radical party.

Club life was fluid and membership voluntary. There were many schisms and splits and these did not take place along exclusively political lines – but also involved class, personal and geographical issues. So the late Socialist League, split so swiftly from the SDF, had a precedent – quite a few actually.

The Clubs became propagandist and set up a publishing house 'for men of small means'. The concepts of Science and Reason were often combined, the former for enlightenment, the latter a hammer against those with vested interests who wanted to keep the world as it was. Some clubs, such as the Elensis Club, had 1,000 members. They organised 'Art Distributions' first used by the Chartists, to raise funds. Members would bring their own work to sell at the Club, a shared exposition with money made for the cause.

In the Clubs were also people like Dr Trans, friend of Robert Owen and Dr Gammage, the historian of Chartism. The terms of reference were broad and included, according to the veteran Frank Kitz, secretary of Manhood Suffrage League and a journeyman dyer by trade, thinkers and doers such as Owen, Henry Hunt, George Julian Harney, Ernest Jones, Bronterre O'Brien, Fergus O'Connor and William Lovett. So the historical continuity that brought Morris to socialism was bringing others too – through the club network and via an Anglo-Irish gathering of the deepest thinkers on social questions, who pre-date Marx.

Many of the club leaders, such as George Shipton (secretary of the London Trades' Council) and George Odger took part, especially in the Manhood Suffrage League. The League was lecturing on Marx's Communist Manifesto as early as 1881. All this refutes Webb's reasoning that socialism was imported into the working class from the middle class and that it barely existed before the 1880s. Maybe, instead of conducting research into the condition of the poor, one or both of the Webbs should have gone to a club.

The most advanced of the Metropolitan Clubs did not need to be begged to join when the Democratic Federation was formed.

Democratic Federation

Into the ferment provided by this established network of myriad organisations strode Morris, bringing with him his innate sense of historical perspective and his unshakeable enthusiasm. He brought experience, practical knowledge and leadership qualities too. He needed to think things through for himself for there were few volumes of ready-made solutions on the shelf and he was already asking questions that were way beyond their scope. Some of the socialist thinking in Britain came from outside the network, from the sizeable community of talented agitators and exiles who had taken up residence in England since 1848. They were being continually topped up by the actions of people like Metternich and François Guizot and later by Bismarck. Few in this community truly integrated or, as Marx had done, made Britain their permanent home. The dream was always to return home and many did.

Alongside such socialists was another community, homespun. They came from the club network, from the unions, and from organisations such as the London Trades Council, grappling with how socialist ideas might be given clear shape when fused with the newly discovered power of a growing working class. It was to this circle that Morris gravitated. This working class was itself feeling its way forward in the dark, growing in power, but unevenly distributed, making an inroad here at a level of local council or school board, and at times, as with the American Civil War between 1861 and 1865 and the Russo-Turkish War in 1878, even having an influence on foreign policy.

The strength of Morris's contribution to this socialism was in the way he accepted influence of how things actually were. Many a time he referred to "so called society" as if it had yet to live up to the standards expected of it by its supporters, let alone, its detractors. Describing capitalism, he wrote of "its mastery of and its waste of mechanical power, its commonwealth so poor, its enemies of the commonwealth so rich, and its stupendous organisation for the misery of life! Its concept of the simple pleasures, which everyone could enjoy, but for its folly? Its eyeless vulgarity which has destroyed art, the one certain solace of labour."

In later years Morris was to oppose Fabianism, on the grounds that it had made a generalised notion of 'Equality' the main aim of the workers' movement rather than rebuilding their relationship with production. Morris wrote, "I have advisedly used the phrase *equality of condition*; for of course I admit that it is no more possible that men should be equal in capacity or desires or temperament than that they should be equal in stature or weight: but in fact if there were not this inequality in this sense I doubt if we could have equality of condition." Equality of condition was the aim not a watering down into 'equality of access'. It would be based on society taking account of everyone's different contributions. If each person made contributions based on his individual capacity and differing interests and standards, there would be a new basis for exchanging products other than through the medium of buying and selling. A worker who made good forks but no toothbrushes could enter into a direct relationship of exchange with one who made poor forks but good toothbrushes. A 'market' would be artificial and superfluous when this form of direct exchange was freely available.

For a man supposedly given to medieval romanticism he brought a realistic and tangible construction to socialism that was rooted in production. In a period where it was not possible to point to a single local parliamentary constituency or authority under working class majority, let alone a country where an attempt was being made to implement any form of socialism, where else could one turn? Where else would one draw one's rationale? Morris himself saw a logical basis in everyday life, in production and in nature. His earlier rejection of Huxley's distortion of Darwin helped here. By unpicking the fabric of exploitation, as it existed, he could begin to stitch together something that was new and different. Not, 'alternatives' or the visionary and experimental communities of Owen or Fourier, but taking things as they were and making them work in a different way because they were now motivated by a different sense of purpose. Morris's turn to socialism represented a conscious break with Liberalism and he quit the liberal party. As we have shown, he had never felt fully comfortable with it, but this did not mean that he rejected the idea of party politics altogether. To his recent Liberal allies he wrote, "My Radical friends, which will you keep, the name, or the thing?"

Socialism seemed to settle in Morris little by little and as this happened he readily accepted it as if it had meant to be that way all along. There was no great Damascene conversion based on a reading of Marx. According to Thompson, "In a certain sense he had already in his lectures advanced the theory of socialism in relation to the decorative arts beyond the point which any other theorist had yet reached." His attitude and practice towards the wide range of disciplines he engaged in was already 'socialised', indeed politicised. His attitude to the political was now catching up. Where Marx did make an impact on him was through his reading of *Capital*. Morris had despised 'civilisation', but seen his role primarily in raising the condition of the working class. Marx posed a different challenge – if Morris accepted that the 'hitherto history of existing society is the history of the class struggle' and if the stagnant Victorian society, that so haunted Morris, was to be reinvigorated, one class could only raise itself to supremacy on the broken back of the other. Morris did not baulk at this conclusion.

He began to read economics in the same way as he had once read to get to grips with the 'history from below' of the medieval period. He read William Cobbett, Robert Owen, Marx and Henry George. He joined the Democratic Federation on 13 January 1883 and the same week was made an Honorary Fellow of Exeter College, Oxford.

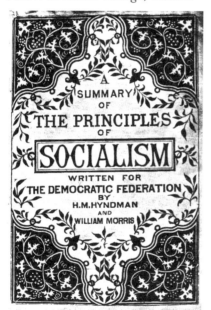

The first statement of broad principles. Despite the inclusion of such people as Friedrich Engels and Eleanor Marx Aveling in its ranks only Morris had the stature to rival Hyndman. Each was too quick to reach for his gun when hostilities broke out. A later list of essential reading for socialists, drawn up by Engels, listed Morris and Belfort Bax *"Socialism – its growth and outcome'* as number one.

When Morris came to call himself 'socialist', he did so against the backdrop of a decade when there was no discernible centre or focus for working class organisation. It was a time of accumulating ideas and of gathering power. The TUC had been formed in 1868, a qualitative and big step forward. But there was little agitation that could have an impact on the nation. Radical and Republican clubs existed but their reach was local and partial. It was sometime before an attempt was made to link them organisationally. What passed as socialism, at least up until the founding of the Democratic Federation and the Emancipation of Labour League was a series of loose associations on a range of issues such as: universal manhood suffrage; defence and extension of democratic rights, especially of assembly; land nationalisation, Irish Home Rule and solidarity with those struggling for freedom or nationhood – the Italians were very popular – on the continent.

The period between the demise of Chartism and the 1880s was rich in the struggle of ideas and experimentation in different forms of working class organisation. Out of the struggle for trade unionism – continually facing legal threat to its status – secularism and Parliamentary reform, came the move towards a workers' party – the Democratic Federation.

(Reproduced courtesy of the TUC unionhistory.info)

Chartism long past, was now little more than a memory. The Establishment had in fact been forced, albeit tentatively, to accept aspects of the demands of the Charter, whilst attempting strenuously to avoid its underlying ethos. In many ways the period between 1850 and 1870 represented the gradual erosion of Chartist ideas as the dominant and most progressive of working class aspirations. Much had been achieved. Workers previously motivated by the shock effect of industrialisation were beginning to chip away at the power of capital. Chartism itself ended divided into a number of camps. Some sought change through exertion of 'moral force' and others advocated 'physical force'. There was also a division between those who concentrated on aspects of the Chartist project rather than the fuller picture and others who saw no possibility of further advance until the aims of Chartism were drawn into a broader scheme for social liberation. In some parts of the country, Chartism had slipped effortlessly into trade unionism. It had a strong local culture, especially in London, Birmingham, Lancashire and South Wales. In other areas, it had barely taken hold. While in Birmingham it represented the political aspirations of the mechanics, some of them quite well-to-do, in the East End of London or in Glasgow it represented the same, but for the poorest communities. When Chartism came apart in 1850, the glue of the six-point charter came unstuck, and these forces spun off in different directions. Some would survive for many years to meet in secret in backrooms of public houses, others, especially the craft unions, thrived to lay down permanent roots. Some opted for cooperation and Owenism. Others put their faith in Gladstone.

Morris was therefore far from being the only one seeking alternatives beyond capitalism. We need look no further than Fergus O'Connor's Chartist Land Company to ascertain that, but 'socialisms' that looked back could not survive as Morris was well aware. His socialism had to have relevance to a future that was not rooted in a romanticised past but in the realities of the day. Therefore, it should come as no surprise that the changes in the 1870s of which Morris was a part, were driven forward by a new generation. He wrote in *Justice* 16 June, 1894, "Think of it! Was it all to end in a counting-house on top of a cinderheap, with Podsnap's drawing room in the offing, and a Whig committee dealing out champagne to the rich and margarine to the poor in such convenient proportions as would make all men contented together, though the pleasure of the eyes was gone from the world, and the place of Homer was to be taken by Huxley?"

New faces of Labour set to become household names (left to right) Tom Mann, John Burns and Will Thorne. (Reproduced courtesy of the TUC unionhistory.info)

The Labour Emancipation League drew many of the new and old together. Formed in 1881 it restated as 'Programme', what it was convinced was the unfinished business of the days of high Chartism. It sought, "Establishment of a Free and Social Condition of Society, based on the principle of Political Equality, with Equal Social Advantages for All." The last point of the programme pressed for the nationalisation of the land, mines and means of transit. It went on to state that the "Emancipation of labour requires the transformation of the said Instruments of Production and the Means of Employment into Collective or Public Property for the benefit of All Members of Society." In the East End of London where the League enjoyed substantial support, it campaigned for Equal Direct Adult Suffrage and Ballot, Direct Legislation by the People and opposition to emigration. The League led a parallel life to that of the Democratic Federation and there was dual membership of both organisations.

Eighteen-eighty was a time of great hardship as a result of trade depression. The political economy of the Liberal party was all at sea, a reflection of its uneasy relationship to its new and increasingly radicalising working class constituency. Its younger radicals were drawing away. The Democratic Federation took up some and drew together a number of radical clubs. Its leader was Henry Hyndman author of *The Social Reconstruction of England* published in 1884. His writing converted many to socialism. Morris joined the Federation in January 1883 before it declared for socialism, but he was clear from the outset where he wanted it to go. The title of Hyndman's book is interesting, in that it concurs with conclusions that Morris had drawn. England, it reasoned, was a great country, driven off the rails as a result of succumbing to capitalism. The basic ideals that had guided the people of England for so long had been perverted. Socialism then, was not seen as a destructive force, but one that could stand Britain back up on her feet again.

At its first major conference, the Democratic Federation had declared for socialism, but why did Morris take to the new thinking so quickly? As we have seen he was fairly well acquainted with it before he joined and he played no small part in pushing it in the direction that it took. However, there was something much more organic to the process. Morris was a designer and therefore used to being the originator and in on the things that counted, from their inception. To design well, as opposed to just competently, it is necessary to understand the whole concept and the pivotal points, of any given process. Morris was a craftsman, accustomed to embracing both process and detail and able to deploy his skill to change raw matter into something both useful and beautiful. As an artist and a visionary he saw not just the 'immediately tangible' but the context, purpose and interrelationship between thought and deed. His characteristics as a designer were historically evolved and determined, and this enabled him to put the sweeping ideas of whole generations together. His emphasis was on the collective nature of all work and human endeavour, and although he was associated with individual genius (he was acknowledged as such, both in his day, and now) he always gave precedence to the collective over the individual.

The whole may be greater than the parts, but in complex arrangements, if each does not fit or coordinate, counterbalance or coincide, the parts never become the whole and the point of culmination is not reached. All these factors instinctively informed his socialism. He was alive to machinery – how it had changed and evolved and what it was capable of. Because of his historical scope and his knowledge of times past, he brought 500 years of perspective to the new way of thinking, where most people struggled to bring a decade.

Morris brought his expertise to all of the processes he was involved in, from textiles to printing. He had a rare and intimate knowledge of materials. Through running a company he was aware of the advantages and shortcomings of business. In Iceland he observed what future generations were to see in the USSR in the 1920s and 1930s – the possibility of something other than capitalism. He had a sense of historical continuity and saw in 'new thinking' the opportunity to redraw the relationship between human beings and the rest of nature. Morris wrote that this would be, "By us, and not for us". In focusing on relationships in production he was really analysing relationships between people. It was much more than a project based on political economy.

He immersed himself totally in every new challenge he met with, and this enthusiasm was one of his greatest strengths.

The socialism of the 1880s was quite different from the romantic socialism of his youth in the 1830s. The new socialism was infused with science and had an air of certainty, precision, and modernity that imbued it with confidence and made it attractive. One of the great strengths of 1880s socialism was that it set out not to oppose, but propose, and to speak for the majority. As 'new thinking' it was of course, untried, untested, and without blueprint or precedent – a perfect challenge to one like Morris who was used to leading and thinking things through for himself. Socialism was soon to attract the very brightest of the workers' movement. James MacDonald, John Burns, Will Crook, Tom Mann, Ben Tillett, Ernest Bevin, who went on to found the TGWU, and Annie Besant. The adhesion of such men as Thomas Barclay of Leicester, a self-taught draughtsman, or the tailor Tom Maguire of Leeds, affirmed for

Morris that he was going in the right direction. Other older and more experienced leaders such as Alexander Macdonald, the Lanarkshire miners' leader, drew new inspiration.

The new unionism was also about a remaking of the working class. In the East End of London, Catholic dockers from Stepney organised alongside Jewish cabinetmakers. The Great Assembly Hall was a popular venue for Labour Movement meetings. (Reproduced courtesy of the TUC unionhistory.info)

He was not alone with his experimentation in ideas. Many, and especially those such as Joseph Dietzgen, Ferdinand Lassalle, Louis Boudin, Ernest Untermann, James Connolly, George Plekhanov and Karl Kautsky, were developing ideas that sought a meeting point in a combination of attachment to nationhood, craft, science and nature and the opportunities thrown up by the new organisation of the working class. In the Radical clubs it was not uncommon for many hundreds to attend lectures on diverse subjects, all dealing with scientific issues. Everywhere: in all industries and in all localities talented and cultured trade union organisers were at work.

It grows and grows — are we the same,
The feeble band, the few?
Or what are these with eyes aflame,
And hands to deal and do?
This is the host that bears the word,
NO MASTER HIGH OR LOW —
A lightning flame, a shearing sword,
A storm to overthrow

Chants for Socialists (1894)
William Morris

Party man, non-politician

What is clear is that as Morris's new thinking was becoming absorbed into socialism, he found new energy. He said that socialism had made him feel fifty years young rather than fifty years old. He described himself as an "unpaid professional agitator". It was associated with the new, with challenges to the old set ideas and to an order that, from the point of view of justice, was indefensible. The old sense of a 'pecking order' was breaking down reinforced by the historical shift from countryside to town and from cottage-based production to factory. Both capitalism and socialism became associated, with "newness" in the eyes of differing and contending classes. The grievances were all too apparent. Most workers did not yet have the vote. Few of their children had formal education. The old faced ill health as a result of factory conditions. Slums were the norm. In 1883 Britain lost her monopoly in the world market. For Morris, and so many others, the first faltering task of socialist agitation, was to complete the work of Chartism, but the socialist programme adopted by the Democratic Federation went way beyond the most advanced Chartism of Bronterre O'Brien, George Julian Harney and even the radical editor of the 'Red Republican' Ernest Jones.

The Democratic Federation had learned lessons from previous attempts at working class organisation. It sought federation as a means of uniting disparate groups around a common platform whilst encouraging local cultures to flourish. In the 1880s there was little media that could be classed national and working class. Propaganda was essentially face-to-face: at street corner meetings and through the sale of pamphlets. When the Democratic Federation opted for socialism at its first major annual conference, it set about establishing a newspaper, *Justice*, launched in January of 1884, which became the national voice of the Democratic Federation.

Morris stepped forward to become the treasurer and to bankroll some of the organisation's early activity. Hyndman said of the adhesion of Morris to the Democratic Federation "His great reputation and high character doubled our strength at a stroke." Many thought that his membership would be merely tokenistic. But Morris approached it with his customary zeal. He was prepared, insofar as it was possible, to accept the rights and responsibilities of an ordinary member.

The now famous cartoon Beehive produced in 1867 by Cruikshank. The queen appears above the constitution as Cruikshank was an opponent of Parliamentary power and an extended franchise. In reality as the nineteenth century unfolded, it was the mass of people who turned the beehive upside down.

One leader said that Morris brought a young man's enthusiasm to his membership, although he was then well past his youth. If he brought energy, he also brought a wise and experienced head. Morris had a wide circle of contacts and as well as seeking to recruit them he also touched them for donations. He wanted to listen and learn from the people, but had to keep an open mind because the Democratic Federation was a Party without a programme. He could not even use the Communist Manifesto, as it was not then in mass circulation in the English language. Morris made new friends, big characters that he came to respect for the rest of his days. Andreus Scheu, a designer and maker of furniture, came close to Morris and was struck by his motivation. Morris was driven to socialism he said, not by the poverty around him or by social dislocation, but by moral revulsion and as a result of an intellectual rejection of capitalism. Morris's socialism had to have substance. In a way he now came to it not as a result of his critique of the influence of capitalism on art but as a means of reconstituting art and liberating it. For

Morris, the workers had to be free before they would indulge in art as an organic feature of their work.

Each time Morris gave a lecture it was news. He became something of a marked man as the proponents of capitalism tried to understand how one of Britain's greatest craftsmen – one called him the most important since the decline of the Middle Ages – and cultural icons could jump the capitalist ship. His books had been a staple in every middle class home since the late 1850s. His speeches were reported. Newspaper leaders and letters denounced his 'defection'. The criticism that stung him was that his views were unpractical. This implied that his energy was wasted on a project that he was incapable of seeing as impossible to implement and also that he failed to see that this socialism somehow challenged the laws of human nature. On the surface such criticism had the effect of making him redouble his effort, but fundamentally it made him determined to ensure that his socialism was both accessible and practical. Indeed the peculiar or unique contribution that he made to the development of socialistic thinking was precisely in this kind of fieldwork, making the basis of socialism a *practice* of life.

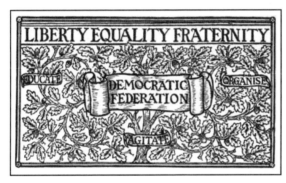

Democratic Federation membership card designed by William Morris. Morris signed his card 'Designer'. He had associated with the cause of the workers for years. But for Morris the project took Liberty, Fraternity and Equality as its starting point rather than its ultimate aim.

One further effect that the censure had on him was to determine him to switch his chosen field of lectures from art and medieval craftsmanship, where he was both detailed and authoritative, to political economy. In this early period it is interesting to note that Morris used the words socialist and collectivist interchangeably.

The question of class, which no self-respecting Victorian bourgeois felt comfortable with, imposed itself in his lecture *Misery and the Way Out*. He wrote, " I yet want to impress the fact upon you that as classes you and they are and must be opposed to each other. Whatever gain you add to your standard of life, you must do at their expense, and they will and must resist it to the utmost of their power." In response to further criticism he even considered turning the Firm, his company, into a cooperative, though this was not pursued.

His main activities were writing for *Justice* and lecturing. How will socialism be brought about? he asked. First, "by educating people into desiring it, next organising them into claiming it effectively." He shared the general description of socialism drawn up by Edward and Eleanor Marx-Aveling. "The approaching change in 'civilised' society will be a revolution ... The two classes at present existing will be replaced by a single class consisting of the whole of the healthy and members of the same community, possessing all the means of production and distribution in common". It was one that most calling themselves socialistic, from Henry George to the Fabians would have agreed with, but differences as to how it could be achieved were soon to surface. Hyndman had a slightly different approach.

The strike committee of the matchgirls at Bryant and May in Bow, East London. This strike led by women became a turning point in the organisation of labour.
(Reproduced courtesy of the TUC unionhistory.info)

Within a year, in December 1884, Morris was to lead the majority of the national council in a breakaway to form what became known as the Socialist League. This disastrous action, which appeared to go against the grain of so much working class activity at a time when organisations were either merging or seeking unity, was one that Morris came to regret.

The root of the disagreements over strategy, tactics and organisation were an inevitable reflection of the different constituencies of the Federation. The fact is, at an early stage, no real internal democratic processes were established which would have allowed a meeting of minds, ideas and opinions. In terms of working class input, the structures of Parliament and local government were also weak and unformed. So, in the absence of any democratic forum they 'took to the barricades' against each other. Each of the constituencies had their own traditions and ways of working. There were those who had only recently made a break with Gladstone – Morris included – who were steeped in parliamentary politics and used to being part of a firmly established Liberal party that could expect its share of government. There were the supporters of the Paris Commune and radical London trade unionists. All too often the Democratic Federation leadership mistook its own break with Gladstone for a break by the mass of workers, but this was not to come for another generation. The same kind of apparition plagued the Left movement for many years. It gave rise to all kinds of impatience and brought the party into policy distortion, and a political cul-de-sac. There was a sense of immediacy where the party came to substitute itself for the working class constituency it claimed to be seeking to mobilise.

As a new political force it found itself opposed to much that did not need opposition. Even the trade unions were attacked. According to Hyndman they were a "hindrance to that complete organisation of the proletariat." 'Limited' reforms were treated in the same manner. Socialists, it was thought, must, if they are to convey the correctness of their ideas, stand aside from the mass and act, not as an organiser or educator, but as an agitator, a tragedy many have been destined to re-enact to this day.

Resolution of the Irish Question, the abolition of the House of Lords, the municipalisation of slum clearance and house building, the eight-hour day-known popularly as the 'short-time movement' – were all seen as mere 'palliatives', best left until after the revolution, but for some, the neutrality towards 'palliatives' was not enough: one had to oppose rather than tolerate them. So, strikes or union building all delayed The Day, and were frowned upon. In this way, the Democratic Federation cut itself off from its own lifeblood. Where would it draw new members from if it did not seek out the opponents of capitalism, then build unions and strike against the employers?

It is probably fair to say that Morris never truly found a place for trade unions in his scheme. He understood the notion of class as well as anyone, as well as craft, skill, industry and community and was constantly working out the core principles and architecture for a British version of socialism. He was never a member of a trade union though he would have immediately recognised their *modus operandi* as he was normally 'a joiner' and an active member of various trade societies. It is more likely that he was happy to let other socialists, probably better suited, take the lead in union building. His idea of a socialist party was one which represented many different currents of working class reality. Trade unionism at this time was one such course and only dominated in certain trades such as coal mining, engineering and work in the docks, and even then, only in certain parts of the country. Elsewhere, it competed with Lib-Labism, co-operation, Owenism and religion.

The Socialist League announced itself with a Manifesto and Morris co-edited a series designed to expand on different sections of this. The series included: *Socialist League Address to Trades Unions* (1885) by Belfort Bax; *True and False Society* (1888) *Useful Work versus Useless Toil* (1885); the *Factory Hell*, by Eleanor Marx-Aveling and Edward Aveling (1885); and Thomas Binning, *Organised Labour: the Duty of the Trades Unions in Relation to Socialism* (1886).

This series illustrates how dominant the Labour component had become within the social question: it clearly draws together the issues of the nature of work, factory life and the unions.

Each pamphlet was written by Morris or a close confidant. Binnings for example became a key figure – head of the compositors – at Kelmscott Press. Together they give us the clearest exposition of the thinking of the League – before it fell to anarchism and a reactionary position on the trade union question.

The *Address to the Trades Unions* was written by Bax, though it carries the clear mark of Morris as it is peppered with references to "shoddy wares".

Bax thought his readers saw socialism as a 'theory', a 'foreign import' and quite impractical as it did not immediately put food on the table. He asked trade unionists how far their practical English trade unionism had got them. He also asked them to contrast their current situation with that of the craftsmen of the industrial middle ages. This craftsman, he contended, sat at the master's table and was his social equal. Then, class distinction, was only a nightmare-in-waiting, work was honourable and pleasurable, and when, "exaction by the fraudulent system of wages, which conceals from the victim the fact that he is plundered, was unknown."

The subtext was not too subtle. Unions might be essential and able to advance against the most direct forms of exploitation, but could do little to influence production. The pamphlet aimed at showing how different from the unions, the Social Democratic Federation and the Socialist League were, actually affirms how much common ground they shared.

According to Bax, "The original achievements of the trades unions were entirely due to the fact that British capitalists had the run of the foreign markets". Unionism, he contended was limited to a narrow 'aristocracy of labour', able to sustain itself because members were employed in making machinery for export. This apparently put them in a privileged position in relation to other workers, but with the growth of competition from abroad after 1870, this advantage evaporated. There was nothing the unions could do about this as the, "success for unionism lies in its ability to limit competition".

The battle of Trafalgar Square, 'Bloody Sunday' (13 November 1887), in which the SDF mobilised a march against unemployment. Viciously assaulted by police, armed with long truncheons and cutlasses, and cavalry, resulting in two deaths and many injuries. Morris recognised immediately that the path to socialism would be a long one, dotted with setbacks amidst advances.
(Reproduced courtesy of the TUC unionhistory.info)

How he could draw such conclusions is disturbing and shows how far removed some members of the socialist movement were from the workers. Even a cursory glance at early union history shows that they were built in the teeth of capitalism rather than with its connivance. They were at their strongest and most durable, in industries like coal mining, on railways and in some localities in agriculture: that is industries at the centre of the domestic market rather than those concerned with export. Bax concluded that the, "trades' unions do not grow in strength or numbers, but appear to have reached their zenith and to have achieved all they are capable of under present conditions."

This was written at the same time as the mass union recruitment drives in the docks and agriculture, and just a year before the breakout of mass general unionism amongst the unskilled and in the ports.

It may be that Bax's pessimistic approach to unions was an attempt to differentiate socialist from trade unionist. Perhaps he saw them as rivals. Many of the old school unionists were diehard Liberals and opponents of socialism, but to the newer generation such as Mann and Burns, socialism and trade unionism were inextricably linked. "What could unionists do?" asked Bax, "Constitute themselves as the nucleus of a socialist commonwealth". The logical inconsistency is all too evident. Trade unions he reasoned had "stalled" – this was in 1885! – because they could not achieve anything but elementary tasks. So he charged them with the simple task of bringing down capitalism.

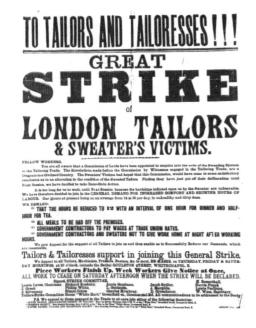

New unionism swept up skilled and unskilled alike. This new growth of power and confidence challenged and moved on, Morris's 'new thinking' of the mid 1880s.

(Reproduced courtesy of the TUC unionhistory.info)

Each struggle for advance and material improvement in the lives of workers threw up new groups who were challenging the reality of the system that the Democratic Federation wished to do away with. By turning its face away from these groups, it was, in effect resisting new forces that could expand its own ranks. Indeed most working class members of the Democratic Federation did engage in such struggles for limited reform 'palliatives', but the lack of support they experienced from their party often led to their resignation or giving up the fight.

There are many versions of why Morris and his supporters broke away to form a new organisation. It is commonly believed that the division was about whether or not to engage in parliamentary activity and the extent to which parliament could be seen and used as a stepping stone, away from capitalism, towards greater democracy. There is an element of this in the sense that, had there been room for discussion and dialogue within the SDF he may not have left, or at least not so quickly. There was also a feeling that Hyndman, originally a Tory, was finding it difficult to break with his early views and ways. In fact it went far deeper than that and one should beware of the many superficial excuses often cited and based on differences in personality. For it is true to say that if personality clashes alone led to division there being so many big personalities in this early socialist movement, expressing a range of sometimes conflicting outlooks, any form of unity or party organisation would prove impossible.

Some in the Democratic Federation concluded that it was precisely such limited reforms which were the key to laying roots in the working class communities and securing, through an alliance with radical workers and unions, a gradual move away from capitalism. This approach had worked on the continent. The concentration on reform, they argued, could be contained within a revolutionary strategy – so reforms would be reduced to a question of tactics and only impinged on strategy in a limited way. To such members, the question of reform or not was not a point of principle. Across the world, in countries as far apart as Japan and Serbia, as well as places where workers were already well organised along party lines like Italy, France and Germany, workers' organisations were discussing the very same issue: reform and revolution versus reform or revolution. But in Britain, this same question led to an organisational split and appeared to elevate the issue to one of principle, formalised into party policy. Henceforth and throughout the middle and late 1880s, if socialists put reform above revolution they joined the Fabians, and if they were for revolution above reform – or to the exclusion of it – they joined the Social Democratic Federation or the Socialist League.

Unsurprisingly, Morris maintained a foot in each camp, though in terms of organisation he put his heart into building the Socialist League. He was not the type George Bernard Shaw had referred to as "socialist or smash". To Morris there was a mutual and radical interrelationship between the old and the new, the now and future and between the immediate and long term. Workers needed to breathe the air of greater freedom, with food on the table, if they were to embrace socialism as their own. So Morris clearly understood the nature of palliatives, and disagreed with Hyndman about them.

He was pretty much for anything that brought workers together and raised their sense of confidence and power. Some 'palliatives' he thought were dead ends – yet he promoted others. The nearer it was to his own heart the better he felt able to promote it. Therefore, although the Socialist League turned its back on reform, Morris was an ardent supporter of socialised housebuilding and the eight-hour day. In this respect, the 'palliative' was an affirmation of his socialism in the here and now and each consideration of the subject opened to him the opportunity to make his 'big point'. It also served to reinforce the practical – or provable – nature of socialism, when he was being accused of simply promoting dreams for generations to come.

The gap between the reality and the rhetoric became most apparent in the struggle over unemployment, which was to reach new, and publicly very visible heights, in the mid 1880s. "Our immediate aim," Morris wrote in 1884, "should be chiefly educational ... with a view to dealing with the crisis if it should come in our day, or handing on the tradition of our hope to others if we should die before it comes."

Where other national leaders of the Democratic Federation, now renamed Social Democratic Federation, saw party growth as a means of entering the bargaining table of local and national politics, Morris saw education of workers for social change as the priority. Where workers were not educating themselves politically or where the voice of socialism could not or had not yet been heard, these should be found in the Social Democratic Federation. In opposing Hyndman and taking off into the Socialist League, Morris showed questionable political judgement. At one stroke, despite securing a majority of the national council, he handed the organisation over to Hyndman and weakened those who stayed there. Why else would they leave a bare year after they had joined? At the same time Morris took with him many of those implacably opposed to any kind of limited or even tactical reform, making him a prisoner of 'impossibilism' and the anarchists who came to dominate the organisation.

The rift is even less excusable when one considers that it was the first organisation of its kind. The word 'Party' meant a body of men and women subscribing to broadly similar aims and philosophy, but for one thing there was as yet no socialist philosophy to subscribe to: it was more a hybrid embodying different strains of working class thinking and remnants of older outlooks. Nor was there a historical requirement for the formation of a political party let alone a model on which to base one. The socialists of the day opted less for parties and more for federations and Leagues with each constituent part maintaining and respecting the integrity of the other's internal processes.

There was an outline constitution, with local by-laws and different ways of operating because, in some localities, the branch functioned as an agitator, and in other an educator. Turnover of the few branch officers was high, as members were often out of work and away seeking. Many were victimised and forced to travel away to find work. There had to be a room for dialogue and for compromise. All parties of the time, including Liberal and Conservative were much looser federations of groups and interests than we are used to in political parties today. If the SDF could have adopted this model, it is likely to have been better able to keep mind and body together.

Morris was no enthusiast for division and resisted it until inner party relations were so poor that their combined energy was being used in squabbling, and not the reason that he and most other members, had joined. Even after the split had taken place, he hoped for and expected some sort of reconciliation. Once the heat of passionate debate and intrigue had cooled, perhaps he had begun to consider that their differences, based on style of operation rather than principle, were not so important, after all, or at least they were containable.

Engels, with whom Morris had established regular contact, warned him straight away, urging him to take a slower pace and to ensure that when the organisation moved, it took workers with them. The split was really an untidy fissure. Political differences were fought out behind the closed doors of the national council and were never explained to the membership, let alone attempts made to bring them into the discussions. So some of Morris's supporters stayed with Hyndman out of loyalty to the organisation and some supporters of Hyndman's ideas left to join Morris because they believed that he would create a more democratic and tolerant internal regime. Some branches such as Manchester and Sheffield, remained untouched or refused to take sides and new ones were soon established where members had never even met the protagonists and saw the division as backward looking. The real problem was that it was tending to look inward rather than spread the 'new idea' outwards.

It is now clear that Morris disliked something much more in Hyndman than his personality or style of leadership. He was increasingly uncomfortable with his attempt to formalise Marxism into a kind of schema and raise it to a credo. Morris saw Marxism as a historical method capable of development because it confronted and sought to incorporate what was new and challenging in a broad range of disciplines in addition to politics: especially science and the arts. His book *Socialism From the Root Up*, serialised in the Socialist League's new newspaper, the *Commonweal*, is one of the first attempts in the English language to develop a

Marxist critique of capitalism and present a vision of what might lie beyond it. Its influence was wide, with pressings as far away as Chicago in the U.S.A.

Explaining his split from Hyndman, Morris wrote, "I want an educated movement. Discontent is not enough, though it is natural and inevitable. The discontented must know what they are aiming at … my belief is that the old order can only be overthrown by force; and for that reason it is all the more necessary that the revolution … should be, not an ignorant, but an intelligent revolution." If only his own members had been listening! Within the League was a group in great confusion. As many were trying to balance the reform revolution dichotomy, others followed a trajectory inherited from the extreme wing of French revolutionary Jacobinism. They mistook a struggle by workers against the machinery of the state for one against all forms of statehood.

Morris too was no enthusiast for the type of society advocated by Edward Bellamy in *Looking Backwards* (1887), which saw a role for the state in all aspects of life. He readily understood that for a long time, socialism would require a central force to keep matters together. The impossibilists did not. He was increasingly unable to moderate the views of this group as it gravitated towards anarchism, or to get his own ideas across, even as editor and financier of *Commonweal*. As a result, it grew extremely difficult to keep the organisation together.

Membership of the League was a small, but a genuine cross-section of the working class throughout Britain. It brought together the poorest crofters, a fiercely independent group of workers who were also amongst the first to embrace socialism, steelworkers from Sheffield, and the engineers in heavy industry from the West Midlands. Although some of the league's brightest members such as Thomas Binning, were union men (there were also a few union women), it did not go out of its way to attract trade unionists, most of who stayed with the SDF. For an organisation that defied 'palliatives' on paper the Socialist League took up the fight for free speech with gusto. This was probably an unavoidable task as the only media open to a small, new working class organisation were, in newsprint or speaking on the street corner. There is no doubt that the police and local authorities systematically sought to deny the right of free speech to both the Socialist League and the SDF.

As the organisation grew more solid it began to attract pockets of local supporters to its ranks, some of them from most unlikely places, such as Torquay. In some areas such as East London, Glasgow and in the Northeast generally, it showed signs of gathering even greater support. The authorities took this shift seriously and endeavoured to control the audience available to the organisation by denying permits to hold street, park or public meetings. The threat was both serious and national, there being very few working class representatives on local authorities at the time. It is a tribute to both organisations that they were able to support each other in the numerous and famous free speech struggles that broke out. Many of these were won and the model of action they used was adopted and adapted by those who fought for and established new unionism a few years later. Having literally sat in the same cells together as arrest followed arrest after each fight for free speech, and with Morris spending most weekends providing bail for members of the different organisations (as well as getting arrested himself), it seems inexcusable that they were still unable to share the same room in order to discuss a common approach to politics. The division had a long-term effect on working class party politics in Britain.

Branches would come into being and disappear again because they had little sense of common purpose save selling their newspaper. Some did this as a means of earning a living. Others were able to sustain a limited amount of activity, usually following a meeting called together by a speaker sent from the national office, only to see interest wane again shortly after. Branches were also unclear if they existed to agitate or educate. Morris wanted a small membership party based on educators but sometimes meetings such as those in the Durham coalfields, would attract hundreds and even, as in Northumberland, thousands. However, the audience had come along to listen and imbibe, not necessarily to join and become active. They took in the new ideas, but mostly expressed their class-consciousness by joining or organising a trade union.

The dominance of trade unionism over political activity is an accepted feature of this period, although this is not necessarily a negative factor. Most of the union leaders of note during the First World War and inter-war years came from the SDF or the League. The list read like a 'Who's Who' of the great tide of unionism that developed before 1921. Ben Tillett who led the gas and dockworkers, Tom Mann, leader of the Great Dock Strike of 1889 and later General Secretary of the Engineers' Union, Ernest Bevin who as a porter and member of the SDF, went on to form the TGWU and sit opposite Stalin at the post war conference in Potsdam, and Will Thorne, founder of the GMB. There were many more such as Annie Besant who led the match girls strike at Bryant and May in London's Bow, and went on to become the General Secretary of the Indian Congress Party.

Some said that Morris gave too much of his time and effort to the socialist movement, yet while he was touring the length and breadth of Britain – lecturing, organising, letter writing – he also found time to attend to the Firm and write some of his most famous works including *Dream of John Ball* and *Pilgrims of Hope*. He also translated Homer. Indeed, in 1883, Morris & Co opened a new shop in John Dalton Street in Manchester's town centre.

DOCK LABOURERS' STRIKE! RELIEF FUND.

Fellow-workmen—An earnest appeal is made to you to help your fellow-workmen, the half-starved, under-paid Dockers, in their great struggle. The men MUST win, or so much the worse for all of us. It will be our fault if they do not. Their cause is the most righteous and reasonable in modern times.

GIVE LIBERALLY & SECURE THE VICTORY!

Public Relief Fund Sheets supplied to duly authorised Collectors. All Clubs and Institutions are asked to co-operate. Shops and Factories should appoint their own Collectors.

SUBSCRIPTIONS RECEIVED at the OFFICE OF COMMITTEE, 23, RUTLAND STREET, every Evening at 7.30 ; 4 on Saturday.

COMMITTEE

John Potter, (Leicester School Board), Harry Woolley, (New Co-op. Shoe Works), Hipwell, (Vine St. Radical Club), C. O'Sullivan, (Irish National Club). Messrs. L. Brown, Staughton, Warner, Gorrie, Barclay, Richards, &c.

The big breakthrough. There had been many previous attempts to organise the docks. By 1889 the opportunity to seize a chance of sustainable organisation was grasped.
(Reproduced courtesy of the TUC unionhistory.info)

Critically, when the working class movement did explode onto the scene of national politics between 1887 and 1889, both socialist organisations were theoretically and practically ill-equipped, to give as much help as was needed. The organisations were both divided and locked in recruitment rivalry. Too often, development of trade unions had its root in one or other organisation because of the individual initiative of one or more members – unsupported by their party which, as we have shown, subscribed to theories that viewed such class organisation as an obstacle to any advance towards socialism. The SDF was anti-union, anti-strike and pro 'one big union' – just about opposing everything positive about the growth of trade unionism that was then happening in so many working class communities. It offered a fatalistic message – that there could be no advancement until socialism – and put off all except the most committed. Many working class leaders like Burns and Mann who were pivotal to the Great Dock Strike, simply left and both the SDF and the Socialist League began to disintegrate. It was the bickering that often disillusioned these workers, who undertook all their party activities voluntarily and after a hard days work. Naturally, they went to where their efforts would have the biggest impact.

It was during this upsurge that Morris came into contact with a new generation of trade unionising workers. It was the first time that socialism had been put on trial as it came into contact with a potential mass constituency. Morris unsurprisingly drew the conclusion that the tone and content of the Great Agitation had to be modified. The experience pulled him up sharp. He never watered down what he said, but did find different ways of saying it. Thompson believes that Morris was simply too far ahead of the average worker and opted to talk to them through people like Mann. It is certainly the case that Morris's approach to socialism required an educated working class (which he had) but also an experienced one. German socialists faced a similar problem and it was quite a different one from those faced by the labour movement in Czarist Russia, or Italy, where many workers were still illiterate and worked the land. The working class in these countries had more in common with the working class found in Britain in 1815, than that of 1890.

Unionism of skilled workers had a history spanning generations. Until the 1880s sustainable organisation for the unskilled and seasonally employed remained elusive.

(Reproduced courtesy of the TUC unionhistory.info)

There was a material reality to contend with that was quite unlike any we could imagine in Britain today. Workers could only work when the colliery did. They had no welfare, no safety net and no wallpaper. Meat was less regularly on the table than it had been a century before, and hours of labour for adults extended up to twelve a day, and in the majority of industries, often for six days a week. The luckier ones, or trade unionised workers, may have had a half-day on Saturdays. These people, according to Morris, "worked to live in so much as they lived to work." They had little time for 'hope', 'liberty' and 'reflection' – but they found it somehow. Tom Jackson recalls in his memoirs *Solo Trumpet* how the printers of Fleet Street would disappear under the bridges behind Bouverie Street in their lunch breaks with a volume of Shakespeare or Dickens in one hand and a dictionary in the other. They were self-taught in history, learned reading and writing only until they were old enough to go to work, when they continued their education in less formal ways. Although it may not fit the early model laid down by the socialists it was precisely when such people joined unions, went on strike or engaged in struggles to improve their communities, that they had time to reflect on their condition.

The unions quickly became crucial to the socialist project in the sense that the struggle for food and housing, work and education would create a kind of elevated stability. Only then would workers have the space for reflection and the collective power to grapple with the kind of challenges Morris posed. Workers were organising into unions quite naturally and no-one had to compel them to do so. Yet too many socialists stood aloof. Trade unionism was not pure enough socialism for them. This was a tragic misconception.

Morris saw much that was positive in this new working class. For a start they were numerous. He said, "we are many and the masters are few". They had a historically deep sense of justice, and were collective in production, with a good and increasing proportion of the labour force possessing higher skills. Some had the vote and all wanted it, including women. They had a strong sense of community. True, there was little by way of cheap transport until the bicycle and tram appeared and little time to use it. They rarely travelled and this was usually when looking for work, but travel by train or canal and migration, both internal and abroad, widened the perspective of the average worker and reinforced a sense of national identity. Union conferences began to bring members together from across the country, where they would recognise common challenges and conditions.

Where organised, there was what Morris called, a growing "sense of combination" and after 1890 a growing 'sense of purpose', too. It was this generation of worker that provided the leaders who went on to build the organisations that were able to establish municipal ownership of utilities, pensions, an elementary but free education and health service as well as locally controlled sanitation and mass housing. When Morris told the striking Northumberland miners that, "to work to live be not the work of men but of machines" he was readily understood.

The Socialist League was doomed from the beginning. Looking back, it is difficult to ascertain why the issue that did so much damage to its internal cohesion became an issue at all, though perhaps this became inevitable as soon as some self-appointed people decided to view it less a question of tactics and more one of 'principle'. How the decision whether or not the League was to be in favour of participation in parliamentary elections could take up so much time and become so fratricidal, when the total number of votes being cast for socialist candidates was numbered in the dozens, is rather depressing. However, it is symptomatic of the pettiness and self aggrandisement often resident in small political parties that become separated from their root beliefs. They seem to specialise in turning issues that should be relatively easy to resolve, into lofty principles.

With little attempt made to see off the anti-parliamentary wing of the organisation or defeat it politically, it soon became apparent that the Socialist League was going nowhere. The predominant position was one of hiding from the mass to ensure purity of programme. Engels quickly turned away from it and it is possible that those around Morris thought about forming a different kind of organisation based on new unionism. Certainly some who had been associated with new unionism did go down this road. Others, such as the Northumberland socialists, mainly coal miners, refused to join either the SL or the SDF and instead put up independent candidates. Journals to rival *Commonweal*, such as Keir Hardie's *The Miner* and HH Champion's *The Labour Elector* began to appear.

Morris was wary of parliamentary politics though not opposed to it in principle, but he thought that those entering parliament would turn their backs on the electors who had sent them there. However, it was the unions, not the socialists who instilled some discipline into working class representatives in the House of Commons. At this stage, the socialists had many questions but not too many answers. They could see what was wrong with capitalism and party politics but had little to replace them. Therefore, they offered little practical for their supporters to do that could help develop a power base and decision-making centre for the country, outside of parliament. Intelligent workers and they were two a penny in the leadership of the new labour movement, as well as being streetwise, knew where the decision-making was going on and decided to get into parliament to throw their weight around. In other words they embraced socialism but also decided to chip away at capitalism.

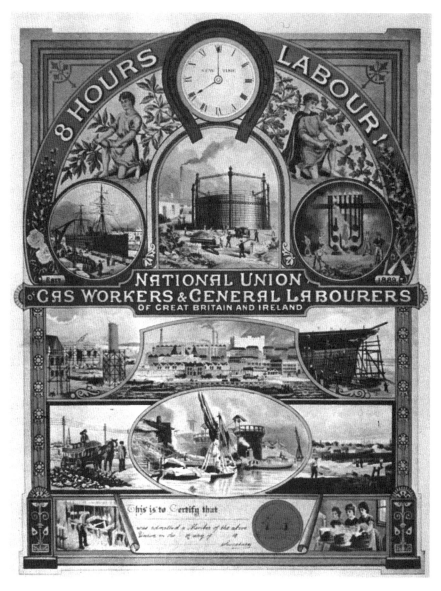

A membership certificate for one of the main 'new unions'. Note the symbolic inclusion of the ancient guildsmen and pride of place given to the campaign for an eight-hour working day. The inclusion of guilds is significant because it demonstrates that the new unions also included pockets of the old stable unions who provided a history, consciousness, regular subscriptions and discipline during disputes.   (Reproduced courtesy of the TUC unionhistory.info)

One of the first significant campaigns of the new labour movement was over the eight-hour day. It was established and promoted by the Labour and Socialist International, known popularly as the Second International. After 1887, a new leadership began to emerge within the TUC under Keir Hardie, to challenge the older and more cautious leadership of Broadhurst. This challenge crystallised around the eight-hour day campaign. James Connolly wrote that Hardie "was to the Labour movement a prophetic anticipation of its own possibilities".

These days it is difficult to realise what an eight-hour day campaign really meant. Morris was quick to seize on its significance and give it a particular twist. He began by questioning what impact an eight-hour day might have. If it was to become the norm in a society not unused to working life beginning at ten years of age, with hours extending from 12 to 14, six days a week, the question became: what would a worker do with the residual 16 hours? The campaign for an eight-hour day was actually much more than it seemed, for it centred not on shorter hours, but on a changing lifestyle and pattern of life: eight hours work, eight hours rest and eight hours for leisure and the pursuit of knowledge. True it was not what Engels said socialists should call for: 'abolition of wage slavery', but it was a huge step towards transforming the lives of workers and was made possible because the unions were becoming more assertive and combative.

The number of hours that an employer should be allowed to exploit a worker would be no more than one third of the hours in a day. The remaining two thirds would belong to the worker for rest, for his enlightenment, and to build family and community. So Morris saw that it was not possible to palm off the eight-hour day campaign as a 'palliative'. Indeed, if successful, it would have captured a sizeable part of the working life back for the employee away from the employer. Significantly, the most prominent advocates of the campaign came from within the membership of the the SDF and the SL. Of course they soon left these organisations when they felt the cold hand of Hyndman or the blank gaze of the SL 'impossibilists'.

Herein one can glimpse the reason for the failure of these two early pioneer organisations of socialists. At a time when the working class was getting organised and its confidence was high, the socialists would go to them with a rigid and preconceived platform – the workers would have to adapt to the socialists when the opposite should have been the case. Whilst publicly, the SDF opposed the eight-hour day campaign, its local branches, especially in East London, took it up. In addition they called for programmes of public relief to alleviate hardship and unemployment and for public works schemes to get the unemployed back to work.

Morris was deeply suspicious of the lingering Blanquism that saw the establishment of a new political power – socialism – as a single act or exercise in insurrection. The march of the unemployed that resulted in Bloody Sunday, where the marchers greatly outnumbered police and troops with their fixed bayonets, yet were easily dispersed, proved to him that violence was not the way forward. His conclusion was that socialism would be a steady and incremental progress established primarily through education. Although he poured scorn on Parliament, he did recognise that it was necessary to have working class representation there.

This was a big leap for Morris and a brave one. Hitherto he and many in the movement would talk of socialism in their lifetime, but after Bloody Sunday he quickly came to the conclusion that this would not be the case. He wrote that, between socialism and the present society there, "must be a transitional condition, during which we must waive the complete realisation of our ideal".

If socialism was to be successful one would have to acknowledge the power and capacity of the state to intervene on behalf of employers, develop means of communication and a national press outside the control of the capitalists, have greater organisation of workers into trades unions, and an overwhelming majority of the working class would need to have an educated acceptance of its principles. In the chapter *How the Change Came* in *News From Nowhere* he suggests 1952 as a date for the revolution, which must have seemed a long way off at the time of writing. Did Morris turn his back on revolution that he said would have to be a decisive and qualitative break with what had gone before? Not at all. One need only read *What We Have to Look For* first written for *Justice* in 1895, or *The Present Outlook for Socialism*, published just a few months before his death.

All things new in the realm of ideas appear shapeless at first, and seem to develop like 'Topsy', with myriad influences. Morris recognised this. Did he not write in *Dream of John Ball* "Men fight and lose the battle, and the thing that they fought for comes about in spite of their defeat." As we have shown, socialism developed in the 1880s, first, as 'new' thinking, then, gradually settling into a distinct groove on points of principle and only later, emerging as a clearly defined set of strategies and tactics. This was an exciting period in which new ideas were unfolding and were tested practically by a growing working class. Many ideas fell by the wayside, such as nationalisation of the land and Henry George's Single Tax. Part of the problem with the SDF and the SL was that they sought to canalise the development of such ideas and give them fixed parameters. Where the working class did not fit the ideas, to paraphrase Brecht, the early socialists sought to select a different working class. Anything that deviated from the new wisdom, as laid down in *Justice*, was damned as appeasing capitalism. Ideas were judged by who said what rather than what was said and this personalisation of politics played a large part in the disunity of the early socialists. It is a tragedy for example that Morris was unable – not because he as a person did not see but was organisationally precluded from welcoming a development from outside of the SL ranks – to acknowledge the significance of Hardie's election campaign in 1888. How powerful it would have been if they had put their heads together instead of having them knocked together.

A rare foray into song. Morris wrote this to be performed at the funeral of Alfred Linnell, a young radical clerk, one of two killed during a demonstration against unemployment at Trafalgar Square when the march was attacked by police and Life Guards with bayonets fixed. The funeral was reportedly one of the biggest gatherings of the nineteenth century.

Morris believed that the revolution was not imminent, when others in the SDF were predicting the date. He saw that capitalism had reserves and that, with the development of imperialism, it still had a lifespan of decades rather than days. Surveying what has become known as 'the scramble for Africa', Morris deduced that capitalism was expanding and changing shape, "It is quite conceivable", he wrote, "that the present stage should be prolonged in a slightly changed form even for another century." In any case, he could see that capitalism had first emerged and really taken hold in the parts of the world where Roman Law had only a tenuous hold – in Holland, Belgium, Sweden, Northern Germany and the USA, and, above all, in England. Others, such as France and Italy were catching up. Some, like Spain and Portugal, were still 'under starter's orders': whole areas of the world were waiting to start on the path towards capitalism.

Drawn by Walter Crane. The top banner referring to the 'old and new world' emphasises the enormous sums of money sent from Australia to support striking dockers and their families.

Morris saw another threat in the growth of the Empire. He gave a great deal of time and effort to the South Kensington Museum, where he acted as advisor on the authenticity, origins and value of rare artefacts from all over the world, especially tapestries, furniture and ceramics. He knew that, although paid for, they were effectively being removed from their country of origin. In imperialism he foresaw the eventual destruction of the ancient arts of India, China and Africa at a time when they were being praised aesthetically and copied for reproduction and sale in Britain. It jarred on him. With Empire reasoned Morris, went war. It is no surprise that he emphatically opposed all sorts of foreign adventures and stressed this through the pages of *Justice* and the *Commonweal* and the letters pages of the *Times*.

A number of people had an influence on Morris – often those who worked with him on a day-to-day basis and when he was editing the *Commonweal*. He wrote well with both Ernest Belfort Bax and Eleanor Marx-Aveling. There were also Edward Burne-Jones his dear friend and lifelong confidant, John Bruce Glasier who went on to become an MP and John Mahon. He was especially close, politically and professionally, to Thomas Binning, a working class craftsman compositor with whom he worked at Kelmscott Press, and also to Charles Faulkner who had been with him in the Brotherhood back in their Oxford days, the architect Philip Webb and the craftsman Frederick Lessner, who was the only non-family member to accompany Marx's daughters when they spread Engel's ashes.

By the time the Socialist league was declining, socialism was spreading rapidly throughout working class communities. Many a time Morris turned down the opportunity to stand for parliament for one or other community. But he had enough of the SL and left at the end of 1890. It was precisely at this time that new unionism exploded onto the scene and under the marginalised and fractured socialist groupings.

Morris's view of socialism was tempered by his extensive, indeed exhaustive practice, especially in party political and organisation matters, yet for all this he could never be a politician. On his application form to join the Democratic Federation, he simply described himself as a designer. He had concluded that there was a maturing process under way, whereby new layers of the working class were coming to the fore.

For Morris, socialism was a movement of a whole class and the formation of unionism amongst unskilled and semi-skilled workers, who had previously been unable to sustain organisation, seemed to confirm his view. Of the Great Dock Strike in 1889, he wrote," No result of the strike is more important than the effect it will have as a blow against the class jealousy amongst the workers themselves." This could be said for any number of strikes then spreading nationwide.

When the strike first broke, Morris was at an International Congress in Paris and then at Kelmscott. But he soon warmed to it and would have been able to recognise its significance anyway, as he knew so many of the strike leaders personally. To Morris, the strike was a much greater blow to capitalism than the 'riots' that had taken place three years before in Trafalgar Square over the unemployment issue. Firstly it involved bigger numbers, mobilised a whole community, and was ordered on a sustainable basis into a properly constituted trade union organisation. It was also disciplined, for there was almost no strike-breaking and the processions moving daily into the square mile were peacefully conducted. For the first time in a stoppage of its kind, workers were joined as one against the employer, and it was this that gave the strike its inner cohesion and special character.

It brought together the poorest of the poor, casually employed in an 'on-call' system, as well as the highly skilled lightermen who helped vessels move through the difficult Thames waters. It united the north Thames districts with the South Side led by Harry Quelch, also a member of the SDF. Many of the dockers had served in the navy or were ex-servicemen. But while new unionism burgeoned a sea change also occurred in 'old' unionism. And for Morris, whatever strengthened labour in united action strengthened socialism too. He wrote, "although a mere combination amongst the men, with no satisfactory ulterior aim, is not itself socialism, yet it is both a necessary education for the workers, and it is an instrument which socialism cannot dispense with!"

In the wake of the strike, thinking about socialism changed. Fabianism began to bear influence. To Morris's horror the Fabians advocated state intervention to put its power alongside that of the workers in order to force through change. The unions liked the sound of that. Had not the Government already enacted legislation such as the Land Acts, Employers' Liability Acts and Acts on education and Artisans' Dwellings. Why not more?

After 1890, because of the spread of Fabianism, Morris moved closer to Marx. He emphasised in his lectures and writings as well as in countless letters written to friends, comrades and enquirers that a legislative and parliamentary programme would only be successful if it recognised the irreconcilability of the classes. He refers to the power of the working class as "the coalminers … plus the intelligence of labour." Edward Thompson has shown that, to Morris, "socialism did not necessarily imply large scale industrialism as an essential condition of its existence." In *Where We Are Now* he aired his reservations about substituting state for the self-management of affairs, "For the rest, I neither believe in State Socialism as desirable in itself, or, indeed, as a complete scheme do I think it possible ... Nevertheless some approach to it is sure to be tried, and to my mind this will precede any complete enlightenment on the new order of things." Morris differentiated between the mass of people new to socialism who wished to 'compel the masters' and those like himself who wanted 'to do without masters.' Though he broadly, if a little reluctantly, came to believe that people would have to work through the former consideration before they would entertain the latter.

Of course, state socialism was to become as associated with Bismarck as it was with the Webbs, and this made it even less palatable to Morris. Indeed capitalism in all the major competing trading nations was reaching the point at which the state would intervene to boost and shape the accumulation process. It was the state that increasingly took responsibility for establishing technical schools, for developing infrastructure such as rail, road and coastal ports and establishing large peacetime standing armies of soldiers and civil servants. In Britain it was possible to dress up state socialism as a national version of municipal socialism, but none of these carried the kind of changes in social relations with production, and relationships between people, that Morris's version of socialism found necessary.

In response, he said the answer was "Make socialists." In short, society could not move to socialism until it was ready for revolutionary change and so the task of socialists was to prepare for that eventuality. In their absence, others, including to their credit, the Liberal party, went on to lay down the kind of measures that led to major material advancement and the strengthening of the working class. The concentration on 'making socialist propaganda' at the expense of direct intervention in improving working lives left a legacy to socialist organisations, who had become separated from the daily struggles of workers.

Morris was aware of being left behind, writing "So many of our hopes in small matters overthrown; and on the wider scale of things going on so much faster than we dared to hope." The campaign for the eight-hour day to which he had served as an inspiration exemplified his feelings. It was the centrepiece of the first official labour May Day Demonstration in 1890. The unions opted to march on May 4th, the first Sunday of the month and a day when most workers would not be working, but the Socialist League held aloof, its purity demanding that the march be held on the first itself even though it was a workday. So there were two demonstrations. While a few thousand people marched on the first, the fourth brought the largest turnout since the days of Chartism.

Walter Crane draws Morris speaking from the 1894 May Day platform. An elder statesman described as one "above the movement", he was in truth still very much a part of it, more interested in bringing its different, sometimes dislocated parts, together.

The League only lasted for six years. As it broke down, Morris lost none of his radicalism, but instead of reaching for his gun – some members of the League were arrested for this offence – he reached instead for his pen. He began to write *News from Nowhere* to be serialised in *The Commonweal*. An interesting choice of journal as the organisation was sinking fast. However, Morris knew that those he most wanted to influence, his corps of socialist educators, still read it. Morris's own branch of the Socialist League split away in November 1890 to form the influential Hammersmith Socialist Society. His last years were spent in a more open frame of mind. He was acutely aware of the dramatic changes that had occurred throughout the 1880s: if anything they were accelerating at the same time as imperialism was becoming the norm and the danger of war on a scale previously undreamt of was growing.

The Hammersmith Socialist Society was blossoming in its new arena, without the need to engage in factional politics or toe unsustainable party lines. It built its own meeting place on the Thames and provided a public platform for all strains of socialist thinking – even the old adversary, Henry Mayers Hyndman. In some ways and certainly in the realm of political theory, this local society had a national influence. In 1891 as a highly respected elder of the movement, Morris spoke at the most tolerant yet of the May Day marches – speaking on the same platform as Engels. He also moved much closer to Engels belief that a broad Labour Party was needed. In 1893, the Independent Labour Party had absorbed most local socialist groups. Morris lived to see Keir Hardie returned for West Ham, John Burns become MP for Battersea, Havelock Wilson in Middlesbrough and his old friend Ben Tillett standing against Liberal and Conservative in East Bradford, a contest lost by the narrowest of margins. But he warned that, "A rise of wages, shortening of hours of labour, better education ... all these things are good even in themselves; but unless they are used on steps towards equality of condition, the inconvenience they will cause to the capitalists will be met by changes in the markets."

Engels wrote in 1889, "Here in England one can see that it is impossible to drill a theory in an abstract and dogmatic way into a great nation, even if one has the best of theories ... " Morris added, "The business of progressive minds is to recognise the coming change, to clear away obstacles to it, to accept it, and to organise it in detail."

At the death of the Poet Laureate, Tennyson, a poet Morris greatly admired, Gladstone arranged for Morris to be unofficially approached to see if he would consider taking up the vacant post. Morris refused, though no doubt, he was aware that in the eyes of the public there were few others who could step into Tennyson's shoes. The offer and its refusal tell us much. No Victorian bourgeois, including Gladstone, who knew Morris quite well, could quite get their heads around the fact that 'one of their own' had gone over to the other side –

socialism. Many attempts were made to draw him back into the fold. Morris for his part had not exactly turned his back on capitalism, but having enthusiastically embraced socialism, he could never see why people could not just accept that. It would have been easier for Victorian society if he had turned his back on socialism in favour of capitalism. Others had done that and made a lot of money. Some even gained high office. But Morris eschewed these riches and trappings in favour of afternoons spent chatting with craftsmen about the art of dyeing fabrics. No wonder the newspapers fulminated against him. However, the workers were clear. Robert Blatchford wrote of him in the *Clarion*, "Morris was not only a genius, he was a man. Strike at him where you would, he rang true."

·A·GARLAND·FOR·MAY·DAY·1895·
· DEDICATED·TO·THE·WORKERS·BY·WALTER·CRANE ·

May Day 1895 and the outlook of Morris is ever present. 'Hope is Work', 'The Plough is a Better Backbone than the Factory' and 'Art and Enjoyment for All' all complimented the main theme of a shorter working week. Morris spoke from the rally platform. Illustrated by Crane for the cover of the Clarion, best known of the new breed of mass circulation socialist weeklies. Its editorial office was in Fleet Street.

With the national press largely barred to them, this was a time when workers and their organisations established journals of substance that lasted. The famous *Clarion* and the *Labour Leader* were established alongside *The Labour Elector*, the *Workmen's Times* and Keir Hardie's *The Miner*. For many workers, their first contact with socialism came through Morris: his speeches, his pamphlets and his innumerable newspaper articles. There could have been very few of those who established the greatest labour movement in the world between the 1880s and 1914, who had not heard, read, spoken to or shared a platform with Morris. This is true in towns as far apart as Yarmouth and Aberdeen and Dublin and Norwich. George Lansbury, worth volumes in his own right was one such, who fought his first election as an SDF candidate in Walworth and ended his days as President of the Labour Party. Between 1892 and 1896, despite his failing health, Morris became, in the words of Edward Thompson, a figure "above the movement."

Morris's analysis of and acceptance of palliatives became much more sophisticated, so, he maintained his revolutionary position as a point of principle. It is an irony of his life that, the lecture he gave and later reprinted as a Fabian tract, entitled *Communism*, which some thought put him beyond redemption, is actually his most measured appraisal of socialism yet. Removed from direct involvement in party politics he no longer had to fear offending the sensibilities of his reform hungry comrades or compromise with the increasingly tangential 'anti-parliamentarians.' He could now begin to combine the theoretical – because socialism was beyond its infancy – and the practical as it had a mass movement to relate to. What is more, he thought that as the gains of this mass movement grew so would responsibilities on the Socialists. Where once the task of socialists was to preach socialism, "in season and out of season, where we were wanted, where we were tolerated, where we were not tolerated … " it now had other action "forced on us by the growing … practical acception of the theory of socialism". The workers, he observed, "have started to claim new conditions of life which they can only obtain at the expense of the possessing classes…". The Parliamentary road was not the one of his own choosing but, the workers having chosen it, he would not abandon them.

'Dreamer of dreams, out of my true time, why should I strive to set the crooked straight?"

The Earthly Paradise 1868-70

The Power of Labour

The pioneer socialists are often criticised for not laying down a blueprint for socialism. However this was quite deliberate and the reasoning was sound. The challenge to the likes of Marx and Morris was to develop an understanding and critique of capitalism, to strip it down and take a good look at the gubbins. Morris wrote in 1883, "… I do not believe in the world being saved by any system – I only assert the necessity of attacking systems grown corrupt, and no longer leading any whither." Marx was very much his own man but also a disciplined thinker within a movement. At times he also led practically. As we have seen, Morris came to socialism through a range of influences and experience. He was a socialist before he could call it by the name and came to Marxism only after he turned fifty and was therefore unconstrained by a prescribed and rigid set of ideas. He was a deep thinker, with wide tools of reference and, rather bravely given his reputation, often thought out loud and publicly. He was confident enough to develop and change his ideas in the same way and used a whole battery of media to think aloud as to, 'After Capitalism, What Might Be?' By the 1880s, he had been ready to move on from 'new thinking' to socialism.

Morris had a fear of being accused of being impractical, and being a socialist did not help at all, for in the middle and late nineteenth century the constant criticism of the idea of socialism was that 'it is a good idea, but it could never work in practice'. Nowhere was Morris able to point to the existence of socialism or even a suggestion of it at a town council level. He could not draw on examples from abroad either – which became a sort of shorthand for future generations in relation to the USSR. As a craftsman of great repute, the charge of being impractical seems to be the only one that hurt him. However, we are the beneficiaries of this as, in order to prove how practical his socialism was, and unable to draw parallels elsewhere, Morris had to look deeply at the functioning of his own country's political economy and find some answers. These he found in an analysis of class. This energising force would serve to underpin his writing, his analysis of empire and art and shape his own practice. The burden of moving society forward was great, for, as he wrote, "the civilisation which does not carry the whole people with it is doomed to fall".

FLOWERS FOR LABOUR'S MAY-DAY
'ALL A' BLOWIN' AND A' GROWIN'

A unique and distinctive style; a brilliant designer and book illustrator, Walter Crane was apprenticed to the Chartist William James Linton, worked for Morris at Merton Abbey and went on to become Director of Design at the Manchester School of Art and then head of the Royal College of Art. Crane stated, that only in Socialism could "Use and Beauty be United".

One of the most effective ways in which Morris attracted his audience was to write in the form of romantic prose – a sort of extended dream or, as he called it, a vision. He was so successful that several of his works in this genre have become classics and are still in print today. He was familiar with the work of the great Utopian writers and had actually written an introduction to the work of Thomas More, perhaps the greatest of all, but utopianism was not down to earth enough for what he wanted to do as they "had their roots in the air". By adopting romantic prose Morris was able to abstract and reflect, but in a way that allowed no room for meandering. In *Dream of John Ball* [1886-7], he reflects on the nature of history, *News From Nowhere* [1890] allows him to project on the character of life in a society where the class division has been abandoned and *The Pilgrims of Hope* [1885] is a tribute to the defenders of the Paris Commune. In a *King's Lesson* [1887] he exposes the inequality of class society with great irony.

It takes a rare and special skill to write in this way, especially as he was then weighed down by family grief and day to day pressure. In addition it must be taken into account that he was writing for workers for whom daily life was a constant struggle to survive and feed their families. Not an easy cohort to transport out of the day-to-day. Morris had actually displayed an uncanny ability to step outside the mundane from an early age, a talent he used throughout his life. Although he employed it in different ways, the quality of one of the handful of truly great nineteenth century writers, up there with Dickens and Tennyson, never fails.

For Morris the class war became the essence of his society. A *King's Lesson* ends with the King telling his serfs that if he was as poor as they and so unfairly treated, he would arm himself, gather to him his community, and rise up. He then returns to his castle to eat his fill, but rest uneasily. Morris's every word and action was aimed at increasing a similar unease in ruling circles. A key is what he called "the struggle of the working classes for citizenship".

As we have seen, he loved England and displayed an unbroken record of pride in his country but an equally implacable opposition to imperialism throughout his life. "The men of our labouring classes, therefore, should turn a deaf ear to the recruiting sergeant." Class interests in Morris's world were divided and only the victory of one over the other would remove the impasse. Like Marx, Morris was not driven to provide a blueprint because he felt that it would tie the hands of future generations and lay down schemata that could then be artificially elevated, and for all the wrong reasons, to heights of principle that they were never meant to be. He was also bluntly realistic about the expectations and limitations of each successive generation. In 1887, in *A Dream of John Ball* he brought the Commonweal of the fourteenth century craftsman and later, elsewhere, of Cromwell's Republic to socialism. This was no historical slight of hand, for both Levellers and Diggers had established cooperatives of production and the exchange of services, not based on money, but on 'equal labour time'. In many ways, this Commonweal was a reality and did not just exist in unions or cooperation. In the print industry, for example, the composing room was referred to as the 'ship' because its title amongst compositors was 'the companionship' or, the coming together. However, Morris would not force his Commonweal as the only way, on those who would one day take up his struggle. They would have to work things out for themselves.

In projecting life as it might be, rather than telling others how it ought to be, Morris drew his inspiration from the life and work of Robert Owen. Owen was a brilliant organiser, a visionary thinker and a man way ahead of his time. Like Morris, he had a rare practical talent for working with production processes, and a commitment to uplifting the hearts and minds of working people. Even today, Owen is considered one of the founders and most original practitioners of management technique, which he combined with production, based on a form of cooperation. However, Morris saw that in Owen, the attempt to do things differently and better than capitalism led to a blurring of the difference between capitalist and non-capitalist property relations. Morris was at pains not to sanction this. For him it was either capitalism or socialism, and there would be no halfway plans or palliatives to blur the divide that existed between the two. In *Dream of John Ball* he reasoned, "What else shall ye lack when ye lack masters? Ye shall not lack for the fields ye have tilled, nor the houses ye have built, nor the cloth ye have woven: all these shall be yours".

Morris used the dream-world of romantic prose as a tool for reflection. By this means, none of his readers would be handed tablets of stone nor compelled to swear allegiance to a fixed set of ideas. Reflection excused Morris from saying 'this is how it must be': instead he was saying 'this is how it might be'. This meant that no one could say of Morris as they later did of Marx –'this is how it has to be because *he* said so' even though *he* was no longer alive to clarify things. In *News From Nowhere* (1890) he wrote, "If others can see it as I have seen it then it maybe called a vision rather than a dream."

Morris's socialism is an emphasis on the communal as a means of enhancing the unique contribution of each individual. He placed emphasis on the things that brought people together. Every aspect of his socialism, from how people were housed, how streets were built and towns planned, to where they ate and how they were educated, was but a variation on the same theme. The common good, or what he called the Commonweal was just an extension of the fullest flowering of each individual. He was convinced that every man or woman had a positive and unique contribution to make. He believed that any young person of average intelligence was capable of becoming an artisan or a craftsman, and backed this thought up with appropriate action. Pieces submitted by his company to the 1893 Arts and Crafts Exhibition were made by boys, "trained in our own shop … they come to us with no knowledge of drawing whatever, and have learnt every single thing under our training. And most beautifully they have done it".

Community was superior to any other form of social existence, "men will at last come to see that the only way to avoid the tyranny and waste of bureaucracy is by the Federation of Independent Communities". Remarkably, four decades before Morris wrote this, in unpublished notes for the Communist Manifesto (which he had not read), Marx and Engels concluded that society would take the form of a federation of "free-standing communities".

So, socialism was more than the Commonweal or a matter of equal opportunity. It meant unravelling the division of labour as it was and reconstructing production on an entirely different footing. As a matter of course, managers should spend time working on the shop floor, not as a punishment, but to gain an all-round knowledge of processes, so that they could venture beyond existing ways of doing things. In the same way, workers should spend time working as management. Craftsmen should work closely with designers: that is, from the very inception of each production process and should be allowed full freedom to use their initiative throughout. In Morris's view, whoever set copy, aligned printer's plates, wove at the loom or laid bricks, was the one best placed to help with the design. The division between the designer and craftsman, between those paid to conceive and plan designs and those who carry them out therefore would become redundant. They should be teamed up to experiment, away from the actual production process. He himself continually worked with craftsmen to experiment in new techniques and the development of new materials like fabric dye and inks. Morris would have been thrilled to find how popular he, his ideas and his work have become on the internet. I say thrilled because in many ways, the success of the internet and of networked communications and manufacture – resting as they do on individual creativity and a high degree of collective interplay – are precisely Morris's way of doing things. He would have been delighted.

For Morris the division of capitalism from socialism was one between 'true' and 'false' society. This was not entirely new thinking in nineteenth century Britain but it raised criticism of a failing social system to a new level. 'False' denotes property relationships and the laws that underpin capitalist rule. 'True' society focuses on human relationships and class-based morality.

In opposition to the anarchists who sought to take over the Socialist League, but succeeded only in destroying it, he developed a depth of analysis rarely matched. Of human relationships, he wrote, "That true society of loved and lover, parent and child, friend and friend, the society of well-wishers, of reasonable people conscious of the aspirations of humanity and of the duties we owe to it through one another – this society, I say, is held together and exists by its own inherent right and reason, in spite of what is wrongly thought to be the cement of society, arbitrary authority."

What he seems to be saying is that, despite arbitrary rule, the media machine, the law and an alien code of values, the working class generates its own culture, thought, necessities and value system and these represented the basis of socialism. Touched by the influences of capitalism – yes, but suffocated by it? Certainly not! He sought to enhance the educated and disciplined aspect of workers' culture. Twenty years after the Paris Commune of 1871 he expressed a fear that a revolutionary change might be sought by a working class, "which, though it shall have attained knowledge, shall lack utterly the refinement and self-respect which come from the union of knowledge with leisure and ease of life". He thought that a working class in search of violent redress for its demands would be no nearer to socialism. "All history shows us," he wrote, "what a danger to society may be a class at once educated and socially degraded."

A notion common among socialists even today is that workers believe everything they are taught or read in newspapers, so all one needs to do is alter the charge sheet and they will believe something different. This was not Morris's way at all. Even though the working class in his time was accumulating power and was then a mere shadow of what it has become today, he could see that socialism would only come if it was consciously embraced free of compulsion, and as a result of increased knowledge and a full flowering of intellect. For this reason he projected, not a finished scheme or blueprint but a series of challenges that would, once implemented, begin a process of exploration, self-awareness and change – a sort of modern renaissance.

Morris recognised, partly because he saw continuity with fourteenth century craftsmen in nineteenth century proletarians, that he was dealing with a body of independent thinkers. In this sense socialism faced a much bigger challenge than if it were a set of ideas to be written on a fresh page. It would have to struggle to make sense of historical continuity and would be more a question of education than anything else. Of all the senses finely developed in workers is feeling for history. It provides them with a legacy, standards which they must seek to better if they are to progress, and a wealth of ideas to define, protect and enhance their lives and workspaces.

It so happened that the people Morris used as his model laid down very strong and fertile standards and ideas. These included the natural rights of freeborn Englishmen, equality before the law, judgement by jury, habeas corpus and patriotism based on the needs of the nation rather than on a monarch or a narrow ruling caste. Especially important were the Commonweal and ownership of their own means to life. The more lettered, cultured and worldly-wise the potential audience for socialism the more they could challenge it. No one could cajole workers to think in the way Morris would prefer nor would any demagoguery achieve results. They would only embrace socialism when they could accept that it was right for them and they were ready for it. It would be a process of self-realisation and popular sovereignty. Only workers could decide for workers.

Socialism was no 'truth' to be handed out at factory gates. As the growth of new unionism and the Great Dock Strike of 1889 were to prove, workers were often way ahead of the self-appointed 'leaders'. In struggling against the ideas of the anarchists, Morris was quick to spot the value of Marx's concept of the withering away of the state. The anarchists wanted to abolish the state – which may once have sounded great, but with nothing superior to replace it with, is somewhat meaningless. Morris reasoned that socialism would need a state in its early phase, but it would soon be superseded by a reassertion of the ancient ties that existed between people as friends, family, community, and as producers. These bonds were far deeper and more historically defined, and were more powerful and superior to any that could be generated by any form of state. The state was an easily recognisable expression of nationhood but did little for the basis of socialism, which was really a new way of producing and distributing plenty. Morris was not a state socialist and of course looked with distaste on Fabianism. His socialism was based on a much closer interrelationship between producers, free from excessive regulation and intervention.

Begun as "a little typographical adventure", the revival of fine book publishing in Britain flows directly from Morris's decision to establish the Kelmscott Press.

The bonds between family, community and producers would be voluntary; they would arise out of a common identity and a shared vision. It is Morris's use of a concept of the people, and the people as a constant source of reference for his socialism, that gives it substance and meaning. Nothing, be it machinery or the state, could replace the fact that life was engaged and enhanced by a combination of individual character and collective endeavour, expressed through art in labour with labour as an art form. In *Dream of John Ball* he wrote words that were to become famous, "… fellowship is life, and lack of fellowship is death: and the deeds that ye do upon earth, it is for fellowship's sake that ye do them, and the life that is in it, that shall live on and on for ever and ever …"

"Therefore, granted well-designed type, due spacing of the lines and words, and proper position of the page on the paper, all books might be at least comely and well-looking: and if to these good qualities were added really beautiful ornament and pictures, printed books might once again illustrate to the full the position of our Society that a work of utility might also be a work of art, if we cared to make it so."

William Morris, *The Ideal Book*

Most agree that Morris's views on how society would develop were both original and exceptional, but he did not dream them up in the gardens of Kelmscott Manor or at Kelmscott House. They came first from his own enquiry into life and what made it work, and as a result of daily dialogue with leading working class thinkers such as Burrows, Burns, Mann and Tom Maguire.

On reading *News from Nowhere* we might disagree with many of the points raised, but the real strength of it is in the big picture. Morris's uncanny ability to set aside a crushing schedule of work and meetings in order to write, was rewarded in the sense that, he penned a classic and influential book. It excels because it does not dwell on what was rotten in capitalism but envisions that something better could emerge in its place. He, himself said that, "it should be read as a vision, rather than a dream." Few writers then or since would dare assert that anyone taking a boat trip up the Thames in 2136 would see London transformed into a garden, with apricot trees growing in Trafalgar Square, and where the primary duty of her citizens would be to enjoy themselves!

Some of the similarities between Marx and Morris are uncanny. In a series of writings (1845-46) later bundled together and published under the title of *German Ideology*, Marks wrote,"The division of labour offers us the first example of how, as long as man remains in natural society, that is, as long as a cleavage exists between the particular and the common interest, as long, therefore, as activity is not voluntarily, but naturally divided, man's own deed becomes an alien power opposed to him, which enslaves him instead of being controlled by him. For as soon as the distribution of labour comes into being, each man has a particular, exclusive sphere of activity, which is forced upon him and from which he cannot escape. He is a hunter, a fisherman, a shepherd, or a critical critic, and must remain so if he does not want to lose his means of livelihood; while in communist society, where nobody has one exclusive sphere of activity but each can become accomplished in any branch he wishes, society regulates the general production and thus makes it possible for me to do one thing today and another tomorrow, to hunt in the morning, fish in the afternoon, rear cattle in the evening, criticise after dinner, just as I have a mind, without ever becoming hunter, fisherman, shepherd or critic…"

Morris took up Marx's challenge of going further; to portray a life beyond the division of labour and of 'intellectual' and 'manual' labour, through his chosen specialty of the arts. In so doing he created a body of thinking that continues to have resonance and relevance today. He reiterated that art was not to be the preserve of an individual, producing artefacts for the few who could afford them. Even so, the artist, no matter how gifted, often ended up in poverty and the greatest poverty was in the lifelessness of the subject matter. Art was the lifeblood of the mass of people and was at its best when it reflected their travails and ascendancy, their loves and accomplishments. The division between intellectual and manual labour, to the extent that it then existed, was, in his view, only transitory because it rested on the existence of the division of labour.

In order to advance, society needed to strip away the idea that 'manual' labour was somehow degrading. In the same way it needed to reduce the loftiness which separated the 'thinker' from the 'doer'. This was simply a narrow veneer, to disguise exploitation, by those who dealt in profit rather than work. In moulding 'manual' and 'intellectual' back together, by annihilating the division between them, social advance would appear natural so that "socialism will melt into society".

Billed as, "An Epoch of Rest" in the form of a Utopian Romance. News from Nowhere soon developed into "a vigorous statement by various friends of their views on the future of the fully-developed new society." Said one, "If I could but see it!".

News from Nowhere was written in instalments throughout 1890 for the Commonweal as was the custom of the age. Although it was written in the form of a 'vision', Morris never intended to take his reader out of this world. It was more an invitation to share his journey. It was written to reduce the dreamer from a state of semi consciousness to full consciousness and to enlightenment. Generations have been nurtured on its storyline and it remains one of the most frequently read books of its kind. With Morris, the reader straddled each state of consciousness, producing a creative tension that grips and prods him into thinking, "What if this were me?"

News from Nowhere was wasted on the membership of the Socialist League, which by the time of its writing had been reduced to a group of anarchists and another loyal to Morris, but the burgeoning labour movement beyond had need of it. It very quickly became a top seller in these circles and a 'must read' for the generation of Labour leaders who emerged after the First World War. Ernest Bevin, who founded and built the Transport and General Workers' Union, Ben Tillett and Will Thorne leader of the Union now known as the GMB, all referred to the lasting influence that the book had on them.

The twist Morris employs is very clever indeed and quite disarming. In the 'dream' one is not looking forward to a society that might be, but back to one that has already been born. The revolution took place in 1952 – and it was not uncommon to ask (tongue in cheek), in labour movement circles at the turn of the twentieth century – "Where were you when it [the revolution of 1952] happened and how did it happen?"

Morris was unable to read even a small portion of the published works of Marx, for the simple reason that they were not in print during his lifetime. *Origins of the Family, State and Private Property, Anti-Duhring*, and the *Theses on Ludwig Feuerbach*, were published after his death although he may have been shown a copy of the *Critique of the Gotha Programme* by Engels at one of their weekend teatime gatherings – an important document dealing with matters of principle inside the German workers' movement. This was then circulating secretly and to only a handful of people.

In the absence of documentary support and direction, Morris fell back on history, but he was clear about its limitations, "… We cannot turn our people back into Catholic English peasants and Guild craftsmen, or into heathen Norse bounders, much as may be said for such conditions of life … " He did not seek out Orders in Council, records of Kings and Queens, but information on everything that could give him a picture of the daily lives of the ordinary people: their work and crafts, how and where they lived, how they worked and divided their communal life, what made them ill and well again, how they divided their land and worked it, what they wore, what they adorned themselves with, how they ordered and decorated their homes, their beliefs and religions, their customs and, above all, their art. Marx had of course done something similar. *Capital* serves as a huge directory of prime sources about life and the political economy of Britain. Where Marx had looked to Ricardo and Saint Just and the experience of revolutionary France, Morris drew from the radicalism and lyricism of William Blake, the industrial drive of Robert Owen and Ruskin's critique of capitalism based on the necessity of art. In approaching what became known as scientific socialism, Marx had to draw from his sources and then break with them, famously adopting the dialectical method of Hegel and then standing it on its feet. Morris never criticised Blake, Ruskin, Owen or Thomas Carlyle, but he did eventually break with them and make a new socialism.

His constant benchmark for socialism is 'the raising of the craftsman to be master of his own destiny.' This stems from his grasp of the role of the craftsman in the Middle Ages from which he draws heavily on Ruskin – who was a significant influence on the early labour movement. The craftsman was the only force in society, he reasoned, who alone had an interest in restoring art to labour. He therefore had a vested interest in rolling back the division of labour that so emasculated the craftsmen. Fiercely independent, patriotic and with an intellect fashioned through his role as controller of the labour process, the craftsman was to be the shock trooper of Morris's socialism.

In the quest for such control, the craftsman came to define his dignity, a character that shone through his role as worker – stoutly defending the quality of his product and developing a whole value system of relationships amongst workers and between workers and those who bought his goods. These became systematised into rules and constitutions first for the guilds and later the unions. He wanted workers to be, "neither master nor master's men, neither idle nor overworked, neither brain-sick brain workers, nor heartsick handworkers … "

One of the things that attracted Morris to socialism was that its historical approach and terms of reference matched his own. History could not be reduced to a static timeline of names, dates and events: it was developmental, passing through incremental and then qualitative change. His activism meant that he could sympathise with history without wishing to return there. Many people are nostalgic for a return to Morris, but he was nostalgic for nothing. In the lecture he gave in 1877 entitled, *The Lesser Arts* he was unequivocal. Speaking of ancient work he said "Let us therefore study wisely, be taught by it, kindled by it; all the while determining not to imitate or repeat it; to have either no art at all, or an art we have made our own."

Did he lament the beauty that had been lost? Obviously so, as when one loses a loved one and must bleakly accept that they can never be replaced. Addressing the Society for the Protection of Ancient Buildings that he founded, in 1877 he said, "It cannot be, it has gone! They believe that we can do the same sort of work in the same spirit as our forefathers, whereas for good and for evil we are completely changed, and we cannot do the work that they did. All continuity of history means is after all perpetual change, and it is not hard to see that we have changed with a vengeance, and thereby established our claim to be the continuers of history."

When he compared the condition of the craftsman of the Middle Ages with that of his counterpart of the industrial revolution he did not do so in order to put the clock back. He knew that was impossible. What he wanted above all was a future where the status of the craftsman was raised beyond that of his forebear, the craft worker of feudal England.

Ford Madox Brown's "Work" (1852-65). Thomas Carlyle appears in the painting along with women distributing temperance tracts. Brown was a member of the Brotherhood, a business partner of Morris and an influential artist who, late in life, painted twelve frescoes to decorate Manchester Town Hall.

The original manuscript of Morris's 'Communism' first produced as a Fabian Tract (number 113). It was in fact a spoken address to members of the Hammersmith Socialist Society in 1893. Its editor, George Bernard Shaw, says Morris is doing "what he could to economise the strength of the movement between its jarring sections". In it he refers to Communism as 'socialism ceasing to be militant, becoming triumphant' and 'workpleasure'.

Reproduced courtesy of International Institute of Social History, Amsterdam

It was much more than a question of condition. It was impossible to go backwards because life had moved on and change had been profound. There was no peasantry now in England and a return to a rural idyllic past had been made impossible by the enclosure of the land and the growth of industry and urban centres. Socialism was about workers and they had changed too. They had emerged as a class, had considerably gained in number, engaged with complex industrial processes, and found new skills and lost others. They had moved away from religion and, to an extent, embraced and learned to bring the new sciences into their lives.

Necessity was defined differently and morality had changed too, as had the communities themselves and dominant working class values. Some core values had endured and become strong, especially those of class association, especially in unions, community identity and patriotism. All this rings true when we study the people of Britain over the six hundred years between the high point of medievalism and the first Industrial Revolution. It is even more certain when we contrast the working class of 1885 with that of 1835. Indeed, the workers had come a long way since they were portrayed in *Work*, a painting by Ford Maddox Brown, in 1852.

In his latter years Morris took exception to the growth of reformism and state socialism or Fabianism as it was then called. He contended that, "Individual men cannot shuffle off the business of life on to the shoulders of an abstraction called the state, but must deal with each other; that variety of life is as much an aim of true communism as equality of conditions and that nothing but a union of these two will bring about real freedom … " It was only when people were brought face to face with the responsibilities involved in making work really *work* that they learnt "to be resourceful and self-reliant", and could take their place, "consciously and intelligently in the great enterprise of providing for the needs of mankind".

Morris referred to himself as a communist and refused to be bracketed with factional terms such as Fabian or social democrat. As a communist, he believed the end of class was the condition where all enter into the fellowship, "They will come of themselves until the habit of socialism will be fully formed, and no one will have to use the word any more, as it will embrace the whole of human life". His was a kind of bare bones socialism, stripped of pretension and superfluity. He focussed on the relationship between labour and capital, and he took up a struggle against the political direction of the Fabian Society. The Fabians had many good ideas as to how society could be reorganised and run, and without wishing to belittle their many achievements, it is true to say they had such good ideas for building socialism that they could not wait for it and so decided to try them out on capitalism instead.

Fabianism reduced socialism to a programme of economic management. It forgot the historical sweep, necessity and values, and for Morris this would never do. He countered, "By political power, we do not mean the exercise of the franchise or even the fullest development of the representative system, but the direct control by the people of the whole administration of the community."

In a moment of great foresight he wrote of what socialism could mean to workers, "The tameness and elaboration of modern mechanical production would be just as odious to him if the plant were in state ownership and the management in the hands of government officials."

Morris's opposition to Parliament was a stand against centralisation. The worker, he thought, could either focus on the faction and party politics of parliament or bring himself "face to face with the actual problem of industrial production and organisation; (he) learns to be resourceful and self-reliant and to take (his) place consciously and intelligently in the great enterprise of providing for the needs of mankind."

In his letters to the Rev. G. Bainton (privately printed in 1894) he defines his government of the future more as "an administration of things than a government of persons". These were core tenets he held to all his days. In December 1890 he wrote, "It is not the dissolution of society for which we strive, but its reintegration." One year before his death he gave an address to inaugurate the Oxford Socialist Union. His last public speech at Kelmscott House was on the subject "One Socialist Party".

In his last years Morris's writing changed. He knew the movement, its men, and the people, and that the old agitation was partly exhausted and somewhat surpassed by events. He feared war so, set about working out how he could economise on the strength of the movement the better to apply it effectively. Feudalism taught Morris much – he could see a shift to socialism would take generations, bearing in mind that the shift from feudalism to capitalism had taken several centuries. Fabianism was merely tinkering, a superficial movement.

On municipal housing and education, Morris wrote, "I freely admit a great gain, and am glad to see schemes tried which would lead to it … but great as the gain would be, the ultimate good of it, the amount of progressive force that might be in such things, would … depend on how such reforms were done; in what spirit; or rather what else was being done … which would make people long for equality of condition; which would give them faith in the possibility and workableness of socialism."

A post-1945 pamphlet produced by the Amalgamated Engineering Union. In it, Morris appears as a ghost from times past but is characterised alongside a union which is "The Voice of the Future".

Equality was not an aim as such, more an emblem of common endeavour. As all are involved in this great project, all depend in some way on each other, and each has a unique contribution to make. Only the conscience of Fabianism elevated equality from emblem to principle.

He wrote of a need to "now take a soberer view of our hopes". He felt that the move towards socialism, "must be a transitional condition, during which we must waive complete realisation of the ideal. It is necessary also in getting working people to raise their standard of livelihood so that they may claim more and yet more of the wealth produced by society". He warned of the dangers of promoting reform at the expense of structural and irreversible change.

"For the social democratic measures ... are all of them either makeshift alleviation to help us through the present day of oppression, or means for landing us in the new country of equality ... And there is a danger that they will be looked upon as ends in themselves."

The consistency in his writing over several decades is remarkable. "Communism does not mean that people would use their neighbours' coats, or homes, or toothbrushes, but that every one, whatever work he did, would have the opportunity of satisfying all his reasonable needs according to the admitted standard of the society in which he lived."

He called upon the movement to come together. "I appeal to all socialists, while they express their thoughts and feelings about them honestly and fearlessly, not to make a quarrel of it with those whose aim is one with theirs, because there is a difference of opinion between them about the usefulness of the details of the means."

Further, he expressed a belief that such unity only found its logic when expressed as a *purpose*, "so let us forgive the mistakes that others make, even if we make none ourselves, and be at peace amongst ourselves that we may the better make war upon the monopolist."

To Morris, when all was said and done, socialism was a question of philosophy. To the question 'What are we doing here?' he could reply, "We are doing much, but we are doing it wrongly and socialism will allow people to do more things and a lot better.' When discussing pattern designing in 1881, he expressed the view that "popular art cannot live if labour is to be for ever in the thrall of muddle, dishonesty and disunion ... I see signs about us of a coming time of order, goodwill and union". In Morris' socialism we find a critique of what has emerged as twentieth and twenty first century capitalism as much as that of the nineteenth century. At the core of his thinking was the view that, "socialism is to substitute the relation of persons to persons for the relation of things to persons". In this sense, to quote EP Thompson, "Morris is one of those men whom history will never overtake." William himself deserves the last word, "... Meanwhile, if these hours be dark, as, indeed in many ways they are, at least do not let us sit deedless, like fools and fine gentlemen, thinking the common toil not good enough for us, and beaten by the muddle; but rather let us work like good fellows trying by some dim candle-light to set our workshop ready against tomorrow's day-light – that tomorrow, when the civilised world, no longer greedy, strifeful, and destructive, shall have a new art, a glorious art, made by the people and for the people, as a happiness to the maker and user."